Contents

Preface

August 15, 1947 is a date etched upon the soul of every Indian. It is the day India won its freedom from the British Empire. Yet it is also the date of Partition, an act which carved up India along religious lines to create the Islamic state of Pakistan, igniting violence which killed more than a million people. 2007 sees the 60th anniversary of these events, unifying the jubilation of Independence with the grief of a nation's division.

The horror of Partition lives on in the psyche of the Indian people to this day, a dark reminder of how the country was forced to pass through the communal fires in order to be reborn as a new nation. Partition has until now remained the defining act in India's post-Independence history: establishing the basis for relations with Pakistan as well as relations between Hindus, Muslims and Sikhs within India. In the days that followed August 15, 1947, India witnessed a kind of collective madness that saw its communities poisoned by the politics of the religious fanatic.

The seeds of this book were sown by reading reportage and fictionalized accounts of the events of 1947. I remember being particularly struck by a slim volume of short stories by Saadat Hasan Manto called *Kingdom's End*, in which the small lives of ordinary men were used to reflect the great issue of the time: Partition and how religion had come to define a person's identity.

These brief, sparely written tales of how communal division destroyed lives across religious boundaries drew me into a subject which resonates in India to this day. Manto was a Muslim Kashmiri who grew up in Punjab and moved to Bombay. Yet he did not write as a Muslim, or indeed as a Kashmiri, nor even an Indian. Instead, his was the humane voice of detached reason that chronicled the societal breakdown that followed India's division.

The most moving story of all is that of Toba Tek Singh, a man from an asylum who cannot comprehend the dismemberment of his country and so flees to a no-man's-land between India and Pakistan, where he stands in protest until collapsing into the dust with grief: "There, behind barbed wire, on one side lay India and behind more barbed wire, on the other side lay Pakistan. In between, on a bit of earth which had no name, lay Toba Tek Singh."

Sixty years after Partition, India and the post-9/11 world at large remain fixated by the dangers of religious division and fundamentalism. While the Western world is newly alert to the threat posed by extreme Islam, India as the world's largest secular democracy has decades of experience of how every strand of religion can be hijacked by the politics of the fanatic and the lessons of India's battles against holy warriors from Hinduism, Islam, Sikhism and even Christianity are more relevant than ever today on a global scale. The de-humanizing effect on the Toba Tek Singhs of this world is now evident, from London to New York, and from Baghdad to Jerusalem. The anniversary of Partition seemed an opportune moment to revisit the issue in India, to discover how the religious divisions in the country have shaped the political and cultural landscape over the last sixty years, and to try to understand what turns a believer into a holy warrior.

Since *Holy Warriors* was first published in India in 2006, there have been a few developments, some positive, some less so. The Congress-led national government has persisted with its policy of seeking to rehabilitate religious minorities back into the Indian family through economic engagement and dialogue in a bid to quell religious unrest. It has continued to pursue peace talks with Pakistan, exploring growing trade, travel and intellectual links as steps towards normalized relations.

That policy has yielded results, with Pakistan hinting that it may consider giving up its longstanding claim to Indian-held Kashmir in return for certain concessions; a sign that *realpolitik* may yet prevail over dogma, as both sides recognize that economic re-generation of the region has become the real issue of the day.

Yet alongside hope, there is continued evidence that the menace of religious extremism remains real in India. Politically marginalized after its 2004 national election rout, the Hindu nationalist movement including the mainstream Bharatiya Janata Party (BJP) and the hardline Shiv Sena have radicalized their rhetoric rather than choosing the path of moderation in their bid to recoup lost votes.

Hindutva's political cadres have rejected pressure to water down their more hard-line anti-Muslim and anti-Christian policies. Hindu nationalist hawks appear to have won out over the doves. After a long period in the political wilderness, the Shiv Sena and BJP alliance recently scored a political comeback in Mumbai by winning power in February 2007's civic elections which put the Hindutva camp in control of the Brihanmumbai Municipal Corporation.

The victory came less than a year after Mumbai suffered yet another devastating terrorist bomb attack in the summer of 2006. Shiv Sena's aging supremo Bal Thackeray was savvy enough to make the link in the wake of victory: "Terrorism has spread across the country and only Hindus can fight terrorism," he said. "Hindutva is still relevant." The message to the Muslims and Christians was inescapable: watch out, we're back.

Last summer's bomb attack on commuter trains by suspected Islamic terrorists killed more than 180 and injured a further 700 and marked a serious escalation in the threat posed by religious fanatics to ordinary Indians, sweeping in from border war-zones like Kashmir to strike the nation's financial heartland. It was the deadliest terrorist attack since the 1993 Mumbai bomb blasts by Islamic militants which had killed more than 250 people. The summer of 2006 evoked a chilling sense of *déjà vu*. At the time, Mumbai reacted by showing the world that it retained its indomitable spirit, its ability to walk through the debris of disaster and go about its business. Such an act of evil was designed to divide, to stoke communal division between Hindu and Muslim, to derail the painfully constructed peace talks between India and Pakistan, to foster insecurity and disunity in an India that is making strides towards becoming an economic powerhouse. India's Prime Minister Manmohan Singh told the world: "No one can make India kneel. The wheels of our economy will move on." Business responded just so. Indian shares rose on the stock exchange and that was the best response Mumbai could have made.

As the UK edition of *Holy Warriors* goes to press in early 2007, India remains top of the world headlines, just as it was sixty years before. After six turbulent decades of freedom, India finally seems set to break free from the shackles of its past and transform itself into an economic superpower for the new century. While there has been talk of the sleeping elephant awakening before, this time things really seem different.

The venerable Indian corporate dynasty Tata has succeeded in taking over Corus, which includes the remnants of the old British Steel giant. The Indian economy is expected to grow by 9.2 percent in 2006/07, the fastest rate in 18 years. Manufacturing output is up, the service sector is expanding, the brain drain has reversed and world economists speak of India becoming a trillion dollar economy which will soon be bigger than Britain's. "The Empire Strikes Back" seems to be the story of the day.

Yet behind the spectacular forecasts, there is a note of caution. India has yet to address the economic apartheid that exists in the country. Large sections of the country remain untouched by the economic miracle that is unfolding in its cities. One thing my journey in India showed me time and again was how religious insurgencies rear like monsters from the bleak landscape of economic stagnation. Leaders of extremist religious movements, including terrorist movements, know that the unemployed provide fertile recruiting ground. In places like Kashmir, terrorism has often been the only job in town and, with a religious message attached, it becomes a holy mission.

When the Bangladeshi economist Muhammad Yunus accepted the Nobel Prize in December 2006 for his micro-credit loan initiative, he said he hoped the award would inspire "bold initiatives" to deal with the problem at its origin: "We must address the root causes of terrorism to end it for all time," he told hundreds of distinguished guests at City Hall in Oslo. "I believe putting resources into improving the lives of poor people is a better strategy than spending it on guns."

In recent years, the world has woken up to India's potential as a real economic force, its political clout as the world's largest democracy and its amazing ability to hold together despite its religious and regional diversities. The ghost of communal violence that dates back to 1947 has a real chance of being exorcised by the unprecedented opportunities for economic stability and growth now opening up in India, which could harness the potential of all of India's people. It's a big prize. One that India cannot afford to lose.

Edna Fernandes, February 2007

Introduction

'I believe in the fundamental truth of all religions.'
—Mahatma Gandhi

Wagah, Punjab, September 2004

Lotan Baba Sai laid his wasted body upon the tarpaulin spread over the dirt, distractedly scratching a scab on his thigh as he recounted the disaster of his aborted holy mission. Dusk had fallen on the makeshift camp near the Wagah border, the frontline between India and Pakistan. Wagah isn't much to look at, but this dustbowl of a town represents south Asia's sundering: the line that separates a people who are the same and yet not the same, divided by religion in 1947.

It had been a bad day and the Rolling Saint was peeved. We squatted in the black dust of the Punjabi countryside beneath purple skies, our faces barely visible in the glowering light of a single gasoline lamp: 'I only wished to ask our leaders to forget all the differences of the past and live peacefully. Every day hundreds are killed in the name of religion by nefarious elements. I wish to disseminate peace,' he declared to an invisible audience, head wobbling gently.

Earlier that year Baba had a vision: he would roll from Madhya Pradesh in the heart of India up to the Wagah border and into Pakistan, right up to the door of President Pervez Musharraf's palace. Once at the Presidential gates he would present a message of peace from India. It was a journey of thousands of miles across inhospitable terrain. He would roll for twelve hours a day, across roads, jungle, stony ground, fields, towns and cities, cheered on by the Indians and then the Pakistani people. It was a beautiful dream.

Sadly, the Saint had not counted on the bureaucracy of passport control. When he set off on his great roll in January 2004 he dispatched letters to the leaders of the two countries, asking them to sort out his travel documents. Maybe it was the election in India, maybe it was the war on terror in Pakistan, but someone, somewhere, forgot. In September 2004 the Saint rolled into Wagah exhausted by the marathon; his emaciated body tumbled down the road towards the military checkpoint, enveloped in a cloud of dust and encircled by a dancing and clapping crowd of devotees. The border security police were unmoved by the religious spectacle. Backs ramrod straight and moustaches bristling, they demanded papers: passport, visa, the usual thing. All the sadhu had was the ragged robes on his back that had shimmied up his thighs during the course of the journey.

So there it ended. The Great Roll for Peace concluded

in pitiful anti-climax beneath the unrelenting gaze of a bureaucrat from immigration. In a babble of fury, the Saint's entourage got on their mobiles to the Prime Minister's Office asking for intervention. But at that very moment the new Prime Minister of India, Dr Manmohan Singh, was at the United Nations in New York shaking hands with President Musharraf, no less. Maybe Baba's prayers had been answered after all.

*

At the time, Lotan Baba's mission impossible seemed a fitting symbol of the disaster-prone peace efforts between India and Pakistan. Six decades on they remain duelling brothers in a house split down the middle.

In 1947 India celebrated its birth as the world's largest democracy. It was the moment of India's greatest victory—freedom from British rule. But it came with the greater tragedy of Partition which resulted in riots that killed more than a million and displaced millions more. The joy of freedom was tainted by the horror of sectarian slaughter and India's future was overcast with the long shadow of communal divide—the politics of the religious fanatic. For India to hold together and forge a common identity, religious tolerance had to form the heart of its political credo. This led Jawaharlal Nehru, India's first Prime Minister, to bequeath India the secular ideal. He saw it as insurance for the country's future unity, protecting it from dangerous religious cross-currents that stemmed from a turbulent history.

Secular India was born to great jubilation. But it was

handicapped by its past. India's multiple-belief system is largely the legacy of 1,000 years of invasion: first by Muslims, then by Christians. At times in recent decades that legacy has had a stronger resonance than Nehru's gift of secularism.

I moved to Delhi in December 2001, when the world was still raw from the events of 9/11. India was gripped by its own terror crisis after its Parliament was attacked by suspected Islamic terrorists. The attack was seen as an assault on Indian democracy. Back then the Indian government was led by the Hindu nationalist Bharatiya Janata Party (BJP). It blamed Pakistan for fostering Muslim insurgency in India, home to 140 million Muslims and the second largest Muslim population in the world after Indonesia. India's army was squared off on the border against Pakistan, with the standoff given terrifying piquancy by the knowledge that both sides possessed nuclear weapons. There was talk among Hindutva hardliners of a holy war to settle the score that dated back to 1947.

The region suffered the unbearable pressure of collective PNT: pre-nuclear tension; staring each other out, neither side would blink first. Aghast at the possible outcome, one by one the foreign embassies ordered their people out of India: non-essential staff at multinationals and embassies were evacuated. The foreign media hung on, pushing back our flight reservations day by day to see how the story panned out. One Reuters hack vowed she would be sitting at her desk filing the first headline when the nuclear button was pressed. These were Dr Strangelove days. The Delhi edition of one Indian newspaper even carried a whole article, with graphics, of what would happen to the city in the event of a nuclear attack. Life had taken on a surreal quality. I remember asking my landlord whether I'd qualify for a rent rebate in case of compulsory evacuation. The retired Punjabi banker dryly replied: 'The lease doesn't specify a refund in the event of *possible* nuclear war.'

Looking back, it might appear that many of us overreacted. But at the time it all seemed very close—to the point where people openly discussed what would happen if India closed its airspace when a border skirmish with Pak forces looked like escalating into a worst-case scenario. This was fundamentalism writ large on the world map: a Hindu nationalist government inspired by an ideology to create a Hindu Raj pitted against an Islamic khaki dictatorship that once patronised the Taliban. South Asia's religious tensions were no longer a domestic problem but a geopolitical one.

It took six months and US mediation for India and Pakistan to pull back from the brink. Listening to the rhetoric in India during those months, I got a sense of what Nehru's ideal was up against. The confrontation with Pakistan was so often presented as a confrontation with Islam: the BJP and its Hindu extremist allies routinely equated Pakistan with all Muslims. Pakistan was a 'terrorist state', therefore all Muslims were terrorists; Pakistan wanted the destruction of India, therefore the Indian Muslim was the traitor within. There was talk of a Hindu Bomb and an Islamic Bomb.

The Western world after 9/11 was obsessed with extreme Islam. But here in India was evidence that every major religion can be hijacked by the forces of fundamentalism.

*

Home to all the major religions, India is also, inevitably, host to virtually every type of religious fanatic. The old and the new have shaped militant movements in Hinduism, Islam, Sikhism and Christianity. A thousand-year history of invasions and colonial rule, Partition by the British and alienation of minorities within post-Independence India sowed the seeds for sectarian divide. Religious insecurity in a modern, increasingly godless world helped that divide grow. India's fundamentalists were radicalized by anger over the past and fear for the future. I decided to travel to the heartlands of these holy warriors to meet them.

My journey took me into the heart of Hindu nationalism. Waking at dawn, I watched the twilight assignations of Hindutva's saffron warriors, goosestepping into the sunrise, writhing in red dust and calling for the Motherland to strike down Pakistan. Their mission was to create a new Golden Age, a Hindu Raj.

The Hindu nationalist movement was born under the auspices of the RSS in 1925, inspired by Nazism. But the source of anger went way back. Centuries of conquest by various Islamic dynasties and then by the British, with pockets of India ruled by the French, Dutch and Portuguese, had scarred Hindu consciousness. India is dominated by the Hindu faith, yet during centuries of foreign rule its believers suffered persecution. Punitive discriminatory taxes were imposed on Hindus and land was stolen from the landowning castes, including my own Kshatriya ancestors in Goa. Temples were destroyed or defiled, brutal conversion campaigns were carried out. After 1857, in the fight for freedom from British rule, Indians of all faiths united to oust the Empire. But in the scramble for power that ensued, sectarian factionalism returned.

Partition was the price India paid for liberty. For the Hindu fundamentalist, the creation of Pakistan was yet another Muslim design to diminish Hindustan. Partition fired a desire to wrest back 'stolen' territory and recreate an imagined Hindu Raj. It spawned suspicion of the millions of Muslims who remained in India and whose loyalty to the country is perpetually on trial.

Nehru's secularism was a talisman, warding off the malevolent spectres of communalism. But by 1992, extreme Hindu nationalism—Hindutva—had captured national consciousness with the destruction of a 400-year-old mosque claimed to be built on the site of a temple to Lord Ram. The act of sacrilege, tearing down one religion for another, marked a dangerous new phase in Indian politics. It was a rallying cry, particularly among poor and dispossessed Hindus who had a new scapegoat for their problems—the minorities. Indian secularism faced its greatest challenge since Independence.

The unmasked face of Hindu fundamentalism was shown to the world in spring 2002 when the BJP state government in Gujarat appeared to be complicit in Hindu riots against Muslims in which thousands of Muslims were systematically targeted and killed. The BJP went on to campaign on anti-Muslim fervour in state elections later that year, winning a thumping victory as Muslim blood translated into Hindutva votes.

But by May 2004 the BJP's fortunes had turned when it was defeated in national elections by the Congress party which led the new coalition government. It was a major setback for Hindutva and a victory for India's secular forces. A battle ensued within the BJP between the doves and the hawks over how to regain power.

Against this backdrop, the Muslim's very presence in India has become politicized. Since Partition the Muslim community has been out-numbered by Hindus, who make up over 80 per cent of a 1.1-billion population. Yet the Muslim has been portrayed as the enemy within.

Alienation has fuelled extremism. The Indian Muslim's identity crisis is most stark in Kashmir, the only Muslim-majority state and the root of enmity with Pakistan. Named one of the world's most dangerous places and a possible cause of a nuclear war between the south Asian neighbours, peace has eluded it for six decades. The Indian Kashmiri was caught in the crossfire between the separatist terrorist and an Indian state crackdown. This blood-spattered paradise represents the ultimate alienation between secular India and its Muslim children.

A different sense of siege is evident in Darul-Uloom, Islam's second-most important religious institution that has inspired scholars and blood-curdling ideologues alike. In the Hindu heartland of Uttar Pradesh, Darul-Uloom is an island of Islam in a sea of saffron; an insular society which recognizes no influence beyond its fortress walls, where all knowledge is instilled within one book, the Koran. Theirs is an Islamic sect which calls for a return to the year zero, the year of the Prophet.

Here Muslim scholars, ambassadors of Allah who will take his Word across the world, return to the austere origins of the faith. It was this madrassa which inspired generations of Islamic scholars and leaders, influencing the thinking not just of ordinary Muslims but the Taliban and bin Laden. I first heard of it during a chat with a senior government spook in 2002. Leaning back in his leather armchair in an office in New Delhi's South Block, glasses glinting in the afternoon sun, he was unequivocal: 'Why should India tolerate this breeding ground for terrorists? Shut it down and if the Muslims don't like it, let them go to hell.' So which was it—the cradle of Islamic militancy or a misunderstood keeper of the faith?

From the bastions of the soldiers of Islam, I followed in the footsteps of Sikhism's holy warriors. The Sikhs throughout history had always been the sword arm of India. The Ninth Guru Tegh Bahadur was executed by the Mughal ruler Aurangzeb for defending the religious freedom of Kashmir's Pandits. It was this sacrifice that led his son and successor, Guru Gobind Singh, to conclude that Sikhs should defend the faith with blood as well as prayers. On an airy hilltop in 1699, the Tenth Guru formed a band of holy warriors, the Khalsa or Pure Ones, who would be charged with protecting Sikhism with words and the sword.

Centuries later, in the 1980s, Sikhism was brought onto a collision course with India as a militant messiah named Bhindranwale called for a separate Sikh nation, Khalistan. He took over the most sacred shrine of the Sikhs, the Golden Temple in Amritsar, and challenged the mighty Prime Minister Indira Gandhi to a showdown. It came in June 1984 when Indira sent her stormtroopers into the Golden Temple to flush out militants. It was a political decision that cost Indira her life.

She was gunned down by her Sikh bodyguards barely four months later at her Delhi residence. Anti-Sikh riots erupted and thousands of Sikhs were butchered across northern India. Survivors named members of the ruling Congress as leaders of the rioting mobs. The anti-Sikh atrocities ignited a new wave of Sikh fundamentalism that raged for another decade.

I ended my journey with a kind of homecoming: Goa, my home state. Today Goa is a liberal mix of Hindu, Christian, Muslim. But it was here that Christian fundamentalism began in India. In 1542 the Spanish Jesuit Francis Xavier landed on the palm-fringed shores of Goa to begin the work of ensuring that new Christian converts did not err from the righteous path. Scandalized by the open practice of other faiths, he wrote to the King of Portugal calling for the Inquisition in Goa. His request was granted and it proved to be more brutal than its dreaded counterpart in Europe.

The horrors of the Inquisition were carried out in a building called The Big House, a place of fear for locals who refused to speak of it by name. Conversion campaigns began against the Hindu population: the teacher classes of the Brahmins were driven out, Hindu marriage ceremonies prohibited, temples desecrated, unbelievers sentenced to torture and death. Today, much of this history is forgotten as Goan Catholics venerate the body of St Francis, the original soldier of Christ.

St Francis won his battle in Goa. But the war for Christ continues elsewhere in India to this day in the dense north-eastern jungles of Nagaland, where one-time head hunter tribes who converted to Christianity are fighting south Asia's longest running war for independence. Nagaland is almost 98 per cent Christian, converted by Baptist missionaries. Far from the world's gaze, a modern-day battle for Christ is waged down the barrel of a gun.

What connected all these stories was fear—fear of marginalization, fear of persecution and fear of 'the other'. Fear of Hindu hegemony has radicalized extremists within all of India's religious minorities, whether Christian, Muslim or Sikh. In turn, the Hindu nationalists have legitimized their fear by posing a basic question of identity: which comes first—faith or country? Remarkably, the Hindu right, whose original ideology took inspiration from Nazi doctrine, has succeeded in defining the political debate of the times: what it is to be Indian.

Yet India remains impossible to define, a kaleidoscope of cultures and beliefs, a country where regional identity over-rides all sense of national character. Talk to a Bengali and he will sniff that the Punjabi is a crude money-grabbing character not to be trusted. Speak to the Punjabi and he will warn you against the vain, self-serving intellectualism of the Bengali. Speak to the Delhi-wallah and he will despair of the thieves in Bihar. Speak to the man in Bihar and he will tell you the biggest crooks reside in Delhi. At times, it seems the only people the Indians hate more than the Pakistanis are their fellow countrymen. Throw into that noxious mix an explosive history of religious, caste and ethnic divides and one begins to get a picture of just how much of a miracle it is that India endures.

India's religious diversity is on the one hand its weakness, in that it has spawned the horrors of communal violence. Yet at the same time it is also the country's greatest strength, because the hope remains that India will not be straitjacketed into one religious identity, whether that is a Hindu Raj or anything else.

The answer to the challenge that India faces is, of course, greater inclusion. During my first visit to Kashmir in January 2002 when India and Pakistan were teetering on the nuclear brink, I met the editor of a local newspaper in Srinagar. Kashmir was at the height of its troubles and as we sat warming our hands around the charcoal burner, sipping saffron and cardamom tea, Mr Mohiddin posed a question he already knew the answer to. 'Why did people join the terrorists?' he asked, throwing the dregs of his glass into hissing red coals. 'The basic cause is not ideological or the jihad factor. Most went because they have nothing here. No future. No job. No hope. If they had hope, they would not go.'

For what is identity without a stake in one's country? In Kashmir, Nagaland, Assam and Punjab, insurgencies reared like monsters from the desolate landscape of economic stagnation. The terrorists were the biggest recruiters in town. Militancy was a job. With a religious ideology attached, it became a mission.

India's traditional response to the threat from religious extremists has been to protect the state at any cost, even if it means sacrificing the rights of the ordinary Indian on the altar of the nation. Human rights is a luxury that was jettisoned long ago in the perpetual war on terrorism.

But oppression is no substitute for engagement. Under Dr Manmohan Singh's Congress-led government that came to power in May 2004 there has been a shift in strategy, an effort not just to dismantle the terrorist network but to implement parallel peace talks and address the economic apartheid that exists within India. A policy of bread, not just bullets.

As a Sikh who grew up in Amritsar and who was born to a place that is now part of Pakistan, he seemed attuned to the insecurities found within sections of various religious groups. To him, economic enfranchisement is the key. It was *this* issue which ejected the BJP from the seat of power in 2004. Hindutva did not provide jobs, electricity, water and schools to enough of India. Also, whereas Hindutva leaders highlighted the differences between Indians, Dr Singh's credo embraced their commonality. His was a policy of rehabilitation into the Indian family, rather than stigmatizing certain communities as the enemy within.

But in India's increasingly fractured political and religious society, which faces the added social challenges of economic change, whether this prevails remains to be seen.

Edna Fernandes
2005

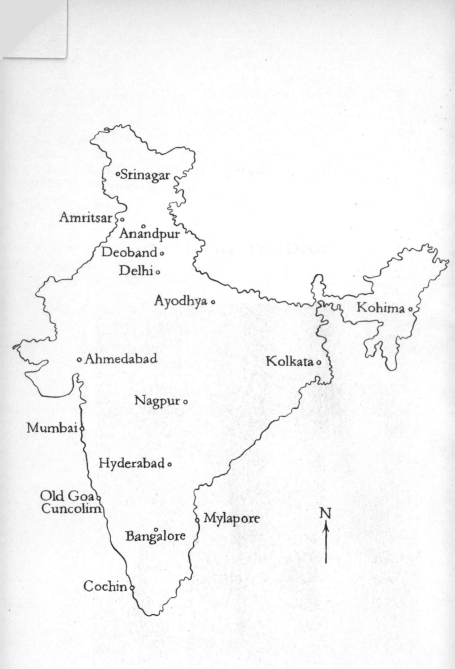

PART 1

Soldiers of Islam

The Mussalmans of Old Delhi

'Behold, the minarets of this mosque bend down to ask you where you have mislaid the pages of your history! It was but yesterday that your caravan alighted on the banks of the Jamuna...How is it that you feel afraid of living today in this Delhi, which has been nurtured by your blood?'

—Maulana Abul Kalam Azad, addressing
Muslims in the Jama Masjid in November 1947,
three months after Partition

Old Delhi, March 2005

Syed Nazar Shamsie's house is tucked within the medieval warren behind the sprawling Jama Masjid. I turned off the main square past the mosque. Screened by shop frontages and hoardings of Bollywood starlets selling cola, this is Delhi's Islamic quarter, a place where worlds collide, home to slum dwellings and the desiccated mansions of old dynasties. It is a city within a city. In these twisted lanes, tin-roofed shacks sell recycled hubcaps and mithai-wallahs peddle sesame-encrusted laddoos the size of golf balls. Fly-ridden halal butchers display chickens dangling from hooks alongside marbled shanks of mutton. The roads are too narrow for traffic, so the only transport is by tonga or cycle-rickshaw. I walked through streams of white-capped men on their way to prayer, followed closely behind by wives cloaked in black burqas that rippled in the breeze.

The entrance to Syed's house was at the end of a lane, up a steep stone staircase that opened onto a plant-filled inner courtyard. Syed, dressed in white kurta-pyjama, greeted me at the door of his room which was furnished with a large bed with silk bolsters, a sofa, two cupboards, a computer desk and an array of knick-knacks. He was in his late sixties but retained a head of thick black hair that rose stiffly from his crown. He had an aquiline face and a mouth the colour of black cherries. He offered me the sofa, and after I was seated, perched cross-legged on the edge of his bed. A servant laid out tea. Sunlight filtered through the blue shuttered doors, throwing stripes of shadow onto the floor.

The Red Fort is just a tonga-ride away from where I sat that afternoon, its vast pink sandstone walls a reminder of the Great Mughals, originally invaders who made India their home and Delhi their capital long before the British. Built by Shah Jahan, in his time the richest man on earth, the Red Fort had been a bastion of power, sanctuary from usurpers and a manicured haven in the tumult of the old city. Today it is the remnant of a vanished epoch, garlanded with gridlocked traffic and piles of stinking rubbish.

Syed's house was a typical middle-class Muslim home in the old quarter: two-storeyed, with upper-floor balconies that opened onto the enclosed garden below. From his bedroom window one could see the lane which marked the old unofficial boundary between the Muslim and Hindu communities. In the days that followed India's Partition in August 1947, mobs of Hindu extremists had surged into these streets demanding that all Muslims quit India or face death, Hindus were similarly hounded out of the newly created nation of Pakistan.

The death of an empire in India was succeeded by the birth of a new political order in south Asia: secular India and Islamic Pakistan. The dissection unleashed a torrent of hatred and led to one of the biggest and bloodiest migrations in history. Hindus and Sikhs from Pakistan and Muslims from India formed endless caravans that crossed the new border into the unknown. It was a political act that lost more than a million lives to religious violence and created millions more refugees. For the Muslims who left India, it was a devastating moment: one where identity was no longer about the place you were born in or an inherited culture, but faith in a foreign land. When Maulana Azad, the Muslim political leader, issued his clarion call from the Jama Masjid in 1947, he insisted that India remained home to Muslims and Hindus alike: 'This country is ours,' he proclaimed to those brave enough to stay. Syed was one who stayed.

Syed was not typical of the ghettoized Muslim; he had lived abroad, he came from a connected family close to the spiritual leader of the Jama Masjid, the Shahi Imam. He could afford a good education for his children, which in turn propelled them into good jobs, all outside India. One worked for the UN, another for the ILO, the third lived in the US and the fourth in Pakistan. It was something to boast about: the only way to escape the burdens of the past in India is to make it. And what better way to escape than to leap-frog India entirely, straight into the first-class carriage of the NGO global gravy train. He counted off his children's achievements on his fingers as he explained that an education was the only guarantee that they would escape the burden of being Muslim in India. 'It *used* to be a nice place,' he said, as he proffered diamond-shaped sweets decorated with beaten silver. 'I felt from the beginning that I had to educate my children well because I feared India couldn't provide a living,'

'So why did you stay?'

'I remember Maulana Azad saying, "Your ancestors migrated here, you were born here, performed ablutions before prayers in the Ganga and the Jamuna. Your culture is the same, your language is the same. If you go to Pakistan, everything will be different." He was right. Those who left for Pakistan, they have no place. They're *still* called mohajirs, "those who migrated".'

The new border was drawn up by the boundary commission and presided over by a British judge, Sir Cyril Radcliffe. As if carving up a continent-sized country on religious lines was not enough, Sir Cyril also had to complete the job within months. It was a cursed task. Whatever he did, the result would be outrage. Plagued by the feverish summer heat and dust storms, Sir Cyril completed the job and departed, vowing never to return. Syed remembered the day when the impact of Sir Cyril's work was felt on the ground. 'I was in this house at the time. My family was against the idea of Pakistan, my father, my grandfather, my uncle all decided to stay. The boundaries had been announced and from this window we could hear the crackle of gunfire. This wall behind us marks the dividing line between the Muslim and Hindu communities,' he said, pointing to the window at the back. The nondescript stone wall was an unlikely religious frontline. 'My maternal aunt was pregnant, she was killed. She hid in the house but they made a hole in the roof and shot her.'

'Who did?'

'The military people,' he said simply. 'One cousin was thirteen years old. When the mob came, her uncle shot her dead to avoid...you know.' Before 1947, the two communities in this district of Old Delhi had coexisted well enough. But as news of the killings spread, the sporadic madness became a communal contagion that consumed both sides. Families would not leave the Muslim district, fearing they may never return. At the stroke of a fountain pen, their world had shrunk to this untidy maze of streets. Yet they remained, believing Azad's exhortation that the Indian Muslim identity was alive. But for Muslims like Syed it marked a turning point, converting India's biggest religious minority into an underclass.

'We're still here. Our numbers are greater than the population of Pakistan,' said Syed. 'But look at these streets,' he gestured with an open palm to his world beyond the shutters. 'The dirt, the rubbish. Would you believe that before Partition our living conditions were better?'

Talk to older Dilli-wallahs who remember pre-Partition Old Delhi and they will smile, sigh and tell you it was so different then. There were fewer people back then Delhi was a city of 300,000 people before Independence and the old quarter was a place of well-kept historical landmarks, broad avenues lined with trees, roads thronging with tongas. There were colonies of gracious family mansions, a thriving multi-religious community and a vocal Muslim political leadership that helped to get things done. Today Old Delhi is part of a greater city of 14.5 million people, a heaving metropolis which cannot bear the burden of its population— in terms of utilities, infrastructure or wealth creation.

After Partition, many of the Hindus and Sikhs in Old Delhi left as this primarily became a Muslim neighbourhood. Muslims flocked to this corner to have safety in numbers. Like much of Delhi, its roads became clogged with traffic, its air choked with pollution, its buildings fell into disrepair. But somehow, Old Delhi, Muslim Delhi, became more polluted, more congested, more dishevelled than other parts of the city. Once, I remember asking a Sikh taxi driver to take me there and he declared: 'Road is closed'. The roads were not closed, of course, but as far as he was concerned Old Delhi was a no-go zone: a heaving Muslim ghetto of poverty, over-crowding, crumbling slums. 'Madam, I am telling you. This area is full of the Mussalman. The cab will not be safe,' he informed me with all seriousness.

The taxi-driver was right about one thing. For the Muslim in India 'the road was closed'. Government statistics on Muslim unemployment levels, education, spending power all showed a section of society that was disempowered.

So isolation gave way to alienation. And in turn, alienation led to a retreat into orthodoxy for some.

By the Nineties, there was a new political development to add to the Muslim problem of economic under-development: the rise of the Hindu nationalist Bharatiya Janata Party (BJP) as a political force in India. The BJP and its parent organizations, the Rashtriya Swayamsevak Sangh or National Volunteers (RSS) and the Vishwa Hindu Parishad or World Hindu Council (VHP), campaigned against the Babri Masjid, a sixteenth-century mosque in Ayodhya, Uttar Pradesh. It was built, they said, on the ruins of a temple to Lord Ram that marked the spot where he was born. Then in 1992 Hindu extremists tore down the mosque, erasing in hours what had survived for four centuries. It ignited communal warfare; riots erupted across the country and the act awakened a Hindu political empowerment that paved the way for BJP-led national rule by the end of the decade.

In early 2002, under a BJP state and national government, anti-Muslim riots engulfed Gujarat in which more than 2,000 people—most of whom were Muslim—were killed. The rioting continued for several days and the state machinery appeared to be complicit. It marked the high tide of Muslim marginalization in India.

Naturally, Syed viewed the BJP with suspicion. And yet, he pointed to the failure of decades of Congress rule to ease the plight of the Muslim. He didn't see politics as the answer. He was urged by people at the mosque to enter politics to lobby for change. But he was done with all that. Politics was now in the hands of thugs and thieves, he said.

'Politics is a dirty game. In the old days, respectable people joined politics. They did so in the service of the people. Men like Nehru, Gandhi, Azad. Now people pay money to enter politics. We're living in a goonda Raj.'

'So if politics isn't the answer, what is?'

'Education,' he said emphatically, forefinger extended in the air. 'We must educate ourselves out of the ghetto.'

It was the answer for exiles everywhere. After Partition, overnight, Muslims had become religious exiles in their own country. Muslim influence and power in India was a distant memory, immortalized in the crumbling ramparts of grand monuments like the Red Fort. The only way out now was a miracle, a fast-track ticket to the top, to a place where status and money relieved the burden of identity. In the West, immigrant families knew that education was the way to escape the past; that nothing succeeded like success. In India, the answer for Muslims was no different.

*

Abdul Ghafoor had not always been a dhobi. Once, he worked in a factory as a skilled worker. It was a prestigious job for an uneducated man and for an uneducated Muslim, particularly so. When the factory closed, Adbul found the options available to him were not good. In this way he became a washerman who went door to door to collect laundry, returning it a day later hand-washed, folded and pressed for the princely sum of two rupees an item. Syed was one of his customers. Abdul had just delivered a bundle of ironing and came to join us, gingerly settling himself on the bed next to the master.

Abdul was lucky: his master was progressive and took an interest in his future, unlike many others who ruled over India's infinite army of the invisible. Syed gave money every month for Abdul's son to go to school—the first in the family. This was *his* politics. Abdul looked as if he were in his seventies, although he was probably much younger, a tiny man with sharp skeletal features and a lean wiry body dressed in crumpled kurta and lungi. Invited by his master to speak, his face became animated as he stood up and rooted in his pocket for a plastic bag; inside were his most precious belongings, things he might need in times of difficulty. He extracted a folded photocopied piece of paper which he handed to Syed to read.

'It says, "Abdul Ghafoor worked as a campaigner for Indira Gandhi's Congress in the 1980s".' His name was spelled out in neat calligraphy and the certificate bore the official stamp of the party. It was twenty-five years since he campaigned for Congress and twenty years since Indira Gandhi was assassinated by her Sikh bodyguards. Little had gone right for him, yet to Abdul Indira's name remained a talisman in times of trouble. Emboldened, he invited me to his house.

It was less than a five-minute walk from that of his master—who accompanied us—but to cross the street was to cross into the ghetto, a medieval slum cluster. The lanes narrowed even further, and the upper storeys leant close enough for a person to stretch out an arm from a window and touch the opposite house. Looking up from the street, beyond the rubbish and decaying buildings, I saw a narrow strip of sky: a blue shard of hope.

Water dripped from washing drying overhead, the

blocked gutters created swirling grey-green pools of water in the walkway and the acrid stench of urine gripped the back of the throat. Abdul scuttled ahead, occasionally looking behind and beckoning with his chin for me to follow. We turned onto a road where a group of labourers were digging with a large hydraulic drill. The scream of the drill assailed the neighbourhood, but Abdul did not notice. He turned sharply into a building on the right. Next to the entrance was a small, open cupboard with a high shelf. A woman squatted in the gutter below the cupboard, slapping wet washing onto the stone floor. She was young and pretty, her head covered with a floral-patterned dupatta. On the shelf above were her three children: two toddlers and a newborn swaddled in cotton and fast asleep. The toddlers sat on the edge of the shelf, watching their mother work, kohl-rimmed eyes wide with fascination. This was Abdul's daughter-in-law. Next to where she worked was the communal toilet used by the occupants of the entire building. At the end of the corridor was a room, home to another family of eight or so people. Abdul lived upstairs. The staircase was steep, with walls that were damp and cold despite the heat.

The room at the top, ten feet by eight, was where Abdul's family lived, ate, worked and slept. At one end was a cooking area with pans and utensils. To the side was a table with a large flat iron and great tied-up bundles of washing. Abdul's wife was tying up one of the bundles when we walked in. He introduced me to her, a tiny woman with a gentle face and wrestler-like arms from decades of graft. Abdul set two plastic chairs for Syed and me in the middle of the floor. Outside, the screech of the drill was deafening so he closed the shutters. Not that it made a difference.

In this single room Abdul and his wife had raised nine

children. 'All married,' he said happily. He came in 1947 after being driven out of his old house which was in a Hindu area. I asked whether he had problems. 'He says he has many problems,' Syed translated with an air of weariness. 'He says a middle-class person cannot afford the expenses of heavy taxes. He thinks he's middle-class, you see,' added Syed with wry amusement. 'He says the position of Muslims in other countries is better. In other countries he thinks people get bottled water for free. He asks if this is so in London.'

'It's expensive—even for Hindus and Christians,' I said.

'*Accha*?' said Abdul, genuinely surprised. His wife stood by his side, eyes lowered and hands clasped as she listened. She was the breadwinner, he said, and had been for decades, washing and ironing people's clothes, as he himself struggled to find regular employment. 'Even if she works morning until night, it's not enough for this,' he said, gesturing with his hand to his mouth. 'But still she raised nine children.'

'You've done a good job,' said Syed. The old man puffed up with pride, grinning and placing his palm on his heart in a gesture of appreciation.

'It can't have been easy,' I suggested.

'I went to the recruitment centre for the armed forces. I introduced myself as Ghafoor. They said to me, "No Muslims allowed. Call yourself Ghafoor Singh and we will give you a job." I left.' He shrugged. The memory stung; behind the resignation was a lifetime of denial that had marked him, corroding the meaning of Maulana Azad's noble words about the place of the Muslim in the heart of the new India.

'Abdul, it's been almost sixty years since Independence.'

'*Haan ji*.'

'Has India taken care of its Muslims?'

'No. Still we have no work. Still the mosques are

broken. The BJP supporters come into our areas, they leave the mandir and break our mosques. They threaten to kill us if we stop them. The Hindus tell us, "*Chup*. Shut up. Do not speak anymore".' He placed his finger to his lips. He spoke of the killing of Muslims in Gujarat in a voice that was barely a whisper. The unthinkable had happened and the message to him was inescapable. 'We are silenced. This is Hindu Raj. There is no voice for the Mussalman. Maybe, I'm thinking, if the BJP comes back to power they'll finish the job and do this to Muslims here as well,' he said. The drilling stopped, leaving silence humming in our ears. 'I have seen a lot,' Abdul said softly, referring to nothing in particular. 'I believe it *can* happen.'

*

Partition was meant to be the solution. Instead, it became the problem.

When India was carved up, the Muslim majority areas of Punjab and Bengal and the North-Western Frontier Province went to Pakistan. But Kashmir did not. It remained in India's hands. Muhammad Ali Jinnah, head of the Muslim League and the man whose iron will secured the Islamic homeland he would one day lead, described the settlement as 'a moth-eaten Pakistan'. Without Kashmir, the new nation was incomplete, and so it remained the unfinished business of Partition. Equally, for India Kashmir gave substance to its multi religious identity. Without Muslim majority Kashmir, what would a secular India really mean?

Pakistan's creation was meant to address the fear that the Muslim could not thrive in a Hindu-majority India, secular or otherwise. For those Muslim leaders who equated independent India with the replacement of the British Raj by a Hindu Raj, a separate nation was the only way to protect their community and guarantee its future. The Muslims had gone from being conquerors to a disempowered minority; Pakistan offered the chance of self-determination. Jinnah, in fact, believed his Islamic homeland would ultimately foster an era of good relations between Muslims and India, stabilizing the volatile south Asian subcontinent. What it did, however, was the exact opposite. The assertion of Muslim identity through nationhood served only to institutionalize sectarian divide on a grand scale. Division along religious lines and the tragic tug-of-war over Kashmir would haunt these estranged brother nations over the decades, resulting in three full-scale wars.

As a consequence, Muslims in India became a target of religious prejudice and violence over the years, painted as the infiltrators in the heart of the nation by Hindu fundamentalists who wished to create a Hindu Raj. For them, the Muslim presence was a hangover from the colonialist past, a reminder that India was once governed for centuries by Muslim rulers who had forcibly converted Hindus and destroyed their temples.

The cost of identity was high for all sides in 1947. But the heaviest price of all was paid by the Muslims who decided to stay in India. Theirs was a conflicting identity, with the question often posed: which comes first—faith or country? With Pakistan's inception, they lost their leadership and swathes of the community, leaving them politically vulnerable and weakened in number. From the Partition riots of 1947 to the Gujarat riots of 2002, the Muslim was not just economically and politically marginalized, but periodically hunted within his own country.

A 2003 news report in *Time* magazine laid bare the great Indian divide and pointed out that in communal riots since 1947 official police records showed three quarters of those who lost lives and property were Muslim. The pattern was the same over the decades, from the Partition riots themselves, through to 1992 in the aftermath of the destruction of the Babri Masjid through to Gujarat's riots in 2002. Although, in Gujarat, the percentage of Muslim victims was a staggering 85 per cent of those affected. Most of these post-1947 anti-Muslim riots took place in the north, which is traditionally seen as a Hindu stronghold and where the Hindu nationalists are most influential. These riots do not even take into account the plight of Muslims in Jammu and Kashmir.

Mr B. Raman, a retired Additional Secretary in India's Cabinet Secretariat gave a speech in October 2004, quoted by the South Asia Analysis Group, which noted that in the first three decades after Independence anti-Muslim violence was led by Hindu refugees exiled from Pakistan. These people were embittered and traumatized by Partition. They lost everything and took it out on India's Muslims. But Raman noted that the anti Muslim violence of the last two decades has been carried out often by people born well after 1947, with no memory or experience of the anguish of those days. Yet they still hate Muslims.

The result has been a sense of siege which manifested itself in different ways—from the alienation of ordinary men like Abdul to the fanaticism of Kashmir's hooded militants.

This sense of siege was most palpable when I visited Darul-Uloom, Deoband, the venerable madrassa in the northern state of Uttar Pradesh which represents spiritual inspiration not just for Indian Muslims but believers from around the world, including Osama bin Laden and the Taliban. Fearing the polluting effects of modern life and rival religions, Darul-Uloom has detached itself from Indian society and modern life, turning inwards and languishing in orthodoxy. This island of Islam gains sustenance not from

Mother India but from the ulema within and beyond national boundaries. Like terrorism-afflicted Kashmir, it has become a kind of shorthand for fear of the Muslim in India. Yet, both Kashmir and Deoband remain equally apt shorthand for what happens to a community left to rot.

2

Audience with the Imam

'After ruling India for 900 years, Muslims today live like slaves. The reason is that the community has been delivered slow poison.'

—Syed Ahmed Bukhari in a *rediff.com* interview in November 2000, shortly after taking over as the Shahi Imam of the Jama Masjid

Days after my meeting with Syed and Abdul, I returned to Old Delhi for an interview with the Shahi Imam of the Jama Masjid, Syed Ahmed Bukhari, the spiritual leader of India's 140 million Muslims and as such a powerful voice. This firebrand preacher had once called for Muslims to form their own band of holy warriors to combat militant Hindus. His language could be intemperate at best, inflammatory at worst: he once stated that the September 11 attack on the US was not a matter for regret.

The Shahi Imam has been courted by politicians of all hues, including the former BJP Prime Minister Atal Behari Vajpayee, who believe he can sway the Indian Muslim vote. The Muslims are still a big enough vote bank to make or break tottering coalitions. At the last election in 2004, the Shahi Imam broke ranks with the traditional ally of India's

Muslims, the Congress, to urge his followers to consider the BJP. It seemed a bizarre move for a man who had condemned the 2002 Gujarat violence against Muslims as 'genocide'— after all, the BJP state government had been accused of orchestrating the terror. But the Shahi Imam's point was the position of Muslims had become so dire, the community needed to demonstrate it had no loyalties to any party. He signalled that the Congress could no longer take the Muslim vote for granted at times of election, only to break promises later. Here was a holy man whose cynicism matched that of the politician.

He had recently warned that after almost sixty years of marginalization the Muslim faced a crisis point. Failure to lift the Indian Muslim from the ghetto of poverty and alienation risked inflaming fundamentalism. The price of failure would be that Muslim anger would no longer be confined in the valleys of Kashmir but sweep into the heartland of India. It was a sobering prophecy. I arranged for an audience with the Shahi Imam. Four o'clock at his residence in the shadow of the Jama Masjid.

*

'More than fifty years have passed since India won its freedom. Muslims wanted freedom. Freedom from tyranny, freedom from oppression, freedom from poverty. They had a dream. After the fight, they wanted the new sunrise. When the first government was formed, they thought it was *their* government. But they didn't realize that one government after another would enslave them. The Indian Muslim has gone from one slavery to another.' After he finished speaking, the Imam cleared his throat with delicacy, pressing a white handkerchief to his lips. 'Let us take tea.'

The Shahi Imam's residence is behind black-painted

steel gates next to the rear entrance to the Jama Masjid. Here, sitting on the sofa in the official drawing room where he receives dignitaries and guests, he spoke with the same rhetorical fire that can be heard from the pulpit at Friday prayers. He is a striking man, a grizzled old lion. He sports a full beard and his head is almost always covered with a brown topi, as it was during my interview with him. His penetrating black eyes gazed with unflinching intensity from behind gold-framed Ray Ban-style glasses. He was dressed in freshly laundered kurta-pyjama made of finely woven white cotton and an unbuttoned black waistcoat. I sat next to him on the sofa, with his brother Syed Tariq Bukhari and the interpreter on adjacent armchairs.

The table in front was laid with meat patties, sweets and tea. It was a grand room, simply yet expensively furnished. A large Persian carpet covered the marble floor and the wall opposite was adorned with a hand-woven hanging depicting Mecca.

An instinctive leader, he combined spiritual zeal and political guile with an oratorial showmanship that played to audiences beyond the mosque and to the Muslim street. I asked whether India had served its Muslim people well since Independence. He answered as if addressing the masses, staring ahead, voice rising and falling in tremulous melody, right hand occasionally punctuating his point with a finger raised to the skies. It was less an answer, more a denunciation.

'In these fifty years the Muslim has been denied justice, employment, education, security. Instead, what has been meted out to him has no parallel in world history,' he said. 'Since Independence we've been oppressed in every nook and corner of the country. If ever we are able to show you our hearts, you will see the wounds—wounds inflicted in this country where religious freedom is enshrined in our Constitution.'

Like a high-performance racing car that had performed nought to sixty miles per hour in seconds, he slipped down into neutral with barely discernable ease and turned his head just a fraction to face me directly for the first time since we had exchanged greetings. The glint of defiance in his eyes softened and there was the hint of a smile as he gestured to the table in front of us, playing the host: 'But Madam Edna, you're not eating. Take something. We brought it especially for you. Do you wish to have ketchup?' I was not hungry, but to please them, I embarked upon a mutton patty the size of a doorstop, continuing the rest of the interview with my mouth ringed with grease like some peasant from the Russian revolution gorging on the spoils of victory. The Imam and his men did not touch so much as a crumb.

The Shahi Imam believed the Muslim had been bamboozled for too long. Almost sixty years had yielded nothing for Muslims: their economic plight had deteriorated and their political influence evaporated. Theirs was now the politics of the victim. Not a pleasant position to be in. Even so, the Hindutva hardliners believed the Muslim had it too good. They accused successive governments of giving too many sops, and claimed Muslim breeding was out of control, hinting that if this was left unchecked India would be swamped by the green tide of Islam. The reality is Muslims in India are at the bottom of the heap according to many key indicators of wealth and literacy, and their population growth rate is actually slowing, not accelerating.

This is borne out by figures produced by the Indian government itself. The 2001 census figures painted a picture which appeared to back the Shahi Imam's commentary. Muslims account for 13.4 per cent of the Indian population of 1.1 billion, and constitute the second largest religious grouping after Hindus who make up 80.5 per cent of the population. Adjusted data showed the Muslim growth rate declined to 29.3 per cent during 1991-2001, down from a growth rate of 32.9 per cent in the preceding decade. Literacy for Muslims was below the national average of 64.8 per cent of the total population in India of seven years and above. Christian literacy was 80.3 per cent, Buddhists rated 72.7 per cent, Hindu and Sikhs 65.1 per cent. Muslims were 59.1 per cent on average, with pockets of Muslim population in areas like J&K, Assam and Bihar falling below 50 per cent.

On employment, Muslims had the lowest percentage of workers within the population. The average percentage of workers to population across all religions was 39.1 per cent. For Hindus it was 40.4 per cent, for Christians it was 39.7 per cent and for Sikhs 37.7 per cent. Muslim workers accounted for 31.3 per cent. Their purchasing power was also lower than other religious groups. The National Sample Survey Organization published a report, 'Employment and Unemployment Among Religious Groups in India'. A *Rediff* news report in September 2002 said the report showed Muslims demonstrated lower levels of consumption or spending on food, clothing and entertainment compared to Hindus. In rural areas, almost 30 per cent of Muslims spent less than 300 rupees a month compared to 26 per cent of Hindus. In cities, where one third of Muslims live, the figure was far worse, with 40 per cent of Muslims spending less than 300 rupees per month compared to 22 per cent of Hindus. On land ownership—a big issue in a country where six in ten earn their living from the land—51 per cent of Muslims had no or very little land to cultivate compared to 40 per cent of Hindus. In cities, 27 per cent of Muslim households had a member with a regular salaried job, compared to 43 per cent of Hindu households.

India had its share of successful Muslims, from President

Abdul Kalam to movie megastar Shah Rukh Khan. But they are the exception, not the rule. Behind every successful Muslim, there is a faceless sea of failure.

The Shahi Imam believed the root cause was the Muslim community's inability to exercise its political muscle. As far as the Imam was concerned, there were no angels in politics, so it was a case of making a pact with whichever devil served the Muslim best. 'Vajpayee said he wanted the Muslim to come close to the BJP. Given the philosophy of forgiveness in Islam, if the enemy of yesterday extends the hand of friendship, we're duty-bound to accept,' he said.

'But this is like the man who has sinned all his life without conscience, only to discover penitence on the day of Judgement.'

'I agree with you,' he laughed. 'But I invite you to scrutinize the record of the Congress. It has also sinned against the Muslim. Since Independence, these parties have used the Muslim community. Muslim ministers are paraded like showboys in the name of so-called secularism. But what role have these parties played in our economic uplift? If a Muslim is made President of India, what benefit is there to the Muslim on the street?'

'So why have the Muslims supported these parties for so long, rather than establish their own party?' I asked.

He fixed me with a long stare and snorted. 'I addressed a conference in 2000. I said there's no way for the Muslim to form a political force in this country without a political party of its own. Almost every community and caste has its political party, only the Muslims don't. Ten years ago it would not have been viable. Now I'm travelling across the country to make this happen.'

Having a political voice was the first step. Tackling Muslim unemployment was the next. In a country like India it was a short road between disenchanted youth and religious fundamentalism. 'Within twenty years these problems will lead to terrorist movements on a large scale within India,' he warned. 'This is detrimental to the country and the world. So the responsibility begins here. If as a reaction to this disenchantment, to this angst, extreme action is taken, it will be the ones who discriminate who'll be to blame.'

In the Eighties the Shahi Imam had called for Muslims to form militant squads to combat the rise of Hindu militants. He had called it 'self-defence'. Yet, despite espousing violent means of self-defence and issuing apocalyptic warnings of mass Muslim terrorism in India, the Shahi Imam has played an unlikely role as peacemaker. Just as it took a Hindu nationalist, Prime Minister Vajpayee, to gamble on peace with Pakistan during his premiership, it took a hawkish Muslim religious leader to talk peace with terrorist group leaders in Kashmir. When peace efforts in Kashmir were still nascent, the Imam said he opened talks with Hizbul Mujahuddin leaders about a ceasefire. He did it because he believed that improved Indo-Pak relations over Kashmir would translate into improved Hindu-Muslim relations.

The concept of people-to-people diplomacy is the crux of the ongoing peace process in Kashmir. Where political grandstanding failed in the past, a series of modest confidence-building measures and establishment of mutual dependency is proving more successful. The building blocks of peace are future trade cooperation, softer borders through bus links between Indian and Pakistan-controlled Kashmir, exchange of visits by media and intellectuals and so on. Upon these small things it is hoped the prize of a lasting Indo-Pak détente can be built. But the destiny of Kashmir itself remains a stalemated chess game of diplomacy and the Imam sees no end in sight.

'It's not possible for the President of Pakistan to give

away Kashmir,' he said. 'It's not possible for the Indian Prime Minister to accept division of Kashmir. This would be another Partition which India cannot accept after the bitter experience of the past.'

I asked how long it could take to find a solution, and this elicited another snort of cynicism as he considered his answer, palms pressed flat against his thighs. 'It's not possible to find a solution in one year or five. Especially when the cards are in someone else's hands.'

'Whose hands?'

'You can understand *that*,' he smiled, leaving me to infer that he spoke of Pakistan's intelligence agencies, the hidden puppeteers in Kashmir's deadly display of violence.

The time for evening prayer was approaching. Outside, the sun was setting. Crowds would be migrating towards the masjid, its sandstone domes a burnished red in the evening light. As he plucked fluff from the corner of his kurta, the Imam checked his watch with his mind turning towards the duties ahead. 'Which will come first?' I asked in conclusion. 'A Muslim Prime Minister in India or peace in Kashmir?' The Imam appreciated the joke, head wobbling as he smiled widely, showing neat little teeth. There was no answer to that one. 'Our priority is peace. If there's peace we can think with an open mind. If no peace, it makes no difference if a Muslim is PM or not.' He paused and turned to look me directly in the eye, placing a hand on the tape recorder which was still running. 'You know, we have been *framed*,' he said, in all seriousness. 'The international community has placed the Muslim inside the frame of terrorism. This has to end.'

3

Kashmir: Paradise Lost

'If there is Paradise anywhere on earth, it is here, it is here, it is here.'
—Mughal Emperor Jehangir on Kashmir

Srinagar, October 2004

Detective Inspector General X was feeling rather pleased with himself. The situation, that is the policing situation in his area of Kashmir, was under control. We sat in his office at police headquarters in Srinagar. He was in an expansive mood, and leaned back in his chair, stomach swelling like a Zeppelin beneath his khaki uniform festooned with medals that went with a tour of duty in India's most problematic state. The DIG was still in his early forties, with a bushy black moustache and thinning hair carefully greased back. He looked like a man who had risen through the ranks the hard way, promoted for knowing how to fight a dirty war.

'The police have now totally become part of the military. If you're a Kashmiri on the roadside you feel afraid of the military, not the militant,' he said with pride. 'When the terrorists came in 1989, we had no support infrastructure and the militant was master. Now the psyche on the street is one of fear.'

DIG X had the weapons and the money to defend the Kashmir Valley and surrounding regions from Islamic militants waging a holy war of secession. He bent to pick up an attaché case by the side of his desk. Putting the case on the desk before him, he placed his palms on the smooth leather and leaned towards me.

'Do you know what's inside?' he asked.

'What?'

'Money.'

The briefcase, he said, was stuffed with cash. Crisp five-hundred and one-hundred rupee notes.

'There's a militant economy. Foreign aid, from Pakistan and others, comes into Kashmir to finance jihad. There's further generation of black money through terrorist extortion and looting. We need to fight back.' He paused for effect.

'This,' he said, tapping the briefcase, 'is for payment. Rewards. Bounty on the head of the terrorist.'

Every month the police force in Kashmir received a slush fund to finance its espionage campaign to find out information about militants. An army of informers across Kashmir was paid from his briefcase for details that would lead to the capture or death of the Muslim terrorist suspect.

'How do you hand out the money, how much does each informant get?'

His face broke into a flashing smile, delighted to have an opportunity to explain his importance in India's war against terror.

'I look at the quality of the information. The amount can be different each time. For example, three to four lakh will be given for information that leads to an encounter with a terrorist.'

Four hundred thousand rupees or six thousand pounds for information that would lead to the killing of a terrorist suspect—an operation otherwise known by the friendly term 'encounter'. The Indian police in Kashmir were renowned for faked 'encounters'. Sometimes, clashes with locals could end in a shooting that was subsequently described as an 'encounter', thereby avoiding any tricky questions. In India's war on terror, a dead terrorist suspect often meant a reward not just for the informant but the officer. It was a useful source of income, a kind of police bonus scheme.

'Are we talking real encounters or fake ones?'

He burst into manic laughter as if I'd told a cracking good joke.

'No, no. For this kind of money, it has to be a *real* one.'

India and Pakistan were going through one of their periodic phases of détente. War-war had been replaced by jaw-jaw and for the moment things seemed better. But they could get worse anytime, almost without warning, as they had several times in the past. The latest phase of the troubles had begun in 1989 when Islamic militancy erupted in Indian Kashmir. A terror campaign began to drive the minority Hindu community, high-caste Brahmins known as the Kashmiri Pandits, from their ancestral land. The purpose was to cleanse the state of non-Muslims. Those Muslims who lived peacefully with their Hindu neighbours for generations suddenly found their local communities broken apart.

They were to start a new phase of living beneath the barrel of a gun. Who were these original jehadis? Some security experts said they were sent from the old enemy Pakistan that never relinquished its ambition to wrest the Muslim-dominated province from India's grasp and ran terrorist training camps along the border in Kashmir. Others said the militant gunmen were veterans of the Afghan War in the Eighties. Having vanquished one superpower— Russia—in alliance with the United States, these soldiers of Islam were redeployed. With India's old strategic ally Russia licking the wounds of defeat inflicted in Afghanistan, Kashmir had provided a new holy war. By 2004, fifteen years since the Kashmir insurgency began, between 40,000 and 100,000 people had been killed, depending on which estimates you believed. But ordinary Kashmiris said the figure was much higher, based on their anecdotal evidence.

In the early years, the outside agitators found fertile recruiting ground in Kashmir's Valley, converting local Muslims to a cause for an independent Kashmir. The 'outside forces' had ulterior motives, seeking to create an Islamic Kashmir territory under the control of Pakistan. But speak to almost any ordinary Kashmiri, ask them, 'What do you want?' And they still say 'Azadi'. Freedom. Freedom from what? 'Freedom from Indian security forces. Freedom from terrorists.' Kashmir for Kashmiris. Did this mean autonomy? In a perfect world, maybe. But this world is not perfect. For now, a job, a home, security would be enough to bring happiness.

At the height of the troubles during the early Nineties, there were at least 20,000 Islamic militants in Kashmir, according to another senior source who asked not to be named. Some of these jehadis were trained in the same terrorist camps as Al Qaeda, according to Indian security officials in Delhi. They were part of an extended Muslim brotherhood of terror that shared tactics and then fanned out across the world to wreak retribution. Some ended up in Kashmir. Now the figure was estimated at around 5,000. The number of sympathizers was not specified. For fifteen years, Kashmir had been a war zone: summary executions by terrorists, bomb attacks, sieges, extortion, rape. The list of tyranny was long. But this was just one of the ordinary Kashmiri's enemies. On the other side of the battle lines was the Indian State. In its fight against Islamic jihad in Kashmir, there had been what the army chiefs described as 'collateral damage' to civilians. Disappearances. Thousands of Kashmiri boys and men between the ages of fourteen and seventy had disappeared into police custody for questioning, never to return.

Caught in the crossfire, a land once worthy of a king's poetry had been turned into a blood-spattered paradise.

I asked the DIG whether the peace talks with Pakistan had improved things on the ground. Had the infiltration of militants across the Line of Control, the de-facto Indo-Pak border, really slowed?

'Infiltration has improved over the last year,' he said, indicating it was now lower. 'It's been noticeable. You don't count the heads of militants, but the level of militancy. And that's improved. I believe there're three stages of militancy. The first is commitment, which we saw in 1989. The second is craziness which happened between 1990 and 1995. The third is criminality of militancy: extortion, rape, etc. It's in that final stage that the ordinary people begin to say "no". We're now in the final stage. Locally-bred militancy is declining. So now what we face is the danger of the foreign insurgent.'

His boss told me later in the day that despite the fall in the number of terrorists infiltrating across the LoC, many Islamic militants remained dormant within the state, waiting to be 'reactivated by remote control' across the border if peace failed. So India had to keep fighting a parallel war: one against the Islamic terrorist and another for the hearts and minds of the civilian. The result was an alienated Kashmiri Muslim who no longer felt like a citizen of India, but a victim.

'Can development make a difference?' I asked.

'What's development? It's a promise to the youth of Kashmir. What do they have now? No jobs, no electricity, no roads. This is all an argument for militancy.'

'The government finally appears to be serious about this,' I said. By pumping thousands of crores of rupees into Kashmir it hoped to ease the pain, erase the desire for independence.

'Correct. You divert attention. If a small kid weeps for something he does not have, what do you do? You provide him with a toffee to stop his tears.'

So this was paradise.

*

The trouble with paradise is that it will always be worth fighting for. Kashmir has stolen the hearts of kings and rulers down the ages. The Mughal Emperor Jehangir spoke of Kashmir as if describing the love of his life: 'The buds of hearts break into flower from beholding it,' he sighed. On his deathbed, when he was asked his dying wish, he replied: 'Only Kashmir'.

Centuries later, Jehangir's desires echoed in the heart of Jawaharlal Nehru. India's first Prime Minister came from a distinguished line of Kashmiri Pandits, so when India was partitioned in 1947, he vowed to hold on to his ancestral homeland. Also, Kashmir became a symbol of secular India. It was India's only Muslim-majority state. Its loss could trigger the unravelling of the country itself if other territories sought secession on the grounds of religion.

Meanwhile, in Pakistan too, everyone from Jinnah to the generals wanted 'only Kashmir'. In 1947 at the time of Partition, Pakistan sent in tribal gunmen to wrest a small portion of Kashmir which still remains in its control. Pakistanis call it Azad (Free) Kashmir; to the Indians it is Pakistan-Occupied Kashmir (POK).

Apart from Kashmir's strategic and political significance, there is, of course, its commanding beauty. Hindu, Muslim, native or foreigner, everyone who sees it is captivated and compelled to return. Jagged blue peaks of the Himalayas melt into the green valleys below. In winter the mountains are frosted with snowfalls that seal Kashmir in an icy casket that does not open until the arrival of spring. In spring and summer, the valleys are carpeted with waist-high meadows of wild flowers and the landscape is tinged with the purple haze of the crocus whose stamen is sold as saffron, a commodity more precious per ounce than gold. In autumn, orchards are laden with apricots, plums and tiny apples the size of cherries with a taste of sour and sweet. The flame-red leaves of the chinar tree set the horizon ablaze in the afternoon. Weeping willows, nodding in the breeze like sleepy old gentlemen, line the banks of still lakes that mirror the mountains.

Flicking through the pages of history, one thing is clear: Kashmiris have always paid a price for their paradise. Protected by the Himalayas to the north and providing the gateway to a continent of abundance in the south, Kashmir has been coveted and conquered routinely through the ages.

Apart from brief periods of invasion, a succession of Hindu Kashmiri kings ruled through to the early part of the fourteenth century. This was a rare time of rule when Hinduism was in the ascendancy, despite the growing popularity of Buddhism. Some great Hindu temples dated from this era and Kashmiri Hindus liked to boast they were built by a race of gods, such was their size and splendour.

Clan warfare and the discriminatory practices adopted by the Brahmins towards the lower castes disrupted the rule of Hindu Kashmiris in the final century of the first millennium. By 1305 AD, in the reign of King Simha Deva, Kashmir had become a country of gamblers, drunks and sexual hedonists. A Himalayan Ibiza. Decadance and elitism set the scene for invasion, and in 1322 AD the Tartar invader Zulzu attacked Srinagar. Its people were either enslaved or massacred. When famine forced Zulzu to leave, he took 50,000 Brahmins with him as slaves. But as he retreated through the perilous mountain passes, a snowstorm struck and his troops and captives perished in the bitter blizzard.

The Tartar attack was shortly followed by the reign of Muslim kings who ruled for five hundred years. It was during this period that Hindus came under oppression: their culture was attacked and people forced to convert, changing the religious balance of Kashmir forever. After half a millennium of Muslim rule, 80 per cent of the Kashmiri population would believe in Islam. Quite a number converted voluntarily, to escape centuries of oppression by the upper castes and won over by the egalitarian tenets of Sufi Islam. Others, especially the Brahmins, were converted by force.

One of the most famous and brutal of Kashmir's invader kings was Sikander the Iconoclast, who reigned from 1394 to 1416 AD, living up to his name by smashing temples and butchering Hindus. On the attitude of Mughal rulers, historians have differing views. While some maintain that the early Mughals, particularly Akbar, were tolerant and enlightened rulers, others dispute this. The greatest ambivalence is about Aurangzeb, who came to power in 1653. A fiercely religious man, austere and distant, he is widely believed to have been a fanatic. Some texts record that during his reign, those Kashmiri Hindus who refused to convert to Islam were tied in sacks and thrown into Dal Lake to drown like kittens.

In 1750, the Afghans swept in to capture the Himalayan kingdom. It was said that they cut off heads with the abandon of a child plucking flowers from a stem. It was of little consequence to them that the majority of those they killed were fellow Muslims. In their desperation, the

Kashmiris turned to neighbouring Punjab for help and asked the Sikh ruler Ranjit Singh, known as 'the Lion of the Punjab', to save them. In 1819, accompanied by Raja Gulab Singh, the Dogra ruler of Jammu, his forces galloped in to defeat the Afghans, ending half a millennium of Muslim rule.

The Sikhs viewed the kingdom as strictly business and the Kashmiris were little more than entrants in the profit-and-loss account of their mercenary new rulers. 'The Sikhs seem to look upon the Kashmirians as little better than cattle,' reported the British explorer William Moorecroft, who visited the Kashmir Valley as Pathan rule came to an end. And like different grades of cattle, the Kashmiris had different prices on their heads. 'Murder of a native by a Sikh is punished by fine to the government of from sixteen to twenty rupees, of which four rupees are paid to the family of the deceased if a Hindu; and two rupees if he was a Mohommeden.'

In 1846, Kashmir was ceded to the British army by the Sikhs via the Treaty of Amritsar and the British later sold vast tracts of the Himalayan territory to Gulab Singh who had been a loyal supporter in key battles. With this deal, history had turned full circle and Kashmir was now back in the hands of a Hindu dynasty, the Dogras. But by now Hindus were a minority community.

Kashmir was sold for what now seems a give-away sum of seventy-five lakh rupees, or less than one year's revenue, plus an annual stipend of one horse, twelve goats and three Kashmiri shawls. It was the bargain of a millennium: while the Tartars, Mughals and Afghans had paid for Kashmir in blood, the canny Gulab Singh bought paradise with hard cash, pashmina and a gaggle of goats.

Under the Dogras, it was the turn of the Muslims to suffer persecution and neglect. Dogra rule was never popular, though it continued right up to the Partition of India, when Raja Hari Singh, desperate for help to repel an attack by Muslim tribal invaders, signed the treaty of accession to India. It is a treaty that many Kashmiris today do not accept as legitimate.

Nor does Pakistan. Jammu and Kashmir (J&K), India's northernmost state, has been the source of almost six decades of enmity between the two countries. Since 1989, the movement for self-determination within Indian Kashmir and Pakistan's proxy war against India in the state have overlapped, and paradise has been brought almost to ruin.

*

Since childhood I had dreamed of staying on a houseboat on Dal Lake. Before the insurgency began, the houseboats were the backbone of Kashmir's tourism industry—the state's main source of revenue alongside agriculture. These were no ordinary boats. Moored on the shores of one of the most beautiful lakes in the world, with views of the Himalayas, these were floating pieces of heaven. Writers, tourists, artists, actors, retired businessmen would hire these boats for weeks and months on end, forsaking the outside world to live the feckless life of a lotus-eater. In October 2004 I realized my dream. While I'd stayed in Kashmir before on work, it had always been at hotels reserved for journalists where a telephone link was vital for filing copy under deadline. This time I was coming to drink saffron tea, eat salty meatballs and curried lotus root on one of Mr Butt's boats.

Gulam Butt's houseboat business dated back to the 1940s and his guest-list was like a roll-call of the great and the good. But the big names stopped coming once the troubles began. Since 1989 most of the guests had been international journalists coming to report on one of the world's most dangerous places. Set amid Mughal gardens, canopied by the flame-red foliage of towering, centuries-old chinars, four boats remained in use out of an original of eight. The others rotted during years of neglect caused by a collapse in business during the worst years of the terrorist insurgency. Sadly, Gulam informed me that the boat on which one of The Beatles once learned to play the sitar was now submerged.

The boats are like old-style colonial barges carved completely from wood. The floor-to-ceiling windows overlook the lake. The interiors are carpeted with the finest Kashmiri rugs, windows dressed with embroidered curtains, the carved ceilings lit by cut-glass chandeliers. Breakfast, lunch and dinner are served by a personal butler. One could spend endless days watching the vistas: kingfishers skimming the waters as kites career across purple-streaked skies; the sun rising and falling over the shimmering lake; the boatmen rowing their shikaras through the blue mist and into the canal network where farmers grow crops of spinach, turnips and marrows on small island allotments.

It was the month of Ramadan and Muslims were fasting from dawn to dusk during this period of religious abstinence. Gulam was his usual ebullient self when I arrived, full of hugs, warm words and gushing enthusiasm. He was a handsome man in his late sixties, a classy dresser who looked like his suits were tailored on Savile Row, London. In fact, his clothes were made by Mr Khan, the local tailor, who could look at a photograph of any suit and replicate the cut down to the last buttonhole. Gulam ran a tight ship and every rupee was accounted for, each employee worked to maximum productivity. During the worst years of hardship, his staff had to double up duties as butlers, cooks and gardeners to keep the business alive. Years passed during which only a handful of guests stayed. Like a Kashmiri Artful Dodger, Gulam had to duck and dive for a living as well as carefully navigate the treacherous waters of Kashmiri politics.

'There was a time when the army made a camp in these very gardens,' he said, pointing to the rose bushes and neatly tended lawns. 'Soldiers everywhere. And you know the mess they make. What could I do? I could *do* nothing. *Say* nothing. Then there were times when the militants would come looking for me. With AK47s on their shoulder they would ask to see me. They wanted money, protection money. I'd tell my staff to pretend I was in Delhi, at the market, anywhere. I'd lock the door and hide.' He covered his face with his hands, peeping through his fingers like a child. 'If the militants came and demanded food, somewhere to stay for the night, what could we do but give it to them? They'd kill us in our beds if we refused. They'd burn the boats.'

The grind of tyranny continued for more than a decade. Everyone knew someone who'd been killed in the troubles; everyone had their brush with death. Ramzana was my butler during my stay. He was a lovely man in his fifties, with grey hair, a small pencil moustache and a flashing smile. He was a man whose nerves and finances had been stretched to breaking point over the decades. He had five children and a wife to support and he had started his working life while still a child. 'I never knew the inside of a school,' he told me. The fasting during Ramadan was a strain for him and sometimes when the hunger pangs hit he would lapse into a fit of frenzied moaning, his complaints garnished with the great Kashmiri flair for high-octane drama.

During the mid-Nineties, Ramzana was kidnapped along with the son of a foreign journalist. He was acting as tracker for a group of foreigners touring the Palgargh valley. The group was cornered by a band of militants and taken to a camp. Ramzana remembers there were around forty militants at the hideout. He was set free after a short while and told to return home and pass on the message that the others had been taken hostage. Because of powerful political connections in India and Pakistan, the journalist's son was freed. But the next group of foreigners to be kidnapped was not so lucky. They were executed; one of them, a Norwegian tourist, was found beheaded in the forests of Pahalgam. To this day, Ramzana hates that valley.

During my stay I had one question in mind. It had been two years since J&K held the first transparently democratic state elections in a generation. It had been almost a year since the start of a peace process between India and Pakistan and the beginning of a dialogue over Kashmir and other bilateral issues. Pakistan's President Pervez Musharraf and the Indian Prime Minister Dr Manmohan Singh had appeared at the United Nations in September 2004 proffering the hand of peace to one another. There were hopes of a breakthrough, of improved diplomatic relations, even an end to the deadlock over Kashmir. Indian troop levels in Kashmir were cut, the Prime Minister visited the troubled state to speak of peace and development, infiltrations across the LoC were reported to be lower. But away from the political spotlight, what had changed?

The 2002 state election had proved to be a watershed moment. After generations of rigged elections in favour of the National Conference Party (NCP)—considered a puppet of the Centre and overseer of corruption and human rights abuse on a grand scale—this one brought in a coalition of the People's Democratic Party (PDP) and the Congress. Out went NCP's Farooq Abdullah, known as the 'Disco Chief

Minister' for his partying ways. In came Mufti Muhammad Sayeed of the PDP. Political observers said the result marked a turning point. Once again Kashmiris had a political voice. The elections had taken place under the scrutiny of the international community and amid unprecedented security: voting stations were patrolled by military, electronic voting machines were kept in wax-sealed iron boxes under armed guard until the count began. Tens of thousands of extra security personnel were brought in for the count, snipers nestled in the hillsides and army patrol boats buzzed up and down the lakes looking for an invisible enemy: the terrorist.

Forty-six per cent of Kashmiris voted in what was largely seen as a clean but bloody election. More than 750 people were killed in the campaign period after separatist militants vowed to derail the democratic process. When the results came in, India portrayed it as a vindication of Indian rule in the Muslim-majority state as well as a victory for the ballot box over the bullet. But amid all the media soundbites, I was struck by the words of one old man in a Srinagar flower shop. Ignoring the defiant jubilation of the youngsters, the retired furrier sucked hot chai through yellowed teeth before pronouncing: 'A black dog has gone. A brown dog has come. What will change?'

Was the old cynic right? Certain improvements seemed evident by October 2004. Kashmir was an effective war zone with heavy troop deployment—usually around 500,000 men belonging to the Border Security Force (BSF), Central Reserve Police Force (CRPF) and the local police. That was a lot of protection for a state with only 12 million people. When I first visited in January 2002, there were bunkers every hundred yards in central Srinagar and the city was dominated by the security presence. A self-imposed curfew kicked in at sunset. It was a place of fear and paranoia, where anyone could be the enemy, where any time a bomb could explode or a gunman open fire. This time, I noticed fewer bunkers, a reduced military presence and a slightly more relaxed atmosphere. It was far from normal. But things had improved somewhat. The staff at Butt's Boats said much the same.

'Things are a little better. For the first time in fifteen years we had a good summer. The boats have visitors, some Indian, some American, some British. The tourists have started to come,' said Ramzana as we went for a drive.

'Killings are less, that's for sure,' agreed Shafi, our driver. Shafi was thirty-five years old and worked as a driver and guide for visiting journalists and tourists to Srinagar. In recent years his duty comprised touring trouble rather than beauty spots. As a tour guide, he knew more than most of the foreign correspondents he escorted. In brilliant sunshine, on roads dappled with shade, we bumped along the mountain passes in Shafi's Tata 4X4, past crystal-clear streams as he pointed out landmarks of terror in a cheerful manner. The hallmarks of militancy lingered. On the way to the glacial valley Sonamarg, we passed some woodland with a small clearing. There were four or five dummies dressed in rags and stuffed with straw, strung up from branches in a row. They looked like scarecrows. But there were no crops.

'Once used by militants for target practice,' said Shafi. 'A few years ago this area was full of militants. They took over many of the houses, barns, land. The people could do nothing.'

'Where've they gone?' I asked.

'They're now mostly in hiding in areas near the LoC.'

India was in the process of fortifying the LoC, creating a kind of exclusion zone and a physical barrier to keep the militants out. This physical barrier had a major impact on terrorist infiltrations from across the border, cutting it to one tenth of the level seen in previous years. In January 2005, the Indian Chief of Army Staff, N.C. Vij, presided over a ceremony on Army Day to salute the completion of the 700 kilometres of LoC fencing in just twelve months. Indian President APJ Abdul Kalam was pictured in *The Hindu* newspaper cutting a giant Line Of Control cake depicting the barbed wire fencing, tiny little bunkers and army check points all in pretty frosted icing. But despite this barrier, some militants were still getting through in 2004.

'How do they get across the border if there's so much security?' I asked Shafi. It was of course a long and porous border. But it was also heavily patrolled and fortified.

Shafi rubbed his fingers together. 'Money. There're stories that 60,000 rupees in cash will buy one Indian jawan who will let through a militant plus one gun. *Plus* one gun. For a militant is no use without his gun. Many people are making big money from the war. Look at all the big houses being built.'

'There're two economies in Kashmir,' Ramzana added, turning his head from the front seat of the car. 'The real economy is dead. Tourism is not much. Then black economy from terrorism. Many people build houses, buy big cars. But where's the money?'

'What's changed under the new government?' I asked.

'Security is less. That's improved,' said Ramzana, referring to the reduced troop presence. It was true that one of the most popular decisions of the new government had been to remove the special security forces from the towns. These special officers had been blamed for many of the human rights abuses and harassment. Their dilution in civilian areas had reduced the climate of fear. The new state government also adopted a more flexible approach to peace talks with separatist leaders than its predecessor. More emphasis was being placed on development. But while the government could pump money into new roads, electricity and other infrastructure, it could not make people come to paradise. It could not even get the Kashmiri Pandits, who had been hounded out of the state by Islamic terrorists, to return. That was a matter of confidence.

Driving around downtown Srinagar it was clear that strangers were still very much a rarity and the deprivation of the local people was of a kind that would take generations to eradicate. It was noticeable in small things. People like Ramzana, who was lucky to have a job, could not afford new shoes even though he worked from five in the morning until nine-thirty at night, seven days a week, during the season. To survive, everyone relied on everyone else to pitch in, even in small ways. Shafi asked me if we could use the car to visit a second-hand shoe store where Ramzana might find a cheap pair of boots for winter. Shafi knew of a store where one could buy used imported trainers and walking boots. The prospect of bargain boots excited Ramzana and he was filled with the expectation of a child on a shopping excursion. The store turned out to be a hole-in-the-wall shop filled with a ramshackle display of stock. There was no light inside as there was a power cut. A group of men groped around in the dark for shoes that would fit, throwing rejects over their shoulders onto the floor. The smell of cheesy feet was overwhelming. After one hour, and some fifteen pairs of shoes later, Ramzana's air of exuberance had evaporated. The price for tatty old trainers was way beyond his budget of 600 rupees. He left disappointed as winter was only weeks away. Shafi patted his arm in consolation and promised to keep a lookout.

We visited the main mosque in the centre of town: a square wooden structure with tall minarets, painted green and decorated with intricate carvings of flowers. The facades were graced with extracts from the Koran. It was more beautiful than any mosque I'd ever seen and dated back more than six hundred years. I could only view it from the outside as women were forbidden to enter. A group of kids gathered round, curious about the stranger in their midst. As we left to walk back to the car, the kids followed. Two small girls took my hands, asking lots of questions as the rest trailed behind. I bought a bag of toffees from a grocer shop and began to hand them out. Ramzana cheerfully took over the role of éclair distributor. But the happy scene swiftly degenerated into a fracas. 'Ungrateful!' he shouted as one teenaged boy attempted to nab the whole lot. In the unseemly tug-of-war that ensued, the bag broke loose, sending silver-wrapped toffees flying into the air, attracting yet more children, a pack of stray dogs and a feral cat. Shafi looked worried and insisted we move on before his car was damaged. Sheepishly, we left the rabble behind, including a small boy sobbing by the kerbside because he had failed to secure a single toffee.

'I know a peaceful place we can go,' said Shafi, deeply unsettled by the bedlam we'd caused. We drove to the Cemetery of the Martyrs. It was one of many that dotted the city, located near some open playing fields. We passed through the gates, marked by a sign that said: 'Lest you forget, we have given our today for tomorrow of yours'. A group of boys played cricket in the adjacent field, watched over by five black crows lined up on the railings like spectators in mackintoshes, their silky heads cocked to the side as they cawed their appreciation. We sat in the sunlight amidst the hundred or so graves of Kashmir's martyrs, from the fancy marble tributes for assassinated separatist leaders to the unmarked tombstones of young militant cadres.

'Before the (2002 state) election, forty-fifty people were killed every day,' said Shafi. 'Afterwards, maybe ten a day.'

'Who's buried here?'

'Militants, victims of militants, civilians killed by army. All are *shaheed*.'

We walked from grave to grave; the tombstones were engraved in Urdu, most naked of flowers or adornment. Shafi translated the inscriptions. 'The majority of militants are under thirty. See, this one, Omar, is twenty. Abdullah is twenty-two. Here's another, Mohammed, aged twenty-seven. Syed, twenty-five.'

He read on for many minutes. It was a testament to the wasted years. In life they lived on opposite sides of the battle lines, divided by ideology, for among the dead were separatists and non-separatists, militants and non-violent civilians. These were public graveyards that included innocents who had not asked to be dragged into this war of terror. But in death they were united, all fallen brothers of Kashmir.

That night I went to visit Sadiq Ali, state secretary of the ruling People's Democratic Party. He was an elderly gentleman with courtly manners, fine aquiline features and bright blue eyes. The electricity had gone off and while we waited for the generator to kick in we sat in his living room in candlelight, eating snacks of masala chicken and laddoos with chai as he talked about the changes under his government. Like everywhere else in life, money talked.

'If Kashmir is to survive it has to survive on its own. Its own revenues are almost nil. The tax revenues here, that's total income for J&K, doesn't even take care of our wage bill. We would starve without Indian central money,' he said.

The big drive now was to revive tourism, turn Kashmir into the Switzerland of the East that it once was, and to persuade the film industry and big business to invest here. Some Bollywood producers were recently in town on a research trip for a new film. But they were scared off because the security of their stars could not be guaranteed in the state even now.

'Everyone's scared of the security scenario. The biggest consideration for the multinational corporation is peace, security, stability. We cannot guarantee that yet. Peace has moved forward. But don't expect miracles.'

'Do you believe peace can be grasped this time?'

'In ten years we may be nearer to a solution. It cannot continue this way.' He pointed out that defence devoured vast chunks of India and Pakistan's budget each year, money that was needed for health, education and infrastructure. 'These are poor countries. They cannot afford this war. But remember, there are doves and hawks on both sides. Let's not forget the main player in Pakistan is the army. And if we have peace in Kashmir would Pakistan need such an army?'

I left his house gloomier than when I arrived. Kashmir was a political, religious and military quagmire. For Pakistan it was a question of territory in the name of Islam. For India, it was a question of territory in the name of secularism. All hopes were pinned on a new dawn. But seasoned Kashmir-watchers had learned over the decades to hope for the best while preparing for the worst. As is often the case, the clearest assessment came from the men charged with providing peace and security on the ground. On the frontline there can be no illusions. When asked about prospects for peace, one of the state's most senior Muslim Kashmiri security chiefs remained sanguine. 'Confidence-building measures between Pak and India is a popular phrase right now. But what about confidence-building between Delhi and Srinagar first? After all, this is ground zero where peace must be constructed,' he told me.

A first step would be to rehabilitate the Kashmiri Muslim in the heart of the Indian nation. For decades the ordinary Kashmiri had been a suspect rather than a member of the Indian family. 'I'm the only Muslim Kashmiri in such a senior position in this state. Yet even in my position I hear prejudice from other Indians against the Kashmiri Muslim,' he said. Such prejudice assumed they were either terrorists or sympathizers. Away from the political grandstanding and warm words, he discerned a lack of clarity about the ultimate end game. As a military man, he sought a clear objective that would define the nature of the peace on the ground. In order to deliver peace any plan had to win over the local people who for too long had been bit part-players in this half-century-long tragedy.

'The Indian government has to decide one thing,' he said, leaning across the table, a chubby finger jabbing at his papers. 'Does it want Kashmir in the shape of a graveyard or a Kashmir of beauty and of people? If India decides it's a matter of territory, then it needs a military solution and Kashmir is a graveyard. If not, India must address the needs of the people. As a security man I tell you, oppression alone cannot win.'

4

Refugee

Nadimarg, Jammu, 24 March 2003

It was late. Suraj had just celebrated his third birthday and been put to bed by his mother. At 11.30 pm, just as sleep was beckoning, fifteen militants dressed in fatigue uniforms stormed into his village, Nadimarg, home to eleven Kashmiri Pandit families including Suraj and his parents. The gunmen broke down the doors, roused the families from their sleep and lined them before a firing squad.

Suraj's mother hid her child behind her. As the gunmen opened automatic fire, she was killed by the first round of bullets. Suraj's father was hit next and then Suraj was shot in the hand and foot. He died just over an hour later.

The midnight massacre left twenty-four dead and news reports of the event plunged India into shock; it was yet another blow to the dwindling Hindu community in Kashmir. Jammu remains a Hindu stronghold in Kashmir, but after the Nadimarg executions more families were deciding whether to pack up and go.

When the insurgency began in 1989, the Kashmiri Pandits were the primary target in what was a new holy war. Fly posters appeared overnight in villages across

Kashmir, warning Hindus to leave or be killed. For the Islamic militants, Kashmir was Muslim territory. The warning was heeded. The insurgency triggered an exodus of hundreds of thousands of Kashmiri Hindus who had lived in the Kashmir valley for a millennium. Fearful of the militant's bullet, a bomb or grenade being hurled into their midst, the Pandits escaped carrying what they could and left everything else behind: property, furniture, memories and a life they would never recover. Within a generation they had gone from being Kashmir's elite to India's dispossessed. Many went to Delhi to start over again and rebuild their lives. Some were successful, starting businesses from scratch and salvaging a new life from the wreckage. Others remain in refugee camps to this day, living in cardboard-partitioned hostels.

On the Sunday after the Nadimarg massacre, hundreds of Kashmiri Pandits gathered in Delhi to stage a silent protest against the killings. A crowd of 200 Pandits dressed in white, the colour of mourning, stood facing the traffic with lengths of black gauze tied around their mouths.

It was here that I met Professor Ambardar. He was a typical Kashmiri—warm, inquisitive and unable to resist a chat. Whispering through the gauze like a naughty schoolboy talking in class, he said I should pay him a visit. The following week, I looked him up. He was one of the Pandits who left Srinagar in 1989. Fifteen years on, he and his wife had a very different life in Delhi. But it was one he did not care for.

The Ambardars' home was on the first floor of an apartment complex across the Jamuna river in East Delhi. I rang the bell and the old chemistry professor opened the door. He was a tall man in his sixties, with fine features: large soulful eyes, a full fleshy mouth topped with a salt and pepper moustache and a large, rather magnificent nose which quivered with emotion. Tufts of grey hair crowned his high forehead. He wore a kurta and his feet were bare, toes splayed from decades of walking barefoot in the countryside.

The door opened directly into the living room—a fair-sized room with a carpet and table in the middle, flanked by sofas. A TV and sideboard were the only other pieces of furniture in a room that was rather Spartan, devoid of the lifetime's clutter left behind in the rush to escape.

The professor sat opposite and his wife, who had brought through some tea and plates of cashew nuts and biscuits, on a divan beside me. She was tiny, almost half his size, and looked warm and cuddly. Despite her reduced circumstances, Mrs Ambardar was still very much the Kashmiri lady, wearing the traditional earrings pierced through the cartilage above the lobe. A red string was looped through the hole and a heavy ornament of gold and gemstones was knotted at the end, pulling the string taut, so the bauble rested on the nape of her neck. Her fine silver hair was tethered into a bun. She wore a lime sari, with a cheery yellow and pink flower pattern. Her pale brown feet peeped out from the edge of the sari. I liked her eyes: a warm brown that sparked mischief. She was slightly older than her husband and joked how she'd been lucky enough to find a toy boy. They had been through a lot together and it was clear that they were still deeply in love.

With no introductions or preliminary chitchat, they launched into their story as if they had waited an eternity to tell it. The words tumbled out; husband and wife finished one another's sentences until it seemed as if only one person was speaking.

'We are genuine Kashmiris, born and brought up there,' said Mrs Ambardar, her legs swinging off the edge of the divan like a small girl's. 'We left our homeland on 22

November 1989 at 1.10 a.m. I remember exactly. We were unable to leave in the daytime. It wasn't safe in daylight.'

'That was a very dramatic night,' said her husband, in deep sonorous tones. He leant forward on the edge of his seat, cup poised mid-air as if mesmerized by the memory. 'There was no electricity, it was the dead of night and there was a huge downpour. Never had we seen such rain. That night the Gods wept: "Why are you leaving your natural place?"'

'We left everything,' said Mrs Ambardar, picking up the thread of the story. 'Sixteen people in a truck, uncles, sisters, sons, daughters, in-laws, grandchildren.'

'My uncle had two children who were mentally unsound. We had to carry them in the rain towards the truck, plead with them, convince them to get in. Then when we were about to leave, one boy broke free and hid himself, so we had to fan out and find him—in the dark, in the rain. Can you imagine?' said the professor.

His wife started to laugh, showing tiny, even teeth. Her laughter set off her husband and that in turn set me off at the thought of this desperate game of hide-and-seek in the midst of a midnight flight.

'The downpour meant we were in a mess, and we couldn't find this mentally challenged boy—Kishanji was his name. When we found him, we slowly made the drive out of town, packed into one car.

'We didn't want to make any noise to let the militants know we were going. But our Muslim neighbours knew we were leaving and we saw their faces pressed against the windows, looking through the rain. As we left under the stars, I thought we'd be back in a few months. It was a miscalculation.'

They were in their fifties when it happened. A growing sense of insecurity descended as the militants tightened their control with each passing day.

'Every day, we heard about the killings of the Pandits,' he said. 'Our vicinity was full of militant activity. Posters were stuck on temples and even on our gate, saying: "Pandits, get out or else."'

The event that triggered the decision to go had happened one night as the family sat playing rummy.

'At midnight there was a knock at the door. It was a group of four militants. They asked for my husband—by name—and all the other men of the house to come outside for a chat. We had no intention of sending our men to them, so myself and my aunt Arundhati went. She was a formidable old lady. She opened the door, stood in front of them and said, "Our men are not here. We are alone." The four militants were known to us and they asked for our men again. Arundhati said, "You have no business coming here at this time. This is not the time to talk." Can you imagine? She was seventy years old!'

Her husband continued: 'These militants asked for us by name. If we'd gone outside we would have been dead,' he said, pointing his finger like a pistol to his head.

'Those were bad days. Bad, bad, bad,' said his wife. The memory had reawakened old fears. Her voice croaked with emotion and she lifted the pallu of her sari, wiped her eyes and blew her nose.

'Now of course we tell the story and the horror lends a romantic air to the whole thing,' said the professor. 'But then we were so scared we dared not open the windows, we dared not open the door.'

The fear manifested itself in strange, sometimes comical behaviour. Gripped by paranoia, the old couple saw assassins around every corner. A simple trip to the bank became a complex affair that necessitated intricate security arrangements. The professor asked his even more elderly uncle and wife to act as bodyguards, shadowing him as he made the trip to cash cheques or withdraw money.

'In the final weeks I felt I was a marked man. Every time I went to the bank I'd ask my uncle to act as my protector, as my bodyguard, and accompany me. Can you imagine? My uncle would sit in the car and scan the horizon as I got out.' The old couple started giggling again.

'When we travelled to the bank I would place a square sheet of metal—four inches by four inches—behind my breast pocket. In case the militants shot at me. It was like the Wild West.'

Mrs Ambardar could stand it no longer. She fell back on the divan, legs in the air, and started crying, this time tears of mirth. 'I said to him: "What's the use of your metal plate? As if the militants will only shoot you there. What if they shoot you in the foot or in the head, will your metal plate save you then? Tell me."'

As tears streamed down her face, the professor protested that he may have survived a shot in the foot. A shot to the head was fatal, yes, but his chest he could have at least protected. 'It made sense. Why are you laughing?' he chided.

Mrs Ambardar laid the coffee table with lunch—rice, dal, subzi, dum aloo and water, while her husband delved into their lost world. 'It was beautiful. Every morning I'd bathe in the stream near my house and go to the temple. The water was pure and clear, the sky was blue and clear. Now I'm stuck here,' he said, mouth twisted with distaste. 'Ants and mosquitoes plague me every night. I'll be honest, I am *miserable*.'

'Musharraf sent them,' his wife piped from the kitchen. 'Musharraf sent his ground troops and air squadrons to torment us even now.'

'Now all we have is heat and dirt,' he gazed unhappily at the dust-ridden horizon. Having lost paradise, the

Ambardars had gained a concrete inferno, descending into the lower circles of hell that are Delhi's crumbling tower blocks. Worse than the physical loss was the emotional deficit of being stripped of all sense of belonging, a common history, a status in society that went back centuries. It was displacement of the worst kind: the kind that destroyed a person's roots. Driven out in the name of a religious war that was not theirs, the Kashmiri Pandits were cut adrift in an India they did not recognize nor call home. I told the professor I planned to visit Srinagar soon and for a brief moment his eyes lit up like lamps, beaming hope. 'Maybe I could come. Maybe your publisher could pay for me to come with you. I could show you the old house, the temple where I prayed, the streams. My old neighbours.'

But even as he said it we knew it wouldn't happen. Even if we did get the money, he was too frail for such a journey and his wife could not leave the apartment. There was no going back. He slipped into the bedroom and after some noisy rummaging emerged with a small pile of photos of his grandparents. They were water-damaged and frayed at the edges. The biggest photo showed his grandfather posing in his best suit, seated on a chair with the extended family gathered around him. It portrayed a handsome family that was well to do. Professor Ambardar laid the photos on the table one by one, recounting the story of each face. It was the only treasure saved from the storm fifteen years ago.

'See. There,' he pointed. 'In Kashmir, I was a professor from a line of teachers, great Pandits. I had prestige. When I got on a bus in Srinagar four people would stand up and say, "Professor, have a seat". Here, I am nobody.' His long fingers softly passed back and forth over the images as if summoning the memories off the page. 'But this has happened throughout history. That's how I console my wife. Many other people have been pushed from their homeland; the

Pandits are not the first to become refugees. So we put up with our destiny. The forces of history are like that.'

*

Not everyone had the astonishing magnanimity of the Ambardars. Other Kashmiri Pandits had been eaten up by a cancerous bitterness. They had lost paradise and been banished to a lesser life. And they could not forgive.

In Jorbagh, a plush gated colony in the tree-lined avenues of South Delhi, there is a refugee camp for displaced Pandits. It is not much known, even to the residents of Jorbagh itself. It is screened from public view down the end of a pathway. Inside a single-storey building more than sixty people live in cardboard partitioned rooms, their entire existence stacked in piles around them, like a bric-a-brac shop. The refuge reminded me of an animal compound, yet these were people crammed cheek-by-jowl into adjacents cells. Cough and your neighbour can hear it, cry and your neighbour can feel it, so close are these people. They had lived for fifteen years in these shelters; conceived, raised and married off children from within these walls. The older ones knew they would die here. They are yet more forgotten victims of Kashmir's Islamic militancy. They faced the indignity of being permanent refugees, hidden away like unwanted children from the indifferent gaze of Delhi's monied classes: these people are powerless to express their anger.

Yet there are others who do articulate their rage. The Panun Kashmir website, which is a forum for displaced Pandits, spells out their situation: 'The cruel killings by Pak-trained militants paled the barbaric and tortuous killings of Jews by Nazis into insignificance,' says one section taken from the site. 'They sprayed bullets from their AK 47s on a minority community victim to their hearts' fill. They enjoyed the torture deaths by causing cigarette burns on the naked bodies of a Pandit victim abducted from his home, office or a village. They teased him by pouring boiling wax on the soft-skinned parts of his body.'

The website details violence even more graphically than this, telling of the murder or rape and mutilation of Kashmiri women. It calls for reparation by the Indian government. The central objective is to win a homeland for the Pandits, allowing the hundreds of thousands who were driven out to return to Kashmir and have the right to live and practice their faith in the state of J&K. Yet their plight is nowhere on the political radar. As I sat chatting with them, on their beds, as they did the washing, as they cooked in this bizarre commune, I had to remind myself that not so long ago, before the troubles began, the Muslim and Hindu shared Kashmir with no need of mandates on how to be neighbours. How times have changed.

5

Messengers of God

'I am standing on the roof of the Noble House of Allah and canals are flowing from the fingers of my hands and feet and are expanding in all directions of the world.'

—Qasim al-Ulum, founder of Darul-Uloom or House of Knowledge, describing an auspicious dream which he interpreted as a message from God to establish a madrassa in Deoband, India in 1866

Peshawar, Pakistan, April 2001

It was a historic occasion. Half a million Muslims from around the world had gathered in Pakistan to pay tribute to a 150-year-old madrassa from the Indian town of Deoband. As wind and rain lashed the tented pavilions during the course of the three-day conference, hundreds of thousands of holy warriors listened to a battle cry for Muslims to rise up against Western oppression. The faithful had come from across the world: Pakistan, India, Bangladesh, Saudi Arabia, Iran, the UK, Libya and Taliban-controlled Afghanistan; Sunni and Shia Muslims in rare allegiance. Banners emblazoned with the slogan 'Death to America and the Jewish State' swayed in a testosterone-pumped maelstrom of mullahs and militants, scholars and clerics.

Darul-Uloom, the House of Knowledge, was established nine years after the 1857 Indian Mutiny or revolt when Muslims and Hindus fought against the British in the first war of independence against the British Empire. Beaten into retreat, that battle had nurtured a hatred of foreign influence and rule among Indian Muslim leaders and inspired the creation in 1866 of Darul-Uloom, which was to become a haven of purity for the Islamic faithful of the subcontinent. Located in the small rural town of Deoband in India's Uttar Pradesh, its influence spread beyond national borders to become the second-most important Islamic academic institution in the world after Cairo's al-Azhar.

Darul-Uloom was more than a school. It was a school of thought, a global movement based on Sunni Islam which believed in a return to the austerity of sharia law, rejected the modes of modernity or Western influence and preached a true Islamic society that could be found in the Koran and the original teachings of the Prophet Mohammed. The credo that began in a small Indian town as a rejection of Western imperialist hegemony in the mid-1800s was now resonating across the Muslim world 150 years later, as many followers of Islam felt under siege from the West in what was viewed by some as a new crusade for the new millennium.

The aim of Deoband was simple: to take a Muslim child and steep him in the ways of orthodox Islam, educate him in Koranic studies, sharia, fiqh, Hadith, Arabic, Persian, Urdu, Islamic history and scriptures until in his mid-twenties he was ready to go forth into the world as a messenger of God. On graduation, these messengers of God established madrassas across the Islamic region, exporting the Deoband message of orthodoxy. Since its birth 150 years ago, thousands of Deoband-affiliated madrassas had been set up worldwide, with particular strongholds in the tribal regions of Pakistan and Afghanistan. Some of these sister schools went on to radicalize the Deoband message further, injecting their own brand of fundamentalism that spoke not just of spreading the message but armed struggle.

The Deoband of India, the movement's founding madrassa, is more moderate than its Pakistani and Afghani counterparts, stressing that Islam is the religion of peace. But the Deoband way of life is also the sharia way. It calls for beheadings and amputations for crimes against society. It calls for women to be kept in purdah and decrees their role in life should focus on the home and child-rearing. It shuns Western influences, whether from television or movies. It prescribes a whole way of life that underscores the literal meaning of the word Islam, which is 'surrender' to God's will.

According to news reports of the meeting, opening the April 2001 Deoband conference in the name of Allah, a firebrand Pakistani cleric from the extreme party Jamiat Ulema-I-Islam issued an ululation of solidarity with 'oppressed Muslims' in Kashmir, Palestine, Chechnya, Kosovo and Bosnia. 'The ulema graduating from Deoband have served the cause of Islam by opening madrassas to enlighten Muslims and prepare them for jihad,' he told the crowd.

Resolutions passed included the call for the US military to leave Saudi soil and for a united Muslim front to 'liberate' Palestine and Jerusalem. The only measure of moderation was injected into the resolution on Kashmir, calling for a peaceful solution to the half-century-old territorial dispute between India and Pakistan over the Himalayan province. That resolution originated from the Indian delegation, conscious that every word was being weighed across the border by the government in Delhi. In the heart of Pakistan, amid talk of Islamic jihad, the elderly vice-chancellor of India's Darul-Uloom was a lone voice in the wilderness. Here was the official voice of the spiritual *alma mater* of the Taliban urging moderation in a conference peppered with calls for holy war. In a scholarly address, the maulana urged Muslims to enter into a pan-Islamist movement of solidarity and stressed brotherhood, not war.

But already the pupil had outgrown the teacher. The message was eclipsed by Darul-Uloom's most famous alumni: the Taliban. These holy warriors had used Afghanistan to put into practice what Darul-Uloom had preached. Across the border in Afghanistan was a puritanical Islamic society shaped by sharia and rooted in Deobandi teachings. The Taliban had taken the puritanical ethos of Deoband and fused it with Islamic militancy to create a society that promised to battle the Western 'infidels' head on. The philosophy born in India was made real in Afghanistan.

Talibanized Afghanistan was a society that most of the world refused to endorse. But it was a society that many Muslims held up as a model state, including the messiah of Islamic militancy himself, Osama bin Laden. Already on America's most wanted list for terrorist acts in east Africa, bin Laden could not resist the chance to address the most important gathering of Islamic leaders and clerics in years. From his Afghan den, he dispatched a recorded message exhorting all Muslims to return to the fundamentals of the faith: 'Afghanistan is the only country in the world with a real Islamic system. All Muslims should show loyalty to the Afghan Taliban leader, Mullah Omar,' said bin Laden in his taped address played over loudspeakers. Local news reports described how Muslim devotees listened in rapt attention in their hundreds of thousands as his disembodied voice intoned over their turbaned heads: 'Do not be afraid. Implement the Islamic system.'

Exactly five months later, bin Laden's act of mass

terrorism would put Muslims on a collision course with the US. It would also expose the secluded world of India's Darul-Uloom to world scrutiny for the first time in its history. The question: is Deoband a misunderstood keeper of the faith or the cradle of Islamic fundamentalism?

*

Deoband, Uttar Pradesh, January 11 2005

It is not easy getting an appointment to visit Deoband. In the aftermath of September 11, the madrassa was bombarded with requests from those seeking to understand Islam and the ideological birthplace of the Taliban. It had taken endless phone calls and exchanging of letters and pleasantries. For months we danced the ballet of evasion and engagement. On my part this required moves of flattery, persuasion bordering on begging, guilt-inducing expressions of frustration and yet more florid flattery. Negotiations had been carried out with Mr Adil Siddiqui, the madrassa's head of public relations, a seventy-three-year-old with a courtly charm and a zealot's desire for precision planning.

'Madam Edna. Deoband does not normally permit ladies to stay overnight, but I am applying for special dispensation from the VC. Inshallah, you will leave Delhi tomorrow at no later than ten-thirty in the morning, to arrive no later than four-thirty. We will then take tea. You are most welcome.' Click. The phone went dead.

The next day I set off from Delhi later than the scheduled departure time. My driver, Gurmel Singh, would accompany me on the journey. Mr Singh is a devout Sikh. If he were to appear on *Indian Mastermind* his specialist subject would be the history of oppression of Sikhs by Muslims through India's turbulent period of colonial rule.

He would recount the story of the beheading of Sikhism's
Ninth Guru by the brutal Muslim ruler Aurangzeb as if it
were only last year. The horrors of Muslim-Sikh clashes
during the 1947 Partition loomed even larger in the psyche.
In India, such history was never far from the surface.

Mr Singh and I arrived in Deoband village just as the
sun was setting. The last two hours of the journey from
Delhi had been hellish. This part of Uttar Pradesh is
desperately poor and renowned for bandit activity. Even the
Taliban would have its work cut out restoring law and
order in the badlands of UP. The road we were on was little
more than stone and dust, interspersed with huge potholes.
Baksheesh-grasping police officers sat in deck chairs by the
roadside, legs akimbo and guns cocked. In UP the police
looked more dangerous than the lowlife. Mr Singh was
desperate to reach the school before dark. 'I am driving
across India for thirty-eight years, Madam, and this is the
sickest road I have seen,' he said unhappily. 'Some roads are
sick two, three kilometers. This road is *totally* sick. UP
politicians are eating the money. Many thief-men in UP.'

There were indeed many thief-men in the state. UP was
a byword for backwardness, crime, poverty, lack of
development and corruption. The only place worse was
neighbouring Bihar. UP was known for its fair share of
communal troubles, too, and was the so-called Hindu
'cowbelt'. It was in UP's Ayodhya that Hindu extremists
had torn down the Babri mosque in 1992.

Deoband itself was a town with a large Muslim
population, comprising fifty per cent of the locals. The town
is dominated by the madrassa. The sun was setting as we
drove into the tight nexus of alleys surrounding the campus
to find the madrassa guesthouse where we would meet Mr
Siddiqui, navigating a medieval-style bazaar, narrow streets
thronged with men on their way back from the evening

namaaz. Darkness had set in and it was difficult to find our way through the labyrinth, congested with carts, sorrowful mules and skittish goats tottering like girls in high heels. Crowds of young men filled the lanes which were lined with Islamic bookshops supplying textbooks, literature and copies of the Koran. Mr Singh parked the car just outside the arched gateway leading into the madrassa itself and looked troubled.

'Madam. they are all Muslims here. These people sometimes do not like Sikhs.' The unflappable Mr Singh was flapping. We stepped out of the car to ask the way and were immediately engulfed by a group of up to a hundred young Muslim men who looked like students, all in skullcaps and long white kurta-pyjama, topped with woolly jumpers, piles of books stuffed under their arm. They stood in a semi-circle keen to find out who these strangers were. Then out of the throng stepped Mr Siddiqui like a vision of salvation in a green camouflage puffa jacket.

Mr Siddiqui was a severe-looking man, with a long face which bore a look of fearsome concentration. He had been with the madrassa for more than a decade, joining after retiring from a career in journalism which included stints at All India Radio. He wore a furry hat to protect his bald head from the cold, sported a neat white beard grown to the regulation length. His dress was a rather dapper ensemble of grey kurta-pyjama, brown jumper and the green puffa that looked like it belonged to a gangsta rapper. His face was wrinkled by age, cold and probably years of austere living. 'I've been waiting one hour, Madam. You're late,' he chastized.

'Sorry, Mr Siddiqui. The road was terrible.'

'The road to Deoband is full of ups and downs. Like life itself,' he said with deadpan delivery. Over the next few days, I was to hear more of Mr Siddiqui's wit. His favourite catchphrase when introducing people to me was: 'This is Mr So-and-So. He is *not* a terrorist.'

He took us through to the guesthouse and to our rooms. The rooms were suitably ascetic and clean. It was absolutely freezing cold and lived up to the Deoband credo of 'high thinking and simple living'. Despite the low temperatures, a couple of super-hardy mosquitoes had survived and buzzed out of reach, promising a night of torment. Mr Singh went off to unpack and adapt to the new surroundings. He emerged from his room looking like a new man. The jacket and slacks were replaced by kurta-pyjama and a long woollen blanket. His turban had been retied in the Muslim fashion. He no longer stood out as the only Sikh in a sea of Muslims, and with his flowing beard and flashing eyes could easily pass for a Taliban.

After Mr Siddiqui left to allow us to rest before dinner, Mr Singh announced that he was going to inspect the cooking facilities and the habits of the cook. Abdul was a typical cook, round as a barrel from snacking round the clock, dusted with chapatti flour and with a cursory interest in hygiene. He would rap at the door at mealtimes, enter without waiting for an answer and announce: 'Brakfast. Dinner. Like?' Unfortunately, Mr Singh did *not* like. He returned from his inspection of Adbul's kitchen and spoke in tones of horror.

'The Muslim kitchen is not good. Very dirty, Madam. I am seeing the pots. Very dirty. I am seeing the preparation. Not pure. Sardarji preparation very pure. I am thinking, what if there is buffalo fat on paratha?'

This was not a rhetorical question.

'They know you're Sikh. I'm sure Abdul will not use buffalo fat. Many top diplomats, professors and journalists have come here and stayed, Mr Singh. They've eaten from his kitchen.'

'I am thinking, they stay one time only. They are not returning if they see the Muslim kitchen.'

That night Mr Singh joined me and Mr Siddiqui for dinner for the first and last time. We sat around a small table, two foot square. Mr Singh could barely disguise his lack of appetite. He later informed me that he would be making alternative arrangements for dinner in future. He went out that night to purchase bananas, a bag of apples, a bottle of Frooti and one paring knife priced ten rupees. Showing me his haul, he happily informed me that he would join me for breakfast, at least.

'Breakfast is safe, Ma'am. I am thinking, chai, bread and boiled egg is safe. Abdul cannot get inside boiled egg.'

The next morning Mr Siddiqui arrived at eight o'clock sharp. He checked that my headscarf was in place and suggested I put on my winter coat, a loose-fitting garment that was a suitable substitute for the burqa. We went out of the guesthouse, across the road and through the arched gateway leading into the madrassa itself. The place was shrouded in fog. The winter season had set in and temperatures were freezing. There was a courtyard, surrounded on all sides by two-storey buildings painted in white and green. Through small doorways on the lower and upper storeys one could see classrooms where groups of students aged from eight or nine through to their early twenties sat cross-legged on the ground in a semi-circle as the teacher gave the lesson. In the courtyard, a group of older students milled around in the morning mist, arms laden with textbooks as they chatted. They were a mixed bunch: some were studious boffin types with steel-rimmed spectacles; others were handsome young hipsters with tinted sunglasses, flourishing whiskers and a sartorial dash reminiscent of Afghan warriors.

An audience had gathered and as we passed through to

the next courtyard through another archway I could see Mr Siddiqui was beginning to enjoy himself. 'Where you are standing, this is a revealed place,' began Mr Siddiqui, voice booming through the square. 'The location of Deoband was decided after it was revealed in an auspicious dream to the founder, Qasimul Uloom Hazrat Maulana Muhammed Qasim Nanautavi, may his secret be sanctified.' He paused to clear his throat, noisily. The students gathered round for this impromptu history lesson.

'Mutiny was an effort by Indians to drive out imperialists from this very place. Since they failed, Indian Muslims believed this fight must continue to be fought in the mind and for that reason this institution was established in 1866.'

Mr Siddiqui said the founders of the school believed in 'composite culture', the Muslim, Hindu, Sikh and Christian living side by side. It was an ethos in line with the original teaching of the Prophet Mohammed. The Koran says 'there shall be no coercion in matters of faith' and called on Muslims to respect the beliefs of Jews and Christians as '*ahl al-kitab*', translated as 'people of the Book' or earlier revelation. This enlightened message had somehow been lost down the ages. In India, most Muslim rulers were remembered for their often brutal conversion campaigns during their hundreds of years of rule. Today, Islamic extremists openly spoke of a holy war against the 'Crusaders and Zionists'.

The boys huddled closer, frosted breath suspended in the cold morning air as they pulled their scarves tight around their throats to keep out the icy wind. Their black eyes danced with engagement, flitting back and forth between Mr Siddiqui and myself, amused by this impromptu theatre. 'What is terrorism?' Siddiqui boomed. 'Terrorism is basically an economic problem. Look at this institution, until now 70,000 graduates have passed out and if you see the crime

graph of the home ministry you will find not a single
student of this institution has ever been proved in any case
of anti-social activity like theft and abduction. But they are
branded terrorists, fundamentalists, extremists and what-
not.'

I imagined a small government official dressed in tank
top and polyester slacks, sitting in his office in Delhi, poring
over a massive chart depicting the criminal activities of
university students across the country. We moved through
the crowd which followed behind. Mr Siddiqui, the pied
piper of Islam, continued rather in the manner of a tour
guide at a grand city museum. It was indeed a national
treasure. While the campus itself was fairly modern, the old
masjid was a stunning testament to Islamic classicism. Built
in pink sandstone, it had a central arched doorway flanked
by two smaller archways. The upper storey supported four
minarets, one at each corner. The cost of building the
mosque soon after the school was established was funded
by a rich merchant who donated 19,000 rupees. The first
students helped lay the foundation stones, carrying bricks
atop their turbans.

Lessons fused worship and knowledge, with the study of
the Koran and Sunnah—the habits and religious customs of
the Prophet, sharia law, fiqh or the study and application of
the sacred laws of Islam. In addition the students trained in
practical skills such as tailoring, calligraphy and bookbinding.
All students are fluent in at least five languages by the time
they leave: Arabic, Persian, Urdu, Hindi and English. Darul-
Uloom believed in returning to the original interpretation of
the Koran. Unlike other centres of higher learning, it
encouraged not independent thinking but unquestioning
acceptance.

The madrassa's official history proudly quoted the
assessment of a Professor W. Cantwell Smith, one-time

Director of Islamic Studies at the University of Montreal: 'Theologically, the school stands for rigid orthodoxy of the classical Aristolean type. The door of ijtihad is closed tight,' he said. Ijtihad is independent reasoning, using contemporary circumstances to interpret sharia law. During the fourteenth century, the Sunni Muslims declared the 'gates of ijtihad' to be closed and decreed that scholars must rely on legal decisions of the past to guide current-day judgments.

No military training is given at the madrassa, say the teachers. Yet when the madrassa was first established, its founders admitted their aim was to create soldiers of Islam, strong in mind and body. *The History of the Darul-Uloom* says the founders 'made arrangements in the campus to teach military arts to the students to maintain soldier-like spirit in them along with knowledge.' As a result, the students lived a credo set out centuries ago. They came as boys and left as men inculcated with a love of Islam and a dislike, even hatred, of all things deemed un-Islamic, modern or Western. So, here we were in the heartland of UP, in an island of Islam surrounded by a sea of saffron.

Here we were in secular India, yet somehow I felt disconnected from the rest of the country. Even Mr Singh recognized this was another land, changing the way he tied his turban to fit in just as I wore the headscarf assiduously. For the students and their teachers, the only world that mattered was within the confines of the madrassa walls and all wisdom was distilled into a single book: the Koran. This island mentality bred an insularity that looked within for knowledge, guidance, inspiration and purpose. Deoband was not about preparing young men for the outside world, but about building a fortress of faith around their minds to prevent the outside world from breaching the boundaries set by Deobandi Islam. It was this rigid, prescribed version of the faith which the young men would then seek to spread to others, as ambassadors of Darul-Uloom.

On graduation, this army of purists would spread the word throughout the Muslim world by setting up other madrassas. It was seen as a political necessity to protect the faith from corruption by the British-Christian influence as well as maintaining a distinct religious identity from the Hindus. This had always been a school born of political strife. After the 1857 revolt failed, there was a clampdown by the British which hurt the Muslim leadership in particular. 'The men of Allah at that time, particularly those august men who had themselves passed through this ordeal of blood and iron and had witnessed the corpses of Muslims biting the dirt and writhing in blood, were beset with this thought and anxiety as to where the caravan of knowledge and gnosis should be given asylum and what means should be adopted to take care of the faith and religion of the hapless and helpless Muslims of India,' says the official madrassa history. It should have been no surprise then that a school born of a backlash against the imperialist West and fear of corruption of the faith should continue to be shaped by these same factors 150 years on.

We passed through rose gardens, set out in the classic design of ancient Mughal gardens that can be seen in places like Srinagar's Shalimar Bagh. Beyond the gardens and the old mosque there were student halls. Washing dripped from the clotheslines. It was an existence stripped of possessions except the books of learning. The students did not pay school fees; that was funded from donations by Muslims from within India and as far as Saudi. Past benefactors included Syria, Egypt and Lebanon. The system of free education opened the school to students from all backgrounds. But the school is not recognized by the Indian government.

As we looped back towards the main entrance courtyard, I asked Mr Siddiqui about his earlier point that terrorism was rooted in poverty.

'If we confine our needs to our income, we are not likely to be deviated from the right path. But since our demands are unlimited, our resources are limited, for bridging that gap we start anti-social activities. Abductions, selling guns to some persons, ransoms, this is all terrorism. Terrorism is, in a way, unemployment,' he said.

'Do you condemn it?'

'Yes, it must be condemned, and should not go on anywhere,' he paused and snuffled into his hanky. 'We should seek the right path. Here in this very institution we seek the right path. Five times a day we offer prayer and in every prayer we emphasize that God should show us the right way, the right path.'

'The Taliban was an interesting example,' I said, fishing. 'They were Deobandis and went on to establish a society based on what they learned.'

'They are Deobandis in the sense that they were taught here and have learned the course of study. They then followed a course of life in their country. But there were local compulsions also. Under this, they were forced to adopt strong measures which should not have been adopted in a civilized society.'

'What measures were excessive?'

'I was told they opposed education of women through and through. We're not against education of women. Education of women is encouraged. But not alongside men, it has its...evil effects.'

He stopped before a steep narrow staircase, leading up to the vice-chancellor's chambers and administrative offices including the Department of Preaching and Propagation. 'Come,' he said mounting the stone stairs carefully. 'The VC will see you now.'

*

The VC did not look like a terrorist, to use Mr Siddiqui's phrase. He was in his eighties, his body bent with age. He looked remarkably frail, as if he had just recovered from an illness. He wore a topi and his white beard fanned out to the top of his chest. His eyes had a slightly rheumy quality and he spoke in a slow, deliberate fashion, each word carefully judged. He was wrapped up in a floor-length dark green velvet dressing gown, tied at the waist with a sash. It looked like something Noel Coward might have worn during evening cocktails. On his feet, the VC wore socks and red velveteen slippers which he slipped off and left outside the room for the duration of the interview. He walked stiffly to the sofa with the aid of a stick. His personal assistant, a huge burly bear of a man, followed close behind.

Maulana Marghoob Rehman came from a wealthy family. When he took on the job he decided to eschew all payment for the post and insisted on paying his own food expenses, according to Mr Siddiqui. He was greatly respected and despite his age and frailty was an active ambassador for the madrassa. The maulana had just returned from a gruelling tour of Arab countries and South Africa, where he no doubt sought endowments to boost the school's coffers. The school survived on the charity of its benefactors

During the interview, he sat next to me on a brown flower-patterned sofa, one hand resting on his walking stick while the other clutched a white handkerchief. He was perfectly charming and soft-spoken, speaking in soft Urdu which was translated into English by Mr Siddiqui. The room was bare, except for these chairs, and painted in white with shuttered doors that opened onto the administrative office next door.

The school has 3,500 students, from India, the UK, Saudi Arabia, Bangladesh and Burma. Its alumni's reach ranged from Africa and America to the West Indies and Yemen. But in recent years, the school said the Indian government had clamped down on issuing educational visas for students from certain countries, including part of the Arab world and Russia. Once again, terrorism lay at the heart of India's fears. For many officers in the Indian external affairs ministry, Deoband was a hotbed of fundamentalism. I began by asking the VC what kind of Muslim Deoband wished to create. 'It is a religious institution which imparts religious education which gives good moral character. So we are making students who are of high character, who give the message of peace to the entire world,' he said.

'After 9/11, Islam was placed at the centre of world attention. What impact have these events had on the world's view of Islam?'

'First. It is not confirmed that the events of September 11 were the work of Osama bin Laden,' he said. 'And the second thing is we don't believe in terrorism. Islam doesn't preach terrorism. Islam is a religion of peace.'

'Has the West misinterpreted Deoband and Islam?

'Not all Western countries, only USA and some Western countries are misrepresenting Islam.'

'Have those events changed attitudes in India towards Muslims?'

He sidestepped the question, keen not to be drawn into India's national politics as the madrassa's existence depended on the tolerance of New Delhi. 'It is already a burning topic in the media. We're constantly preaching that these madrassas are the epicentre of peace and do not preach terrorism in any way. We invited media persons, other foreigners to come here and see with their own eyes that these are not the breeding-grounds of terrorism.'

Islam was facing perhaps its greatest challenge in

generations. Deoband was not a normal academic institution: it was an academy which shaped the minds of future leaders on the religious questions which invariably influenced Islamic countries' search for political solutions. But Deobandi theology was not interested in the building blocks of a modern nation, such as a liberal market economy or democratic principles. As one of the world's leading Islamic institutions, Deoband was in a position to influence the reaction of the global and Indian Muslim community to these difficult times, either helping it to enter a quest for understanding and accommodation with the West or retreating into defensiveness and anger.

'What happened in Iraq and Afghanistan has encouraged terrorism and the action taken by those armies living there are a reaction to what USA has done,' he continued. 'They're raising arms simply to defend themselves, asking for rights. For example, we're asking for our rights in Palestine. It is *not* terrorism.'

'Is this jihad or a struggle for faith?'

'There are some places where there is really terrorism. Islam does not believe in that terrorism. But there're other places where people are asking for their rights. If they are doing so, it is quite justified.'

'Which is which?'

'Jihad is actually in very few places. Jihad is not everywhere. In most of the places, terrorism is there. We don't approve of that. But there are persons who are asking for their rights.'

'So is the militancy in Palestine legitimate?'

'It is justified.'

'Insurgency in Iraq?'

'It is justified.'

'Kashmir?'

'It must be settled amicably by composite dialogue. It is

the only way.' The maulana was careful to avoid any controversy on Kashmir, an emotive political issue for any Indian government, Congress or BJP. His statement on Kashmir was the model of moderation, in tune with the position of the ruling government of the day. The school could not risk being associated with Kashmiri militancy. Yet there was evidence of madrassa students from the overall south Asia region going on to train in terror camps and some of those recruits went on to infiltrate Indian Kashmir which was portrayed as the arena of another Muslim holy war, alongside Chechnya, Palestine and Iraq.

'After 9/11 has there been a radicalization among the students?'

'We don't ask for tit-for-tat. We ask them to lead a pious life, to think everything through on reasonable grounds. My students, I ask that they should pray to Allah the Great that the USA may lead a pious life and go to the right path and avoid this terrorist path.'

'Do you believe America is a terrorist state?'

'All policies of USA are proof that this path leads to terrorism.'

'Terrorism by whom, by the US or by Muslims?'

'Terrorism by the US. Muslims are not terrorists. The US is leading the path of terror. USA has attacked Iraq, USA has attacked Afghanistan. What do you call this activity? It is terrorist. It is obvious.'

'The Taliban leaders in Afghanistan were Deobandi students. Do you believe they were true to the faith of Islam and the teachings of Deoband?'

'I agree with the lifestyle they established there and it was quite in consonance with the Islamic principles of life. They were justified in doing all that and we approved of their efforts. Whatever was established in Afghanistan, the same government is running in Saudi Arabia and is quite successful. It has been able to check crime; it has been able to give justice to the people.' He paused to clear his throat. 'Compare that system with USA, where so many murders and abductions and anti-social activities take place every day.'

'Yet the Saudi regime and Afghanistan under Taliban were centres for Islamic terrorist networks.'

'This is false propaganda by the US.'

'So you believe there were no terrorist networks in Afghanistan?'

'We don't know.'

Another round of coughing signalled the end of the interview and I took some photos as the VC continued to chat. The three men had moved on to the topic of Osama bin Laden again. I asked what they thought of his role in September 11.

'The question itself is confusing,' said the VC perking up considerably. 'USA or anyone else cannot say definitely who has attacked it. It is the false propaganda of USA and the Jews. Only a name has been suggested, just to malign Islam.'

'What about the video tapes showing bin Laden admitting to the attack?'

'They were false, they were fake tapes. Just to win the election. It was under the pretext of these tapes that Bush wanted to win the election. Bush is the biggest terrorist ever,' said the VC. '*He* is the epicentre of terrorism.'

Bin Laden also sought a return to the old purity of sharia law. Yet despite preaching tradition, his own network had availed itself fully of every modern Western device and technology to orchestrate global scale attacks: from sending encrypted e-mails to his men via a laptop to satellite phone communication to using an aircraft as a flying bomb. I asked whether the VC considered al Qaeda to be a dangerous organization.

'Nobody knows what is al Qaeda. Al Qaeda is simply a name in the newspaper. Where is this al Qaeda, where are its headquarters, who are the members? Who are the managers? No one knows.'

'Who do *you* think Osama bin Laden is?'

'Osama bin Laden was the man of the USA. He was used against Russia in the Afghanistan War and after using him they rejected him, threw him out. It is the US policy of use and throw.'

'Al Qaeda is the world's most dangerous terrorist network,' I said.

'We don't know anything about al Qaeda. It is beyond our knowledge.'

*

'What is this famous English writer?' asked Mohammed from across his desk, hands spread over his papers. The other students looked at the ceiling, as if expecting the answer to fall from the heavens.

'Which writer?' I asked.

'Your English writer?'

'J.K. Rowling? You know Harry Potter?'

'Not Potter. Your Jane Austen. What does he write about?'

'I don't think you'd like Jane Austen much. She writes about women, getting married, English society. You'd find it totally boring.'

'No,' said Mohammed emphatically. 'I think I will enjoy it very much.'

The English class burst into laughter. These were Darul-Uloom's most gifted undergraduates seeking to polish up their English skills before leaving the madrassa. English was a relatively new offering by the school and it had been the subject of a bitter internal struggle between the modernizers and the reactionaries. In the end the VC sided with those who favoured teaching English. The students followed the national school textbook, which included conversation, reading, writing and some literature.

They were fairly advanced, able to discourse in a rather professorial, formal fashion about the great issues facing their people. They had limited access to books, relying on donations, which made their choice of reading somewhat random. It was curious that in the middle of rural India, in a centre of Islamic learning steeped in sharia law, one could find a bunch of teenage Muslim boys intrigued by Jane Austen's society of manners in the shires of England. Austen's heroines would have received rather short shrift in the society of Taliban Afghanistan. The penalty for such fiesty independence in a woman would probably have been a good thrashing.

The students sat in the Department of English Language and Literature, a classroom with low-level reading lecterns. Around twenty young men sat cross-legged on the carpet. The teacher was a young man in his early thirties. He spoke very formal English with wonderful crisp diction. The students also spoke beautifully, better than many natives in London, I thought. But the teen preoccupations of Darul-Uloom were somewhat different from their counterparts in the UK. Instead of idolizing David Beckham and fantasizing about Britney Spears, they admired bin Laden and dreamed of George W. Bush.

'Just before you came in we were discussing dreams,' said the teacher. 'One student here said last night he dreamed of going to the White House where he met George Bush.'

'And what did he tell Bush?' I asked.

'He hoped George Bush would invite us into his country

to teach Islam,' joked Mr Siddiqui. The class erupted with laughter again.

So did they enjoy learning the language of the infidel?

'Actually, we enjoy it a lot and we have found this language equal to Arabic language which is the *best* language in the whole world,' said another student, an ardent young man with a downy beard and glittering black eyes. 'After being aware of English language, a human being can reach his every need and he won't fear anything.'

'Before learning English they considered themselves half man. Now they are considering themselves full man,' added Mr Siddiqui with a mischievous glint in his eye.

'My name is Abu,' added another student. 'I believe there are a lot of misconceptions about Muslims outside and inside the country also. So we want to affect the minds of other people who don't know about Muslims and don't know about Muslim ulema. Islam is peace and security. It does not want to be terrorist.'

Did the world misunderstand the purpose of Deoband?

'Yes,' they said in unison.

'First of all America attacked Afghanistan and in that time Afghani people said we are similar to Deobandi ulema. This made people confused. But this war and the war of Afghani people don't mean they are terrorist. American people and Western countries imagined Afghani people and Afghani government are terrorist and they imagined Deobandi ulema are also terrorist,' chipped in another young man at the back.

How were Muslims viewed within India by other Indians?

'They have some problems about Muslims. They are ignorant about Islam. They should read about Islam,' he said.

I asked if Muslims in India had equal opportunities compared to everybody else.

'Nearly.'

'In what way do you not have equal rights?'

'As far as the fundamental Constitution of the country is concerned, we are equal. But underside, the government people who have jobs and are in high posts—they want sometimes to put Muslim worker down. Sometimes this is so,' said one student simply. He said it matter-of-factly, as if that was the lot of the Muslim in India and there was nothing to be done about it.

'What jobs do you want to do?'

'We scholars have a very sacred purpose,' said Abu. 'What is this? To meet you kind of people. Western countries are claiming Muslim ulema are terrorist and Islam is a religion which can destroy the whole world. The West says the holy Koran is a book which teaches terrorism. So we want to talk to you, make you understand. That is our job.'

'I tell you,' said Mr Siddiqui, his hand waving across the classroom, 'these boys can become anything. Anything. Excepting the terrorist.'

It was almost time for prayers and the boys would have to get ready to go to the mosque. There they would participate in the daily ritual of prayer five times a day, from dawn to dusk. During my stay, I would listen to the magical sound of the muezzin, the call to prayer, ringing out across the campus from before sunrise to sunset. As we got up to leave, the students asked me when I was coming back. I promised I would return sometime, but did not know when.

The English teacher asked if I could arrange for some books to be sent for them to practise reading aloud.

'What kind of books?'

'Anything.'

'Maybe this Jane Austen,' one voice suggested.

Jane Austen it would be. When I returned to Delhi I

dispatched a parcel to the Darul-Uloom English Department marked 'Urgent'. Inside were copies of Austen's *Pride and Prejudice* and *Emma*: stories of peach-complexioned heroines encountering love and frustration in the male-dominated world of old-world England; stories of candlelit balls and corseted ladies suffering the vapours; the subtle trials and agonies of the English middle classes. What I would not give to hear the boys breathlessly reading those passages out loud.

*

Talibanized Afghanistan was Deobandi theology made real. The religious police under the ministry for the promotion of virtue and prevention of vice once patrolled the streets of Afghanistan with sticks, ready to beat those who strayed from the path of the righteous. The position of women was particularly depressing. Women were not allowed to work, denied education, instructed to remain in purdah, screened from the world in the billowing black burqa and veil. Even in faith, they were less than equal, instructed to pray in the house, not the mosque. The purpose of all this? To guard against temptation, or what Mr Siddiqui described as the 'evil effects'. In truth, the Koran made it the duty of both men and women to guard against these evil effects:

> 'Enjoin believing men to turn their eyes away from temptation and restrain their carnal desires...Enjoin believing women to turn their eyes away from temptation and to preserve their chastity.'

Any show of 'adornments' or 'finery' by women, which one could take to mean physical attributes, was prohibited in the presence of men other than husband, father, other male relations and children.

Yet the history of Islam shows that the Prophet Mohammed was more enlightened towards women than many non-Muslims imagine. He would consult with his wives and listen to their opinions on current affairs, assist with the chores and even mend his own clothes, according to Karen Armstrong's *History of Islam*. 'The emancipation of women was a project dear to the Prophet's heart. The Koran gave women equal rights of inheritance and divorce centuries before Western women were accorded such status,' she writes. While the Koran did prescribe some degree of segregation and purdah for the Prophet's wives, she adds, there is nothing in it that requires all women to be veiled or to be confined to a separate part of the house.

Polygamy was a sign of the times. One reason was that many women lost their husbands in the series of inter-tribal battles waged during the early years of Islam. Multiple marriages enabled men to take on widows as their second or third wives, giving them financial security within the community. The Prophet himself married several times, and indeed some of his marriages were inspired by the need for political alliances to protect the nascent faith's allegiances within the tribes. Of course that was then, this is now. In the Prophet's time women also had a purpose in the community beyond the home. Armstrong points out women in the first Muslim community in Medina were active participants in public life and even fought alongside men in battle. Many of the restrictive practices imposed on women came after the Prophet's death.

The call for the reform of the position of women in Islam is an eternal cry. I was interested to learn that the majority of queries for advice and guidance from Muslims around the world to Deoband's muftis or religious judges were on the question of divorce. Could this be related to women feeling stifled in the role prescribed by Islamic traditionalists?

In the evenings, while dining on more of Adbul's culinary delights, my conversations with Mr Siddiqui would often turn from work to family. In his work, he was a devout man who sought to introduce some modern elements where he felt they would benefit the school and further the cause of Islam. He was not a man of modern values, so this relatively progressive thinking was probably the result of having educated children, including a highly educated daughter. His conversation would focus often on his daughter Sarwat Jahan. She had recently returned to Deoband from Delhi and all was not well.

Sarwat Jahan was in her mid-twenties. 'She was a journalist like me. She worked in Delhi and did some media work. She also worked at the YWCA,' he said proudly.

'Where is she now?'

'She's in Deoband. I instructed her to leave Delhi to return for family reasons. She had to look after her mother who was ill.' He paused, gazing into his lap as he tied his handkerchief into knots. 'She's a very independent-thinking woman. Broad-thinking. She doesn't like it here. She is unhappy.'

'Why is she unhappy?'

'She thinks this place is too closed-thinking. She wants to see change. She wants to see freedom for women,' said Mr Siddiqui, his mouth twisted to one side. 'It was my mistake to call her back.' Mr Siddiqui asked if I could help her return to Delhi. Did I know of anyone who could find her a job? 'She does not fit in here, you see. She refuses to wear the headscarf, she refuses to remain in purdah, she doesn't wear the veil. She speaks her mind. They make fun of her here.'

He asked if I would meet her before I left, suggesting that we'd have a lot to discuss. I agreed to see her. She worked at the Doon Valley Public School, a co-educational school which was a couple of kilometers away. I had given Mr Siddiqui a book called *The Heart of Islam* written by a well known Muslim academic. He dipped in and out of its pages and said he would give it to his daughter to read. 'I must go now,' he said abruptly. 'I've taken enough of your time this evening.' He got up and left.

Mr Siddiqui spent his days preaching the rigid orthodox Islam of Deoband, but when he returned home he saw such orthodoxy suffocating his daughter. He was devoted to Deoband, yet he was also a father. Sarwat Jahan was representative of the forces of modernization within Islam, the new Indian Muslim woman. Not submissive, nor accepting of restrictions. During her brief stay in the Indian capital she saw a world of possibilities. Potentially, it was a world that promised fewer barriers, fewer parameters of constraint and she was willing to take her chances, even if that meant operating with no safety nets and risking failure. Delhi was just a five hour drive from Deoband, yet it was another universe, from the spiritual and intellectual isolation of Darul-Uloom to the infinite vistas of freedom in a changing India.

During my stay over several days, I was aware that my position was privileged. I was allowed to visit, I was allowed to stay overnight, I was allowed to converse with men on equal terms, I was allowed to openly disagree. I covered my head but did not veil my face. Although covered from head to toe, the exposure of my face was seen as a provocation by some. When I met the head mufti, a cheerful man full of smiles, he informed me that this was not acceptable usually, but since he was an old man and I was young enough to be his grand-daughter, it was permissible this time. For the women of Deobandi Islam these so-called privileges were denied. During a chat with the English and Computer Department heads over afternoon tea before prayers one day, it was clear that something had driven these young men into a fundamentalism which was far more reactionary than Mr Siddiqui's.

'Why can't a woman enter a mosque under orthodox Islam?' I asked.

'It is better that she prays in the house,' said the recently married head of the English Department, as if that was the end of the discussion. 'If a woman is in the mosque she will distract the men from their prayer,' his colleague added. 'A beautiful woman enters the mosque. The man sees her and is astonished by her beauty. Every day he returns to the mosque at the same time to see her, to look upon her face. After seeing her ten, fifteen times he is in love.' His colleagues wobbled their heads vigorously in collective dismay. 'This is why we cannot have women in the mosque.'

'But isn't faith about controlling the mind to focus on God?'

'The Muslim is controlled in mind. But why should a woman come to the mosque when it is said the blessings are greater if she prays at home? If you are told you could get twenty rupees for doing one thing and twenty-five rupees for doing another thing, why not do the thing that brings more rupees? The woman is getting even greater blessings by praying in the house. So why not be happy with that?'

'But if she chooses to visit...'

The young men looked exasperated, while Mr Siddiqui twiddled with the buttons on his camouflage jacket. 'It's for her protection. To keep her safe,' said the English professor. 'We're not saying a woman is the possession of a man. See. A woman is like a beautiful piece of jewellery. It is better to keep this beautiful jewellery locked up in its box. Otherwise, someone will see it, want it and take it.'

I thanked them for the tea, got up and left. Mr Siddiqui held his tongue until we were outside. 'You must excuse them,' he said finally. 'They have yet to learn there is one destination, but many paths.'

Back in the room, Mr Siddiqui and I had more tea. He looked worried again. I asked him if these same issues frustrated his daughter. 'She argues for modern thinking,' he said. 'What you heard today, it is for these reasons she cannot take this place.'

The next day I met Sarwat Jahan. Mr Singh drove to her school, past the religious bookshops, bazaar and down a side road on the outskirts of Deoband itself. Sarwat was unmarried and educated. She had a masters in English and another qualification in education studies. The school had 850 pupils, both boys and girls, and was multi-faith. She greeted me warmly when we met and introduced me to the headmistress, a prim woman in her fifties, wearing a sari and cardigan. I asked the headmistress if she had also grown up here. She seemed mortified by the thought. 'I know nothing of Deoband,' she replied stiffly. 'To me this is a foreign land.'

In the corner of the small reception room by the gates, I sat down with Sarwat Jahan to have a chat and some tea. She looked different from her father. She had a round face, dominated by huge expressive eyes. Her hair was cut short and left uncovered. She was intensely serious and mature beyond her years. I asked her why she wanted to leave.

'I want to get out of this cage of orthodox life. Here the thinking is very limited. People don't want to come out of their shells. They still want to have those old kind of traditions and customs. It's time people in our community started to think in terms of change. All these customs like veils and purdahs and so on, this is just an outward issue. It doesn't have any inward meaning.'

I told her about my discussion with the professors about the position of women. I told her I found the younger ones more rigid than the older ones. She giggled, covering her mouth with her hand, her eyes lighting up for the first time. But in an instant she was serious again: 'They *are* more rigid. God has created everyone equal. When we're born it's not that a boy has two eyes and a girl has four. We all are born equal, so we should all be treated equally. It's a fundamental right. Why do girls always have to stay behind a boy? Suppose a girl wants to go out to the market—her own mother will ask the girl to take her younger brother along. Is this right?'

'Is there pressure to wear full veil?'

'*Haan ji*. It should be full veil. According to the religion it should be a full veil, covering the face,' she said, demonstrating a mask-like covering with her hands.

'How do you feel about this?'

'It's an outward show. We need to move forward, we need education; we need to go out to look for a career. In such a world, there's no sense in a debate on the full veil or half veil. The grace should be within the girl. It's not a matter of I'm wearing the veil or not wearing the veil. What's the point if your eyes are still looking at men? If we are religious-minded, then if a boy or girl is standing before us it shouldn't matter, because Islam teaches us self-control.'

'How do you change things? Even while India changes it seems the religious leaders at Darul-Uloom will never contemplate change.'

'There *must* be change. Women in Islam must be self-dependent, go out, be educated, get a career. And only when we have changed ourselves can we expect change from society itself. *We* have to start the process.' The school bell rang, signalling the next class. Children spilled out into the courtyard to switch classes, chattering loudly. Sarwat Jahan had to go to class, so we shook hands and said our goodbyes. I got into the turquoise Wagon R and as we drove off, clouds of red dust rearing up from the wheels, Mr Singh looked pensive in the rearview mirror.

'This is Mr Siddiqui's daughter?'

'Her name's Sarwat Jahan.'

'Sarwat Jahan. She is married?'

'Unmarried. She works as a teacher.' He nodded with approval.

'But Ma'am, she is looking a little weak.'

'Weak?'

'Ma'am, I am seeing some sadness in her eyes.'

*

The old mufti sat cross-legged on a threadbare rug before a low-level lectern. He was surrounded on all sides by piles of books on Islamic law and piles of correspondence written in Urdu, Persian and Arabic. There was a separate desk for faxes and printed out e mails. Technology had increased the mufti's workload dramatically. Each day the mufti received fifty e-mails from around the globe seeking guidance on everything from the arcane details of religious law to marriage guidance. He had been a mufti for twenty-one years and looked every inch the severe executor of sharia judgement. His rulings were dispensed across the Islamic world and followed assiduously. He was an old man with huge horn-rimmed glasses that engulfed his thin, sharp features, softened marginally by a neat white beard. He wore a woolly hat and a threadbare baby pink pashmina to ward off the cold and damp. He refused to be photographed and listened to my questions with an air of barely disguised disdain, as if conducting the interview under sufferance.

Mr Siddiqui explained that Mufti Habibur Rehman was one of the foremost experts in sharia. His knowledge and experience were excelled only by the chief mufti whom I would meet later.

'Darul-Uloom, Deoband, is the most well-known and famed religious institution which is respected throughout the world for its authenticity in Islamic education,' said Mufti Rehman. 'All the Muslims of the world believe in this very institution. They rely on this institution to acquire the final judgement on religious matters.'

'How do they seek judgement, what is the process?' I asked.

'People from all over the world put their questions to us in writing, on phone, on internet and other ways and we explain to them in the light of the Holy Koran and Hadith. We answer their questions and satisfy them.'

'What are the most commonplace questions asked of the Mufti?'

'People are very much concerned about social life. Marriage and divorce, and all the quarrels among them.'

I asked if he feared that modern life, Western values and consumerism were eroding the true spirit of Islam. He stroked his beard thoughtfully and then with one slender finger extended, as if addressing an audience, he said:

'Consumerism is totally against Islam, it does not follow the principles of humanity and morality. Islam does not believe in consumerism, consumerism is a purely worldly thinking. Islam believes in two ways: one life here and one life hereafter. If we believe in life hereafter, then we have to follow the right path. Islam puts emphasis on that life which will be faced after death.'

The path to salvation in the hereafter lies in the distant past, in the teachings and ways of the Prophet. So a modern reinterpretation is ruled out, he said.

'You see, our way of thinking is very different to the way Westerners think. Westerners think only of the present and the future and they chalk out a plan. We look back to our past, because our elders had proved what is true Islam.

Each and every problem can be solved by true Islam. So we want to follow that path of the past, we are not concerned about the future in this life. Our future in the life hereafter depends on the path of the past.'

The Taliban's way represented that return to the past in order to secure the life hereafter. The old way was the path to salvation and thereby justified the acts that alienated much of the non-Islamic world. Post-Sept 11, many Muslims felt enraged by the retaliatory action of the US and its coalition allies. There was a genuine sense that their very existence was under attack. Even in secular India, under the last Hindu nationalist BJP-led government, there was open talk of Muslims representing a terrorist threat in the heart of the nation. This sense of suspicion simply fuelled the cycle of persecution and fundamentalism. And those who turned to extremism and militancy often spoke of 'jihad', which has been interpreted by non-Muslims as holy war. Its actual meaning is a struggle for faith, including the inner struggle to live life true to Islam. It was this internal struggle for faith of which the mufti spoke. I asked him if this meaning of jihad hadn't been hijacked by extremists seeking justification to resort to mass terrorism.

'Whatever the young generation is doing, it's not truly jihad,' said the mufti. 'They've been compelled by circumstances to defend themselves and all these steps are being taken by them to defend themselves. So it is not jihad in the true sense. It is an effort for self-defence.'

'What's your definition of jihad?'

'Jihad is a religious term. It demands that we have to make an effort for the propagation of Islam. If there is opposition anywhere and we are not allowed to do and perform our religious duties we can raise arms against the enemy. This is jihad. This type of effort is called jihad. Not all that is going on in the world.'

'So what's happening in many places in the world is not a religious battle, but a personal or political battle?'

'It is not for the propagation of Islam. They are doing it in self-defence or for local compulsions.'

'Is violence in the name of self-defence un-Islamic?'

'It is not un-Islamic. It is *necessary*. Every moral law allows for self-defence. They are fully authorized.'

The head mufti was ready to see me now. We thanked Mufti Rehman for his time and he graciously reciprocated. He had warmed towards me by the end to something almost approaching tolerance. His boss, Chief Mufti Zafeeruddin, is one of the world's most influential Islamic judges. He is in his eighties and has been a mufti for fifty years; his pronouncements resonate across the Islamic world. He is the author of thirty-five books and his volumes on Islamic law are consulted by muftis everywhere, his case histories quoted by other judges. He wore a brown woolly hat and was swathed in a royal blue blanket. We conducted our conversation cross-legged on the carpet. There was no heating and it was freezing. My legs were completely numb by now. I had given up trying to keep the circulation going. Despite the temperature, the chief mufti exuded rosy cheerfulness and his eyes danced with a vitality that defied his years.

His sphere of influence extended across the world, but I asked him what concerned him most about the position of the Indian Muslim. Even in this cloistered existence, the problems were evident. 'There are a handful of Hindus who create riots, burn our houses, put oppressions and aggressions against Islam,' said the chief mufti. 'The problem is the handful, otherwise all Hindus are basically good, all Sikhs are good, all Christians are good. I only hope that this government will do something better for Muslims. I want to see the difficulties, the backwardness of Muslims being removed. I want to see relief to Muslims.'

Usually such matters were studiously evaded. But now the mufti said that if the government did not act, the Muslim must act for himself. Did alienation contribute to fundamentalism in India, and at its most extreme, to terrorism?

'Terrorism is un-Islamic. Only self-defence is necessary. To defend themselves, Muslims can raise arms against the enemy. Whether he lives in USA, whether he lives in England, whether he lives in France, whether he lives in Italy or Germany. Wherever he lives he is authorized to defend himself and for self-defence he can raise arms against his enemies.'

He went on to explain that despite the West's criticism of the Taliban, its way of life was deemed to be the blueprint for Islamic society, a model of purification. He disagreed that a society which called for a subservient place for women, for beheadings and amputations had no place in the modern world. Instead, the Chief Mufti pointed to the West's own descent into criminality and decadence as a warning of what happened when the moral reins on society were loosened. Modernity was essentially the slide into immorality. Orthodoxy, then, was the refuge of the faithful, whether in India, Iraq or London. Deobandi Islam was about going back to year zero, to the time of the Prophet.

*

Mr Siddiqui decided I was worthy of a privilege. 'I am appreciating your serious interest in our institution,' he said. 'I am therefore allowing you to see our great library. It has many historic manuscripts, old hand-written and painted copies of Koran. Come.'

The chief librarian permitted entry with an elegant wave of the hand, thoughts consumed by the worthy tome in his lap. The library was a bibliophile's fantasy: chamber after chamber of ancient books and manuscripts on floor-to-ceiling shelves. Corridors branched off from the main rooms, indicating yet more archives. There were texts in Urdu, Persian and Arabic that dated back centuries. This was the depository of learning and law that formed a valuable fount of knowledge for the Muslim world. Clusters of boys sat on the carpeted floor, their bent white-capped heads bobbing as they memorized from books spread open in their laps.

The place smelled damp and musky. We entered the library museum at the back and there, in glass-topped display cabinets, were the madrassa's greatest treasures. These were pieces of Islamic history often presented to the madrassa by dignitaries or heads of state from Muslim countries. There was also a copy of the Koran translated into Hindi and a copy of the Hindu religious epic *Ramayana*, a copy of the Torah and the Old Testament. 'Islam is not against other religions, you see,' said Mr Siddiqui, carefully pointing out one after the other.

When we eventually emerged into the sunshine our eyes took time to adjust from the gloom. It was time to leave and I was sorry to go. I had found Mr Siddiqui to be an agreeable companion over the days. He looked sad and asked when I would return. 'If you're in need of further information, prepare a questionnaire and we shall receive you once again in ten days,' he said. He handed me a parting gift—a press release entitled 'Darul-Uloom Deoband X-rayed'.

The car was loaded and ready to leave. Mr Singh had consulted the locals and found out to his great pleasure that there was an alternative route to Delhi along a modern road which also passed his favourite roadside dhaba. He was already planning his lunchtime stopover, having not eaten a hot meal for days. I said goodbye to Mr Siddiqui, shaking hands warmly. Mr Singh was no longer uncomfortable at the madrassa and had reverted to tying his turban the Sikh way. He and Mr Siddiqui clasped each other's shoulders in a show of mutual respect. After a prickly beginning, it turned out the old Sikh and old Muslim shared more than separated them. 'You shall come again. Inshallah,' said Mr Siddiqui.

*

During the visit, I had been moved by the sincerity of some of the students I met who strived to abide by the ascetic credo of 'simple living and high thinking'. It was in stark contrast to the designer label-devouring youth of Delhi. Here was a disciplined regime of prayer and study, a place where personal fulfilment came second to creating an army of holy warriors with the sole purpose of taking Islam to the world. But what kind of Islam? The purpose of the madrassa was not to create men who would push back the boundaries of the religion and broaden understanding. Both teacher and pupil were sheltered from external influences and viewed the West and modern developments with suspicion at best and contempt at worst. This school was not about expansion of the mind but conditioning it.

Deoband was forged in the fires of a revolt against British imperialist rule. Its formation was a declaration of independence from outside influences, a return to Islamic purity free from the taint of 'foreign' forces, whether those were Western or Christian or even Hindu.

Once again in their history, Muslims in India and those abroad felt under attack. While Bush and Blair stressed theirs was not a war against Islam, their assurances fell on the barren ground of suspicion and anger in the Muslim world. Before September 11 bin Laden and the Taliban had

used the Deoband platform in Peshawar to call for a return
to the austerity of the sharia and a battle against the
polluting influence of the West. Only by purging themselves
and returning to the puritanical essence of Islam could the
Muslim ulema be saved. After September 11, the Deobandi
Muslims of India and overseas believed bin Laden was
unfairly blamed, the Taliban unfairly ousted and Iraq illegally
invaded and taken over by the Americans. It looked to them
like an anti-Islamic conspiracy. The founding principle of
Darul-Uloom, to fight Western imperialism through faith
and education, seemed as relevant as it did a century and a
half ago. The holy mission was given new life.

In India itself, Muslims were among the poorest, least
educated and most marginalized sections of society. They
had gone from being the ruling classes during the Mughal
era to the underclass of post-Independence India. For many
Muslims the meaning of equality under the Constitution,
the fine speeches by secular leaders had little substance in a
country where they were still at the bottom of the pile. The
rise of Hindu nationalism in the 1990s and into the new
millennium had exposed the Indian Muslims to a new form
of politics—one that openly derided the secular ideal and
called for a Hindu Raj under which Muslims must know
their place. The 2002 anti-Muslim riots in Gujarat, where
the state BJP government played a partisan role, were the
worst example of this. It did not help that shortly afterwards
the then Prime Minister of the country, Atal Bihari Vajpayee,
delivered a speech at his party's national executive meeting
in which he all but condoned the rioting as a natural
reaction to the burning of a railway coach that had resulted
in the death of fifty-eight, mostly Hindu, passengers. In the
same speech, he went on to say that Muslims tended not to
live in co-existence with others and wanted to spread their
faith by resorting to terror and threats.

After September 11, India allied itself closely with a 'zero-tolerance' America. India had, after all, suffered terrorism for decades longer. But its complaints about Pakistan's role in this had never been taken seriously in the West. An America suddenly awake to terrorism, especially Islamic terrorism, could now be made to see India's point of view. The right-wing BJP government at the Centre endorsed America's war on terror. Many Muslims felt that it did so a little too enthusiastically and feared they were next in line.

In Kashmir, people had witnessed fifteen years of insurgency by Islamic militants waging what they called 'jihad' to 'liberate' the Muslim-dominated territory from Indian rule. The Indian army crackdown that ensued hurt not just militants but the ordinary Muslim Kashmiri as well. Many Kashmiri Muslims fled their homeland to escape not just the abuses of the terrorists but also of the Indian army. Outside Kashmir, they were viewed with suspicion and often persecuted by an over zealous police. In fact, Kashmir-related terrorism—in J&K, Delhi and Gujarat—coloured mainstream attitudes towards the entire Muslim community in India.

This sense of prejudice and persecution fuelled fundamentalism, whether among Muslims in Old Delhi, Deoband or Kashmir. The Muslim faith was a brotherhood, where pain felt by one part of the ulema radiated throughout the community.

Another factor responsible for the siege mentality I encountered in Deoband was fear of change. Modernity is upon the maulanas of Darul-Uloom. The mufti, arch-executor of sharia law, uses e-mail to disseminate judgements and fatwahs. The VC accepts English as a necessary part of education, even for messengers of God. But modernity stops there. For now. But the change happening in the rest of India is sweeping and cannot be stemmed. India is experiencing one of the highest growth rates in the world, the brain drain to the West has been reversed as jobs relocate from the US and Europe to India. The economy is opening up as never before to foreign investment by multinationals which are altering the nature of Indian society. As Western companies pile into India, it is inevitable that Western values will also be imported into the culture. We now see emblems of modernity in cities across the country: from mobile phones and satellite television to Pizza Hut delivery within thirty minutes and Louis Vuitton boutiques in five-star hotels. But the change in attitudes and values will be more profound, for example, as the position of women in the workforce is strengthened, leading to demands for equality. This onset of change is incomplete, so far leaving vast tracts of rural India untouched. But it has begun. And its effects are inevitable and irreversible.

Darul-Uloom is committed to resisting these influences. The madrassa represents an island of Islamic orthodoxy in India; facing the rising tide of change, it strives to find answers in the past. Its message is this: to live a good Muslim life means returning to a pure version of faith that does not contemplate adaptation to the new. The gates of 'ijtihad' are firmly closed. The result is a fundamentalism that the West and much of India, too, cannot understand.

In Peshawar, the Indian Deobandis—the keepers of the original flame—were studious in their avoidance of any call to arms. Instead, they called for brotherhood. Yet, they allowed their conference in Pakistan to be used as a platform for messages from more militant brethren such as the Taliban and bin Laden as recently as April 2001. Islam forbids war against another nation unless Muslims are prevented from practising their faith. The killing of civilians is also strongly prohibited by Islam. According to the Deoband muftis, much that was happening in the world was not jihad, but self-defence and in self-defence violent struggle is permissible under the faith. Militant insurgencies in Iraq and Palestinian suicide bombings were both examples of justified self-defence, according to the muftis. To the clerics and scholars of Darul-Uloom this was not terror, but a response to state terror. These were the desperate responses of the victim.

The language of the Indian Muslim, whether in Deoband or Delhi or Kashmir, is also the language of the victim. Muslim leaders in India warn that alienation could end in a radicalism of the type seen in Iraq or Israel. And if after years of oppression a victim finally hits back, who is to blame?

During one Q&A session with a bunch of journalism students, one young man asked me the most provocative question he could think of: 'Who do you think is to blame for September 11?' I replied: 'Osama bin Laden.' The group of thirty or so students and professors nodded gravely in silence, deeply disappointed by my answer. It showed how far apart they felt from mainstream opinion not just around the world but within their own country. Or perhaps, how far apart I was from what they considered to be mainstream Muslim opinion. The scholars I met at Darul-Uloom were not violent, bloodcurdling ideologues. Yet their interpretation of Islam justified violence in the name of self-defence. But define self-defence.

Just as the freedom fighters during the Mutiny had been willing to take up arms against the British for the sake of protecting the purity of their respective faiths, Muslims were willing to do so today. The Mutiny of 1857 began because a group of sepoys believed that the British intended to force them to use the tallow of cows and pigs to grease their cartridges. The plan was hugely offensive to both the cow-revering Hindus and the Muslims who considered the pig to be an unclean animal. Such sacrilege was enough to ignite a revolt against British Christian rule that would culminate less than a century later with the Independence of India. Today, those sepoys are not described as insurgents against the nation state, but the first freedom fighters. Indeed, Indians reject the term 'Mutiny' and call it the 'First War of Independence'. To the muftis and maulanas, the abuses of Muslim honour in Kashmir, Guantanemo Bay or Palestine were not so different in principle to the battle that inspired the madrassa's founding fathers.

It is a perspective not often considered in the rarified circles of Delhi's Gymkhana Club or Habitat Centre, cherished haunts of the Indian political elite. I had lost count of the number of times I sat through Delhi dinner parties while some whisky-and-ghee-indulged bore, fat on kebabs and corruption, raged about the 'pampered' Muslim in India. On one occasion I begged to differ, only to be called 'a Muslim-lover'—like 'Jew-lover' or 'nigger-lover'— a term of abuse. And this from a Brahmin Hindu educated in the best Christian schools in Delhi. This anti-Muslim propaganda ranged from the fashionable 'all Muslims are extremists' to the fanciful 'the Taj Mahal is Hindu, not Islamic'. The manufactured fear psychosis about the Muslim in India is at times ridiculous, yet its insidious effect on Indian society is deadly serious. These are scary monster stories, tales of wicked djinns waiting in the shadows to take your heart out.

The fear psychosis ends in a self-fulfilling cycle of suspicion and alienation that prevents the phantoms of Partition being laid to rest. It seemed a reckless way to proceed in a country with the second biggest Muslim population in the world, a disengaged community lagging behind the rest of Indian society. It remains an economic apartheid that needs to be addressed, even more so as India embarks on a journey of rapid economic liberalization that could polarize society still further. Almost six decades have passed since Maulana Azad's plea to Muslims to keep faith in the new India. They did so. Now, Azad's nearest modern-day inheritor to the mantle of Muslim leader, the hardline Shahi Imam, says the time for blind faith is over. It's quid pro quo time. Indian Muslims must have an economic stake in their country's future and assert their identity within India and the first step is rediscovering their political voice. The cost of continued impotence is descent into fanaticism, he warns. But equally, it is India's duty to recognize that tolerating Muslim disengagement is like witlessly listening to a ticking bomb and not expecting to hear a big bang.

PART 2

The Crusaders

Don't Miss !

A spectacular breathtaking

Sound & Light Show on the Life of :

Everyday from 8 a.m to 7 p.m

6

Inquisition and Exposition

'*More than four months have passed since we reached Goa here in India, a completely Christian city that is something to behold. It has a monastery with many friars of the order of St Francis, an ornate cathedral with many canons and many other churches. God our Lord must be greatly thanked for the fact that the name of Christ is flourishing in distant lands and among so many infidels.*'

—St Francis Xavier, writing from Goa to Jesuits
in Rome, 20 September 1542

December 2004, Se Cathedral, Old Goa

'They say it's as if the body is still alive,' whispered Benicia Gonzales, an eighty-two-year-old Goan Catholic who had been queuing since ten in the morning to see the body of St Francis Xavier. She moved closer, conspiratorial voice slipping a notch lower as she extended a hand towards my face. 'They say if you place your fingers in the wound to his side the blood is still fresh. It's a *miracle*.' Benicia crossed herself and began to recite the *Our Father*.

It was just before Christmas and Goa was in the throes of celebrations for the sixteenth Exposition of its revered saint. Four hundred and fifty years after his death from pleurisy in 1552 the body was paraded in its glass casket through the streets of Old Goa from its final resting place in the Basilica Bom Jesus to Se Cathedral where it remained on display for one month.

The Exposition of Saint Francis Xavier is a religious spectacular that comes along once a decade. St Francis remains an icon for India's Catholics: a missionary from the warrior priesthood of the Jesuits or Society of Jesus, who was dispatched to the East to bring God to the unbelievers.

He was the ultimate crusader, the man who brought the Inquisition to India. The Inquisition was the blunt instrument of Christian fundamentalism and an institution of terror that left scars imprinted on Goan society to this day. Its aim was to stop new converts to Christianity from slipping into the ways of their old religion. The converts from Hinduism found it hard to erase tradition, where culture and religion were entwined. The Inquisition aimed to destroy that part of the Goan identity, stripping out the Hindu ways and replacing it with a pure, unadulterated Catholicism. It was a brutal process. Yet centuries on, the majority of the ancestors of these converts venerated Francis Xavier and loved him still.

This Catholic Indian heartland was going crazy over the desiccated remains of a nobleman from Navarre, Spain: memorabilia flooded the state; newspapers were filled with stories of his miracles and Goan Catholics bowed down to secure blessings for the future. Even non-Christians paid respects in accordance with Goa's religious pluralism. Within a fortnight of the opening of the Expo, one and a half million people had visited the holy relic. By the end of the month, the Goan authorities expected that number to rise to three million. Security was tight, with twenty-four-hour surveillance, 1,000 policemen assigned to guard the body, plus twenty plainclothes special officers around the casket itself. Close-circuit television monitored every access point. For those few weeks, St Francis Xavier was probably better protected than the Prime Minister of India.

'We can't take any chances, considering the situation,' said Bosco George, commissioner for the Expo, sitting in his small pavilion on the fringes of the event, sipping iced tea as his minions scurried back and forth with pieces of paper tracking every development. 'Say a blast takes place, imagine the result? Anarchy. All local residents have been screened, all staff security-checked. Even the bishop needs a pass to enter.'

Twenty days before the Exposition started, a blaze engulfed buildings close to the historic Basilica. Everyone feared sabotage by anti-Catholic elements, but in the end the cause of the fire turned out to be a short circuit. Goa has a tradition of religious harmony, a place where Christians, Hindus and Muslims co-exist despite centuries of religious warfare. The Portuguese were ousted on 19 December 1962 when Nehru sent Indian troops into Goa to recapture the territory. It was the last piece of the puzzle to fit into the new secular India.

But the past decade had seen Hindu nationalism on the rise and a growing consciousness of Hindu identity within the state. Things were changing and the nature of the Goan identity—traditionally associated with Christianity—was evolving. Against this backdrop, a nascent movement among the Catholic community is calling for the Church to admit to atrocities committed in the name of faith and for Goan Christians to view their history in context. The forces of Hindu nationalism are right behind this movement which dovetails neatly with their own political strategy of radicalizing Hindus. But the Church calls it communal mischief-making, opening a fault-line within the community.

It was Mr George's job to ensure that the biggest religious feast in a decade remained free of such communal tension.

Tens of thousands of devotees lined up from dawn until dusk, enduring blazing temperatures and heaving crowds to pay their respects. Benicia among others carried garlands of orange chrysanthemum and jasmine as well as a small wax effigy of the body part she wished the saint to cure: her foot. At the Exposition market just beyond the Cathedral perimeter were hawkers bearing raffia baskets filled with wax arms, legs, stomachs, chests, heads. The faithful would buy the effigy which best represented their ailment and place it in a basket before the saint's body, praying for relief.

The market was a fusion of Indian bazaar and Vatican souvenir shop. Stalls selling everything from cut-price pants to towering pyramids of orange ladoos jostled alongside displays of religious icons, statues of Jesus, Mother Mary, St Francis, bunches of rosary beads, carved crosses and holy scapulas to place around the neck to ward off the evil eye.

Benicia and I spent more than three hours queuing in a line that stretched as far as we could see, snaking back and forth. Finally we reached the cathedral itself. The operation was monitored not by police nor priests but a force more forbidding: fierce old ladies in black crochet shawls who looked as if they would take your eye out if you stepped out of line. The Cathedral remains one of the largest in Asia, seventy-six metres in length and more than fifty metres wide. It dates back to 1562 when the King of Portugal ordered its construction, an architectural jewel in his Eastern empire.

Inside its cavernous central chamber the only sound was the low mumble of prayer. We could see the glass coffin just ahead, resting on a rectangular plinth before the altar. A woman fell to her knees, proceeding to crawl the final few feet across the stone floor which snagged her nylon tights. The faithful deposited their wax body parts into a wicker basket near the relic; many had broken into pieces, not the most auspicious sign. Posters prohibited kissing, drooling, leaning on or smudging the glass casket in any way. An eagle-eyed Goan matron, duster in hand, stood by ready to whack anyone who lingered too long and wipe down surfaces besmirched by bodily fluids.

Then the moment arrived. We were ushered forth to view the body. It had been four and a half centuries and, understandably, St Francis Xavier was not looking good. He was clothed in gold-embroidered robes which shielded the shrunken and skeletal body. The feet were terribly deformed with a number of toes missing, trophies claimed by devotees over the centuries. The saint had one arm and his neck and skull were slightly crushed from a mishap during one of his numerous exhumations and reburials. The miracle of the preserved body had long since passed, but Catholics were nonetheless transfixed by the religious experience. Ignoring the God squad watching over the body, Benicia closed her eyes in prayer, clasped the rosary to her lips, then bent over the casket and kissed the glass tenderly as if it were a lover. The whole thing lasted a few seconds before she was ushered on, kisses wiped away with a jay-cloth.

During an earlier Exposition in the days when the body was not encased in glass, a wealthy Goan lady Dona Isabel went to kiss the feet of the saint. Overwhelmed by the occasion she bit off one of the toes on the right foot and carried it home in her mouth. She built a shrine for the toe inside her family chapel and kept her sin a secret. On her deathbed, she surrendered to her guilt and confessed, offering to return the toe together with a silver gem-encrusted crown for the saint by way of reparation.

St Francis Xavier died in China on 3 December 1552. According to a biography written by Fr Luis M. Bermejo, *Unto the Indies: St Francis Xavier*, the body was placed in a coffin and only four attended his burial: one Portuguese, one Chinaman and two slaves. His coffin was packed with lime to speed up the decomposition process. But on February 17, 1553, it was exhumed before being put on a boat for Malacca where it would be reburied. A fellow Jesuit and biographer Fr James Broderick wrote of how the body was 'strangely untouched by the finger of death'. The new grave in Malacca was too short for the body so the head of the saint was crushed into his chest to fit the space.

News reached Goa of St Francis Xavier's death and some old friends journeyed to the grave and in the dead of night exhumed the body once again. There was still no sign of decay, although the face had been battered and bruised. It was decided to bring the body from Malacca to Goa and more than a year after St Francis Xavier died he set sail once again for Goan shores.

The body's arrival was greeted on the white beaches by thousands of devotees, church bells pealed across blue skies and the corpse was received like a conquering hero. To verify the 'miracle' of the preserved body, a medical examination was carried out. Doctor Cosmas Saraiva, physician of the Viceroy, wrote:

'I felt and pressed all the members of the body with my fingers...There had been no embalming of any kind, nor had any artificial preservative agents been used. I observed a wound in the left side near the heart and asked one of the Society who was with me to put his fingers into it. When he withdrew them they were covered with blood which I smelled and found to be absolutely untainted... I affirm an oath that what I have written above is the truth.'

It was deemed to be miraculous. During his brief career

as a missionary leader, St Francis Xavier won a reputation as a priest of extraordinary ability. His crusades took him to Japan and China as well as to India. On his death, with the discovery of the preservation of the body, everyone wanted a piece of him. Literally. In 1614, Pope Paul V ordered the upper part of his right arm to be amputated and sent to Rome. According to the writings of Filip Neri Xavier in his *Resumo Historico*, the story goes that the Holy Hand arrived on the desk of the Holy Pontiff and wrote the name of the saint on the first piece of paper placed before it. The lower part of the right arm was divided into two parts and one was sent to Malacca and the other to Cochin. A shoulderblade was removed and sent to Macau, all former missions of the saint. Following this mutilation, in 1755 a royal order decreed that the body only be viewed by the public once a year to prevent further damage. It was forbidden to open the coffin without the King's permission. The three keys needed to open the coffin were split: one was held by the archbishop, one by the governor and the last by the controller of the treasury.

St Francis Xavier's body was big business through history, not just in modern times. In 1922 local businessmen were keen to capitalize on the religious fervour which represented a selling bonanza. Local merchants B. X. Furtado and Sons placed an advert in the paper boasting of 'Everything in the devotional line...BUY NOW'.

But who was Francis Xavier?

The best guide is probably the saint's correspondence written in Portuguese and Spanish. Dona Maria gave birth to Francis Xavier on April 7, 1506. He was born in the castle of Navarre to a noble family. As a boy he was weak but dreamed of growing up to be a powerful army commander and he would use his collection of toys to practise war tactics.

In September 1525, he went to Paris to study and lived there for eleven years in the Latin Quarter. The place was 'a tangled maze of rough, dirty, winding streets and alleys' of churches, monasteries, wineshops and gambling dens, said Fr Bermejo's account of the saint's life based on the letters. Many students were regular visitors at the taverns and brothels, sometimes accompanied by their college masters. These adventures led to many contracting the 'French disease' or syphilis.

'Francis saw all this with his own eyes and the pus-covered, repugnant sores made him pull back from the brink of the abyss. For we should not forget that when in Paris he was still in his twenties, with hot blood coursing through his veins,' wrote Berjemo. 'But horrified by the loathsome ulcers that he saw both master and pupils contract, he did not dare to continue association with them.'

It was during this time in Paris that he caught the attention of Ignatius of Loyola who came to Paris three years after Francis. Ignatius was a fellow Spaniard and former soldier who would go on to establish in 1534 the Society of Jesus. Ignatius saw Christ as his commander-in-chief and believed it was his divine mission to spread the word of Jesus. The two men did not hit it off straightaway: Francis mocked Ignatius' piety and in turn, Ignatius was disappointed with his protégé's fascination with war games. 'What does it benefit a man to win the whole world and yet lose his soul?' he mused. In the end, Ignatius convinced Francis Xavier to join him and become a soldier of Christ.

He became one of the first members of the Jesuits. Francis Xavier was ordained a priest on June 24, 1537 at the age of thirty-one. In 1539 he was chosen to go to India as the Church's envoy. The mission was a daunting one for the young man, clearly affected by the burdens of his duty. Shortly before departing for India he fell sick and awoke with cries and violent movements as if pushing someone aside. He later explained to his companion Rodrigues who quoted Francis Xavier saying:

> 'God has granted me the great grace of preserving my virginity. That night I dreamt that... a young woman came into the inn and tried to touch my breast. To fend her off, I shoved her away from me with my arms with so much force that I must have burst a vein and this is why I bled and woke up.'

He set sail for India on his thirty-fifth birthday in a fleet of five ships painted black with white sails. The flagship was the *Santiago*, on which Francis travelled, and from the crow's nest fluttered a white flag emblazoned with a red cross. Francis suffered terrible sea-sickness on the journey. Disease and illness gripped the passengers and the only cures available were bleedings, enemas and faith in God. During the journey, as the fleet crossed the equator towards the Cape of Good Hope, there was a terrible storm.

'The sky was suddenly covered with pitch-black clouds...Terrible bolts of lightning rent the awful darkness and icy rain splattered on the deck. The wind howled and the foremast bent like a bow... Mountainous waves, topped with foam, embraced the ship,' wrote Fr Bermejo

After passing through the eye of the storm, the fleet landed at Mozambique and then sailed to Goa, known as Rome of the East. They landed in Goa in May 1542. Back then it was a small walled city which took just half an hour to walk through from north to south. There was already a strong Christian community of 14,000 plus 4,000 Portuguese. The rest were mostly Indian.

'What a sight Goa is from the river.' wrote Joao de Sepalveda, a chronicler of the time in 1541. 'Partly built on hills, partly built on level ground like our Lisbon. It is a sea of red roofs glittering in the sun, emerging from tufts of vegetation and stately palms. Here and there shoots up a tower or spire from some church or cathedral, like a white finger pointing to heaven. The river is brimful of ships and boats... and infinite is the number of coolies waiting at the docks. And the sound of languages and voices is a veritable Babel.'

The main thoroughfare of the Rua Direita was a crossroads for East and West. Along this road one could purchase everything: Persian rugs, multi-coloured bolts of silk and cotton, Chinese blue and white porcelain, precious stones, horses from Arabia and Persia, slaves from Africa.

Kaftan-bedecked bearded Arab horse traders mingled in the bazaar alongside Hindu merchants with curling-toed shoes and gold hoop earrings, Hindu women in saris and Muslim women in veils walked through markets that traded semi-naked slaves. Money-changers squatted at the crossroads, exchanging Portuguese gold cruzados or Venetian ducats for local currency. It was a truly multi-cultural, multi-lingual and multi-faith society. And that cosmopolitan character gave rise to a liberalism that eventually descended into licentiousness.

The Portuguese, including some priests, openly cavorted with mistresses. They kept local women as concubines. When Francis Xavier arrived he was scandalized by the loose morality of the Portuguese locals and resolved to mend their debauched ways. He was equally disturbed by the new Christians who continued to practise the ways of their old religions, whether Hinduism, Islam or Judaism. Faced with these challenges, St Francis decided to write to the King of Portugal asking for the ultimate weapon in the battle for a return to the fundamentals of faith: the Inquisition.

*

'The story of the Inquisition is a dismal record of callousness and cruelty, tyranny and injustice, espionage and blackmail, avarice and corruption, repression of thought and culture and promotion of obscurantism...'

—(The Goa Inquisition,
Anant Kakba Priolkar, 1961)

Amen to that.

The Goa that welcomed St Francis Xavier in 1542 was a religious melting-pot. As well as the indigenous Hindus, there were followers of Islam as a result of Muslim invasions dating back to the fourteenth century. There were 'new Christians' from Europe who had been forcibly converted from Judaism and left their homeland for India in search of tolerance and security—back in Portugal they were viewed with suspicion by the old Christians and suspected of secretly observing their old Jewish traditions. Goa was also home to thousands of Portuguese Christians who had begun to settle here from 1510 and started the process of converting the local population. Like their Jewish counterparts, those Hindus who converted to Christianity found it difficult to wipe out the millennia-old traditions which were inextricably bound up in their culture and identity.

In 1534 it was felt that the number of Christians was still too small. So in 1541 the Church adopted a policy called 'Rigour of Mercy'. Under the auspices of this rather incongruously-named campaign, Hindu temples were destroyed, land was seized and monies forcibly raised to finance the building of churches and missions. There was widespread destruction of Hindu shrines across Goa during this period. Temples were defiled with the entrails of the sacred cow, Hindu images smashed and golden idols melted down to make candlesticks for local churches. Naturally, the local population did not react well and there were pockets of fierce resistance, particularly in areas of southern

Goa in villages like Cuncolim which openly defied the Church and the Portuguese militia.

It was against this backdrop that the great missionary arrived. On witnessing the lapses in behaviour by the Portuguese and the converts, he dispatched a letter to the King of Portugal, D. Joao III, on May 16, 1545: 'The second necessity for the Christians is that your Majesty establish the Holy Inquisition because there are many who live according to the Jewish law and according to the Mohommedan sect, without any fear of God or shame of the world,' he wrote.

This first request was ignored by the King. But Francis Xavier persisted and after the King's death in 1557, in March 1560, Cardinal Henrique sent to Goa the Inquisitor Aleixo Diaz Falcao. By the year end he 'founded a tribunal which in time earned a sinister renown as the most pitiless in Christendom' (H.C. Lea, New York, 1907). The Inquisition of Goa ran from 1560-1774 and was revived in 1778 during the reign of D. Maria, Queen of Portugal. It was not abolished until 1812.

The Inquisition was established in the palace of the former Muslim ruler, Adil Shah, who ran Goa before being toppled by the Portuguese. At first it was used as a grand residence for the viceroy but it was then handed over to the Church for its religious duties. It came to be known as The Palace of the Inquisition. Originally it had been an Islamic structure but those features disappeared and all historical descriptions refer to a classical design. When the building passed from the hands of the Viceroy to the Church it was renovated in keeping with seventeenth-century religious architecture. The palace was built around a square courtyard, with the surrounding buildings converted into prison cells.

The Holy Office came to be known as a house of horror; as Father Nery Xavier wrote in 1903:

'The terrible acts of the Inquisition during the early period of its existence had caused terror to be so deeply rooted in the memories of the people that none dared to name the place where it was housed as the house of the Inquisition, but gave it the mysterious appellation 'Orlem Gor' (the Big House).'

An edict of the Goa Inquisition was issued for new converts, aimed at preserving the Roman Catholic faith. Its requirements included the following:

* A ban on Hindu musical instruments at weddings.
* A ban on sending the bride and groom 'any gift of flowers, betul-leaves, areca nuts or fugueos (fried cakes)'.
* Relatives should not strew flowers or sprinkle scented water on the married couple.
* under the marital bed, the 'natives of India are hereby ordered that under the bed on which the married couple would sleep, they should not place betul leaves, areca nuts or any other edible thing.'
* 'The said natives are hereby ordered that on the day on which the married woman commences her first menstrual period, they should not arrange a bouquet or any other festive demonstration or send gifts or bananas, flowers...'

Clearly, nothing was beyond the all-seeing eye of the Church. This was just a sample of the prescriptive rules which sought to stamp out cultural traditions of the Goan coverts. These were traditions that went to the heart of the Goan identity. Those who suspected the edict had been broken were required to inform the Inquisition within thirty days or face 'dire punishments'. The edict created a culture of fear and mistrust within the Hindu community, some of whom had embraced the new faith. It was followed by a series of anti-Hindu laws in Goa, coupled with positive discrimination for converts. The missionaries were determined to stamp out Hinduism and nurture the roots of Christianity in their Eastern territory.

The Goan historian J.C. Barreti Miranda (1863 *Quadros Historicos de Goa*), said of the Goan Inquisition:

> 'Every word of theirs was a sentence to death and at their slightest nod were moved to terror the vast population spread over the Asiatic regions, whose lives fluctuated in their hands and who on the most frivolous pretext could be clapped for all time in the deepest dungeons or strangled or offered as food for the flames of the pyre.'

Various orders were made to entrench Christianity and bolster the power of the Church. On April 2, 1560 the Viceroy D. Constantino de Braganca ordered a large of number of Brahmins into exile. Many of them lost property and this led to a mass migration of Hindus. On March 23, 1559, an order was made that the children of Hindus who were left without a father, mother or grandparents should be handed to the College of St Paul of the Society of Jesus to be baptised and educated by priests. But there was evidence that some children living with relatives were snatched and it was believed that this was not just to save their souls but to seize their estates.

Torture was used by the Inquisition to make sure the edicts were obeyed. This took place within the walls of the palace. M.V. Abreo's *Navacao de Inquisicao de Goa*, describes a complex comprising a chapel, entrance hall, audience hall, hall for trials, residence of the Inquisitor, a House of Penitence, the Perpetual Prison and the House of Torture. All were contained in one large edifice, the outer walls of which were seven hand-palms thick.

The contemporary French traveller Dellon, who was imprisoned in the palace for three years, described in his account of the Inquisition a place of two hundred prison cells, dark and windowless. He described 'that Famous House, whose very name makes thousands tremble'. The cell walls were five foot thick and secured by two doors. Food was served through a slit:

'Breakfast for Blacks is cangee, or water thickened with rice, and the other meals consisted of rice and fish,' wrote Dellon. The white prisoners fared better, having soft rolls, fried fish, meat and fruit and a sausage on Thursdays and Sundays.

Dr Claudius Buchanan's *Christian Researches in India*, published in 1812, described dinner with the Inquisitor himself at his country residence. Despite a fine meal and cordial conversation the Inquisitor refused a request to allow Buchanan to see the dungeon cells or say how many were held captive. But the Inquisitor did concede that Dellon's account of the dungeons, torture and trials were perfectly true.

Use of torture was governed by the *Manual of Regulations of the Inquisition*. If judges found the evidence of the prosecution and defence inconclusive, they would sanction use of torture of the accused. During torture the accused was simply instructed to 'tell the truth'. But sometimes they were unsure of what 'truth' their inquisitors wished to hear, thereby prolonging the agony until they guessed the right answer.

Typical Inquisition methods of torture included use of pulleys, the rack, thumbscrews, 'Spanish boots or leg-crushers'. Spiked wheels were drawn over the victim's body with weights placed on the feet. Boiling oil was poured on legs, lighted candles held under the victim's armpits and burning sulphur to eat into bare flesh.

The Inquisition finally ended in 1812 and between 1828 and 1830 the government of Goa ordered the palace to be demolished. In 1878, J.N. Fonseca said in *An Historical and Archaeological Sketch of the City of Goa* that the demolition uncovered the chilling secret of what had gone on behind those walls:

> 'The debris was suffered to remain on the spot til it was removed in 1859 on the occasion of the Exposition of the body of St Francis Xavier. The labourers who were employed in its removal discovered a subterraneous staircase and human bones buried under a thick piece of lead of the shape of a whale or a boat.'

All trace of the Palace of the Inquisition has been removed and today one can walk past the spot and never know the dark secrets that lie beneath. It also remains a chapter in Goan history that is buried by the Church and unknown to many Catholics living in the state today. For many Catholic Goans, the era of Portuguese rule will be forever associated with rose-tinted memories of benign governance by European gentlemen who gave this corner of India some of the finest churches in the world, an archive of exquisite religious art, knowledge of Latin and Portuguese, fusion cuisine and a taste for melodrama.

But a band of Christians from the southern village of Cuncolim is seeking to revise the history of conquest. Their aim is to force the Church to admit the atrocities that took place in the name of Christianity during this period, to put Goan identity in context: an identity that has been Christian for almost five hundred years, but one that was Hindu for thousands of years before that.

Levinson Martin is one of the men leading the campaign. An unlikely revolutionary, Martin is a Goan Catholic from

Cuncolim and the chief public prosecutor for Panjim, a family man with a wife and three children. His aim is to seek justice for the Hindu ancestors of Cuncolim who staged the last stand against Catholicism some four and a half centuries ago. The Battle of Cuncolim has gone down in local history as a David-and-Goliath clash between villagers and the Church—a battle that helped arrest the Catholic sweep down the palm-fringed coastline of Goa. Over a lunch of fish fry, curry and rice, Levinson was in a rabble-rousing mood as he described his ancestors' fight against a Christian fundamentalism which changed the Goan identity forever.

7

Fish Fry and Fundamentalism

Cuncolim, Goa, 2004

It was spring 2004 when I first met Levinson and his brother Leicester. Levinson was a big bear of a man in his late thirties, with a black beard and large soulful eyes that flickered with intrigue. His young brother was a sailor, employed on board one of the many steamships that came through Goa. They were the sons of my father's childhood friend and lived next door to my great-grandmother's old house which borders Cuncolim and now lies in ruins. As small children, my father and their father would play carrom together after school, a board game with wooden checkers. Levinson still had the old board and set it up for his small son to play my Dad—a hardened carrom veteran who played the game without pity.

As the eldest son, Levinson inherited the family home, a beautiful green-painted Portuguese Goan mansion, with the traditional large central salon with shuttered windows opening onto a lush garden of tropical trees and plants. Our family was visiting Levinson for lunch and as we went up the stairs to the verandah, my Dad warned: 'Remember, don't bore him about your book.'

As it turned out, Levinson and Leicester were fanatical about the Catholic conversion campaigns. Putting his glass of beer aside, he drew up the shirtsleeve on his right arm and showed me a tattoo: a Catholic cross overlaid with two curved swords which he said symbolized the dual identity of the Goan: Christian and Hindu. Levinson had chosen his tattoo, but many Goan villagers in the Catholic regions of the state were forcibly tattooed within five years of their birth: a small black cross on the back of the hand, just below the thumb. The mark of the Lord was usually given to lower-caste Catholics—for caste remained an issue even after conversion to Christianity. The higher-caste Catholics did not have this particular cross. Levinson and Leicester, from the Kshatriya or warrior caste of Hinduism, had a tattoo which did not represent possession by the Church, but an assertion of self.

Lunch was served by Levinson's wife and mother on a long teak table in the dining room. There was fried pomfret, a favourite fish of the region, pork vindaloo, beef curry, chicken *cafrael*, chilli fried prawns, salad and two types of rice—steamed and pilau. Plus lots and lots of King's beer. The meal told the story of Goa's mish-mash of cultures, where no food was forbidden and everything was good for the pot. The only thing missing was feni, a local spirit usually distilled from cashew nuts, mostly taken with a mixer and strong enough to blow your head off.

The Battle of Cuncolim had become something of an obsession for Levinson who had a locked filing cabinet full of paperwork on the subject which his wife was banned from touching. The episode was renowned in the Catholic Church for the killing of five priests who were attacked by villagers after they came to convert the locals and explore the erection of a church. The people of Cuncolim were having none of it and when the warning to the priests was not heeded, they killed them. The priests were declared martyrs and in its official history of the episode the Church characterized the people of Cuncolim as cold-blooded murderers. A chapel has been erected in Cuncolim village in honour of the martyred priests—warriors of Christ who died in the battle to bring their faith to the unbelievers.

The move triggered a backlash within the community, for the Church's version of that history left out one key fact. In retribution for the death of the priests, the Church invited the village elders to a peace summit where they were trapped and killed. Levinson and his friends were involved in the building of a separate tribute to the 'real martyrs of Cuncolim'—the sixteen village elders. This marble plinth lies adjacent to the chapel, a juxtaposition that represents tensions in the community to this day.

'I'll show you the whole thing. We'll need a couple of days, maybe more,' said Levinson. 'These elders were our ancestors, your father's and my father's. It's our history. So, you should know.'

I took up the offer at the end of the year, during Exposition month just before Christmas. This is the best time in Goa and the season when the state comes into its own. Every house porch is decorated with a white Christmas star lit up by a bulb. Driving through Goa at night, one is guided through the pitch-black countryside by a garland of white stars that seem to have been cast from the heavens. Periodically, the night skies are ignited with explosions of fireworks as families conduct test runs before the big day. Christmas in Goa is about a family party on Christmas Eve, followed by Midnight Mass when the peal of church bells competes with firecrackers bursting as the clock strikes twelve.

The markets were selling Christmas cards and decorations, Konkani renditions of *White Christmas* could be heard tinkling from tinny radios in every store, tinsel and baubles festooned every restaurant. Village churches decorated the altar with Nativity scenes and cotton-wool snow and erected silk marquees in preparation for Midnight Mass and the Christmas dance that would follow. It was going to be a brilliant blue Christmas.

I arranged to meet Levinson on December 19, the anniversary of Goa's Liberation Day. He had a packed day planned but first he wanted me to meet his neighbour Dr Eclito D'Souza, former vice-president of the East Africa Goan League, freedom fighter and Cuncolim village elder.

Dr Eclito had just returned from hospital and was recuperating in his rambling old house. It was a fine specimen of its type with a stairway leading up to a verandah, with double teak doors opening into the lobby of the house. His dog Comet sat on the porch and enthusiastically greeted us with a lick of his tongue. Waddling behind, Comet followed us into the reception hall. The house had seen better days and showed signs of neglect. Paint was peeling, the rattan and teak furniture looked ragged and there was no homely touch in sight. All the shutters were closed, cloaking the house in a depressing gloom even though it was mid-afternoon. Levinson confided that the doctor had hired a housekeeper/nurse who seemed to do little of either duty, turning up late, taking lunch and a nap and leaving early. He was worried about the doctor's welfare but the old man insisted on being independent. Having lived his life on the political barricades, the doctor did not intend to slip quietly into the debilitating embrace of dependency now.

After twenty minutes, Dr Eclito entered from the door at the end of the corridor, bent double and walking slowly aided by a stout walking stick. My father had described the doctor as a tall, imposing man with a fine physique and sharp mind. He had been one of Goa's leading activists, campaigning for the exit of Portugal from Goa. Age and illness had ravaged his body over the decades, but his mind was as combative as ever.

'My father was a freedom fighter and he didn't like the Portuguese much. He was an independent thinker and I was influenced by him,' he said. 'These days people are so indoctrinated. In Goa the people have been turned into morons by the Catholic Church. Too many Goans know nothing of the Inquisition, they know nothing of the battle of Cuncolim. It's all written in our history, waiting to be read. But nobody reads it.'

As he spoke I noticed that his face and neck were scarred with black marks from his chemotherapy, but despite his evident suffering the doctor's eyes still blazed with the mischievous glint of a true provocateur.

'St Francis Xavier,' he said, bashing the stump of his stick on the flagstone floor. 'This year all of Goa is celebrating his Exposition. And what celebrations! But there is no changing the fact that *he* asked for the Inquisition in Goa. His apologists say he wanted to punish the wicked Portuguese who had settled here, those who strayed from God. But there's no record of the Inquisition burning the Portuguese. They burned converted Jews and converted Hindus who had turned to Christianity. They burned these so-called heretics. These were the original fundamentalists.'

Sensing the doctor was a lapsed Catholic, I asked him whether he still saw himself as a member of the Goan Church. 'I was born a Catholic. But I'm what you might call a liberated Catholic. Most Goan Catholics don't know. The Jesuits have assiduously hidden the fact that Francis Xavier asked for the Inquisition. But it is our duty to expose the truth of our history.'

'What do you think Francis Xavier means to Goa?'

'Every nation needs an icon. The French have Napolean, the British have their Nelson. The Jesuits created Francis Xavier as an icon for Goa to rally its people. Today the Church is seeking to destroy our true history. If one reads the official Jesuit history of what happened at Cuncolim it speaks of the Five Martyrs of Cuncolim—the five priests who were killed by the natives. The question is who are the *real* martyrs? It is our Hindu ancestors who are the martyrs. After all, they were the ones fighting for identity. And for freedom.'

Exhausted, his concentration trailed off into various side alleys, including the whereabouts of the slacking servant. Levinson suggested it was time for the doctor to take his nap and promised to send over some dinner that evening. We left him and went to see the resting place of the martyrs—of both sides.

*

Here we were, on the very spot of red dust where in July 1583 a mob of Cuncolim villagers attacked and killed the five Jesuit priests who had come with the purpose of destroying a temple and replacing it with a church. The church was indeed built, but it was to commemorate their ultimate sacrifice. The Martyrs' Chapel is a small, simple whitewashed building. Nondescript, it has none of the baroque grandeur of other churches in the state. It is a rather sorry affair, its doors secured with padlocks and the lights switched off. The chapel is on a junction, surrounded by noisy traffic and rubbish. I peeped through the barred entrance and through the gloom I could see above the altar a large painting of the five priests offering themselves to the arrows and spears of the natives.

In the sixteenth century, the Portuguese state was keen

for the Jesuits to push forward the conversion crusade in villages like Cuncolim in Salcette, south Goa. These villages had been points of resistance which posed a challenge not just to the Church but to Portuguese rule. The Cuncolim villagers had resisted paying taxes on lands which belonged to the ruling castes. When the Jesuits arrived in Portugal in 1542 they were given the task of bringing Christianity to these resistant territories. Goa was an important trading station for the Portuguese empire which was keen to wrest control of the spice route in the region. Naturally, religion and politics went hand in hand. It was a strategy of souls and spices. Looking at this wider picture of trade and economics, the defiance of the Cuncolim villagers was always going to be crushed. The stage had been set for a showdown.

The mission was led by Fr Rodolfo Aquaviva, according to the volumes of Jesuit letters and records set down in *Documenta Indica*. Fr Antonio Francisco, the priest from the village of Orlim, had already informed the Cuncolim elders of the planned visit. The response from the elders was cool and suggested a visit would not be convenient. The Jesuits decided to press ahead despite the far from welcoming response.

On July 15, 1583, the priests said Mass and set off for Cuncolim where rumours abounded that the Church delegation planned to raze the village temple and erect a church. The Jesuit accounts reported the elders greeting the priests. During the meeting a 'wizard' appeared who shouted 'War' in a state of high agitation. 'Now is the time. Here they are trapped in the tent. This is a good present of many heads.'

Undeterred by this rather inauspicious beginning, the priests waited for the villagers to gather. One priest raised two intersected loaves of bread on a palm tree branch and said, 'Wouldn't a cross look good here?' This was reported back to the villagers. Shortly afterwards, the priests were confronted by a baying mob bearing swords, spears and bows and arrows. The mob shouted out, 'Kill these wizards, disturbers of this region, enemies of our gods, destroyers of our temples...' according to Jesuit records.

The priests were set upon without mercy. Fr Aquaviva was wounded in the legs and neck. The *Documenta Indica* described how the 'barbarous' natives then hit his left shoulder and cut off his fingers. The mortal blow was an arrow to his chest. Fr Francisco Aranha was hit in the neck and speared in the back. He fell back into a newly-planted paddy field, his blood mingling with the bright green rice seedlings. He tried to escape at one point but was caught by the villagers who dragged his body around the temple and ordered him to pray to their God. He refused, saying: 'Am I a beast like you to adore sticks and stones?' Their reply was to shoot him with arrows and beat him with sharpened sticks until he died.

But the worst was saved for Fr Pero Berno who was knifed in the head, blinded in one eye with a dart and had his right ear removed. As a final insult, his genitals were severed and placed 'with cruel insolence' into his mouth, according to the Jesuit records. Fr Afronso Pacheco was speared in the chest and beheaded. Lastly, Fr Antonio Francisco died of a series of injuries to his head and body.

The priests had been accompanied by some converts and mercenaries. But the Church's account focuses on the martyrdom of the five Jesuit priests whose sacrifice was evocative of that of their master, Christ. While the high-born foreign priests were declared martyrs, the locals who also died for Christ were not officially recognized. It reflected the hierarchical nature of Portuguese society in the sixteenth century, not very different from that of Hindu society.

At the top of the tree came the *reinoes*, those who were born in Portugal, then came the *casticos'*, those born in Asia of Portuguese parents, then the *mesticos* who were of mixed parentage and lastly, at the bottom, were the natives.

The murder of the priests was greeted with outrage, and retribution soon followed. The Viceroy ordered the village to be razed and when the elders pleaded for peace, they were invited to talks at Assolna Fort. There, they were encircled and killed, with only one of the sixteen elders surviving by jumping into the river and swimming to the opposite shore. Cuncolim fell to the Portuguese and the village elders lost their lands.

Centuries later the Church chose to commemorate the sacrifice of these priests in the name of conversion by erecting a small chapel. The move stung the Cuncolim villagers who remembered their own unsung sacrifice in this history. A group of Cuncolim villagers, including Levinson, campaigned for a parallel monument to the village elders who were murdered by the Portuguese. Defying opposition from the Church, the Cuncolim Catholic Goans erected their own tribute to the sixteen martyred village elders (even though one escaped). That marble plinth naming the Cuncolim martyrs stands alongside the Chapel of the Martyrs. The row rumbles on as this group of Goan Catholics demands recognition of atrocities committed against the village. Cuncolim's struggle to reconcile with the past seemed to embody the dichotomy of the Goan identity.

As Levinson and I peeped into the Chapel we were joined by another member of this campaign and fellow villager Vijay, a teacher at a Catholic school. A tall slim man in his thirties with a neat moustache and amiable manner, Vijay was a Hindu whose family could also be traced back to those villagers who confronted the Jesuits in 1583. Vijay saw the priests not as innocent victims, but soldiers of war, fundamentalists who came to India to purify the Christian community and convert Hindus. It had been holy war in which both sides suffered losses.

'When they came to Assolna and Cuncolim, our ancestors tried to stop them. I'd call this the first war of Independence.'

'Is this how it's seen here?'

'Yes,' said Vijay. He pointed to an invisible God's army marching in the distance, cross held aloft amid the swaying palms. 'When they came, they came with military. And who wrote this history? The Portuguese. They won't give every aspect. The negative aspects they will not highlight. To view these priests as innocent bystanders is a fraud on the Goan people.'

'You can't expect only five priests to come all this way into hostile territory,' added Levinson. 'These priests are casualties of war. They weren't murdered. But if you see the picture hanging in this chapel, they've shown the scene rather differently.'

The painting in the chapel showed no mercenaries, no Portuguese militia, only five unarmed priests, inviting death with open arms. 'See the picture,' said Levinson, incensed by the painting. 'See them willingly taking the blows. But where are the soldiers?'

'You cannot digest this thing,' said Vijay, softly brushing his moustaches with his fingertips. The fall of Cuncolim freed the way for Christianity to sweep further down the coast. The Hindus took action to protect their local deity Shantadurga and took the image from the destroyed Cuncolim temple to safety in Fatorpa. The links with Christianised Cuncolim and its old Hindu deity remain to this day.

'Fatorpa was in the valley,' said Vijay. 'The Portuguese converted along the coast and it was a mass conversion by the sword. Our religious elders came to know they could not fight them, so they shifted the god into the valley. All local gods were shifted to the valley part and there is still a strong Hindu community there. Cuncolim suffered, but others benefited and we're proud of that.'

'Every year, once a year, our old Hindu deity comes in a procession to here,' said Levinson. 'It's known as the umbrella festival, *sotri* festival. People dance and it's carried here with twelve umbrellas. Twelve umbrellas depicting twelve districts of Cuncolim.'

The dual Hindu-Christian identity of Goans continues to this day in other ways. For example, in Cuncolim villagers from the top-to-bottom of society still give a token donation of rice and coconut to the temple priest every year. The Church does not approve, but the age-old practice continues.

'Why raise this now?' I asked.

'What we're saying is our forefathers did everything for this liberation movement. In Cuncolim you'll find in every house a freedom fighter. This is a movement to correct history,' said Vijay. Was it rooted in the rise of Hindu nationalism, I wondered? Even in Goa, a state associated with religious pluralism, the BJP had won power. One of the key strategies of the BJP is to examine areas of local history, conversion to Islam and Christianity, and use it not to enlighten, but to radicalize. The two men vehemently denied any double agenda.

'We don't have any connection to this movement. Look, he believes the Catholic religion,' Vijay said pointing to Levinson. 'If he as a Catholic proudly says these things then I don't think we can be accused of having links with the RSS. We don't have any links to the RSS. Our demand is not to convert them again to Hinduism.'

'So what do you want?'

'We want history in the right context.'

'Basically, a person should be aware of his past,' chipped in Levinson. 'A person cannot exist without his history. Being a Cuncolim man, being a descendant of this village means something. Go to any place in Goa and 'Cuncolkar' means a person who, wherever you have to fight, defend your people, takes the bull by the horns. The Cuncolkar is the person who can achieve this. The battle of Cuncolim helped forge this identity.'

'Is there a risk that in doing this it creates tension between the religious communities?'

'This is not a war with Christianity,' cried Vijay. 'It is a war for our identity. A war of pride. The history written by the Church portrayed the Cuncolim people as criminals, as murderers. This stuff is taken seriously by many people. If someone calls me a criminal because my forefathers fought for their identity, I don't mind. Let them call me criminal. But let new generations be aware of the reasons for this.'

'So you wish to correct the Church's version of history?'

'Exactly,' said Vijay.

'We wish the Church to delete that portion of the Catholic encyclopedia which says the feast of this chapel is being celebrated by the very descendants of the murderers of these priests. This is highly objectionable. We demand it be deleted immediately,' Levinson added, his hand flourishing towards the nodding palm trees and a piglet snuffling in the bushes, as if addressing the bench in court.

Both men deny the Church's charge that this movement is really about land ownership and caste privileges rather than religious identity. The Church has accused the movement of being one based among the Kshatriya castes—whether Catholic or Hindu—over ownership and control of lands which once belonged to their ancestors and now lies in the hands of a church or temple. But Levinson rejected the motive was 'caste apartheid'. I asked whether the Church still objected to Catholic Goans maintaining old Hindu rituals like the umbrella festival.

'The whole Inquisition period was for that, no?' said Vijay. 'As a history student, I say this: you can change your religion. But you cannot change your mother, your motherland, your culture.'

'Haa,' said Levinson, twirling his moustaches in appreciation, head wobbling from side to side 'Tradition and culture you cannot change. Under the Inquisition, what was the punishment for people who would not abandon their culture?' he said, using the lawyer tactic of posing a question he intended to answer. 'If you admitted guilt, you were killed and burned. If you did not admit, you were tortured and burned alive. And *who* brought this to our Goa? Francis Xavier. How much we should venerate him is a debatable question.'

'Why are you still a Catholic then?' I asked. He laughed, a blush appearing in his bearded cheeks.

'Catholic. Hmm... If given a choice, I might have been something else. But the system is, you're baptized when two months old and you are Catholic. Your mother is a Catholic, your father is a Catholic. But being a Catholic is not such a huge liability. The Catholic religion is quite progressive. But let the Church allow Indian Christians to express ourselves, to define our identity our way.'

'Goa's a special case,' added Vijay. 'We have religious harmony here. For any Catholic feast, the feast for Our Lady of Health, I go and light the candles there. I pray also, I don't mind.'

'And I go to a temple,' added Levinson. 'Not just me, right back through my ancestors. Even in your father's time also. Take the Sotri festival. Your father must have taken part as a boy. These traditions go back to before the

Church. The Church says you should have nothing to do with the temple, you cannot contribute to the temple, you cannot even enter the temple. But this is also part of our culture.'

We climbed into Levinson's beaten-up old Maruti 800 and took a drive to the local temple. It is off a dusty track, hidden within a coconut grove, a basic stone building with a bell hanging from the ceiling above the entrance, surrounded by brush and spiky tamarind trees. Outside, women make an offering of coconut and rice before the deity. We entered the temple, ringing the bell twice, three Goans: two Catholic and one Hindu.

'This is the temple of the Original Man,' Levinson whispered as we slipped off our shoes to leave them on the threshold. 'He's the ancestor of one of the twelve Kshatriya clans. The ancestor of our clan. He came from Banda which is the village on the Goa border with Maharashtra.' So, this was my ancestor too.

'Why is he called the original man?' I asked as we watched the priest light incense sticks before the shrine, releasing wisps of grey smoke that ascended like unspoken prayers to the heavens.

'He was asked to bow before an Indian king in Maharashtra. He was very proud. The king was very cruel and this man would never bow down before the king. One day the king called a big durbar and the entrance into the meeting was made in such a way that it was a narrow space and above the entrance a sword was tied. So those coming on horseback would have to bend beneath the blade, bow down before the king and enter. He told his brother I will never bow down. I would rather chop off my head.' Levinson paused for dramatic effect, then, with a finger making a slitting motion across his throat, he continued in a husky whisper. 'He lost his head and his brother took it to settle in a faraway land. He came *here* with the head. We are descendants of that clan.'

The bell rang.

'Come, the priest is about to begin his puja. Let's go eat.'

The story of our decapitated ancestor lingered long after we had left the temple and left me feeling a little dismayed. It seemed a little like empty, foolish pride. And yet it was indicative of the same combative spirit that led the Cuncolim villagers to take on the Church in order to preserve their way of life. Today their ancestors are seeking to preserve the traditions of both parts of the history. One from the indigenous faith and one from the faith of the conquerors. The composite identity was seen not just in the food, architecture and art of Goa but among the people themselves, where Christians and Hindus respected one another's festivals and traditions, prayed in one another's churches and temples, made offerings of candles and coconuts to one another's Gods in the name of a common identity.

But the Church feared that the Cuncolim campaign to expose the sins of the Catholic conquerors was an opportunity to sow religious divide rather than foster harmony. In the run-up to Liberation Day in 2004, a political row had broken out over a 68-minute documentary *Goa Ka Swadhinta Sangram* (Goa's Liberation Struggle). The film was produced and distributed by the state government with the backing of the then BJP chief minister Manohar Parrikar. (That government has since fallen.) It showed the Liberation of Goa in the context of the brutal conversion campaigns of the Portuguese. Pictures of atrocities against Hindus were juxtaposed with the cross, associating it with evil. The Xavier Centre for Historical Research branded it 'intentionally provocative, biased... and insensitive'. But the BJP's brothers in arms, the VHP and

Shiv Sena backed the film which was due to be distributed to schools across the state.

Later, at the Basilica Bom Jesus, I met up with Fr John Pedro Fernandes, no relation, a seventy-something priest who had been preaching for fifty years. We sat in a sun-dappled room off the courtyard to the rear of the Basilica. Fr Fernandes had first-hand experience of Cuncolim as he had been the parish priest there during the 1980s. He resisted the campaign to rake over the Church's past, however good the intentions. The Liberation Day film issued by the BJP-led state government was a case of how history could be exploited to damage the Christian Goan identity and stoke religious tension.

'We cannot be naïve. Sometimes there's a hidden agenda,' he said. 'The BJP is close to the RSS and VHP and these people are fundamentalists. They say India is for Hindus and they consider Goan Catholics to be Western. Because we're Catholic, they question our very Indian-ness.'

'So do you think one should simply bury this history?'

'There were mistakes from the Church,' he said, looking more than a little uncomfortable, as if suffering from indigestion. 'But remember, in 2000 the Pope openly apologized for mistakes of the Church and we accept the Inquisition was a very bad phase. But you cannot blame us now for what happened then. And one cannot tolerate one fundamentalism in retribution for another fundamentalism.'

Fr John Pedro believed the BJP and its allies wanted to use the sins of the Church's past to build a political campaign. I suggested to him that the best way to deal with such a scenario was open discussion of what went on and how to move forward. It was a dirty history, but one best dealt with in the Catholic tradition of confession, followed by absolution and penitence.

Perhaps it is better that we're more enlightened about

the past. These are mistakes from our past. We accept them and apologise. But we can do nothing more. Goans must accept that.' The priest took me by the hand and stood up. 'Come,' he said. 'Let me show you the Basilica.'

The Basilica: a world-famous shrine for Catholics everywhere that houses the remains of St Francis Xavier in between the Expositions. The church was completed in 1605. Its exterior walls are unplastered and with pillars carved from black rock. Inside, the Basilica is a testament to simplicity without losing any of its dramatic grandeur. Whitewashed walls are canopied with high vaulted ceilings. Nestling amid the exposed wooden beams are pigeons and citrus-hued parakeets who periodically take off from their perch to sweep over the heads of the faithful. Behind the altar is a floor-to-ceiling frieze gilded with gold depicting an engraving of St Ignatius Loyola standing guard over a tiny white statue of the Christ child. The tomb of St Francis lies to the right of the altar, on top of a tiered structure inside a silver and glass casket. Standing beneath the towering figure of St Ignatius, founder of the warrior priesthood of Jesuits, and in the shadows of St Francis Xavier's resting place, Fr Fernandes was struck with awe.

'The Jesuits were a very powerful society,' he whispered, turning his head to me and back to the altar. 'Did you know the Superior General of Jesuits was known as the Black Pope?'

'What does St Francis mean to Goan Christians today,' I asked.

'For Goa, St Francis is very important still. After all, he's the one who brought the faith to our people. He started the process of evangelizing. He believed in a pure life. He condemned the morally objectionable life. He came to purify us. We are Christians now and it's due to *his* efforts. That's why we honour him and venerate him as our patron.'

8

Last Tango in Goa

Mario Miranda, the cartoonist, captured the Goan nature better than most. His raucous cartoons are a visual satire of everyone from the local church padre, to dandy aristocrats of Portuguese descent to the feni-fuelled goings-on of the *kunbi* labourers. Who better to ask about the nature of the Goan identity? We'd met at a Christmas party in Delhi three years earlier. In a room full of networking Delhites, Mario stood apart, like a silent observer watching a play from backstage. When we met again on the steps of his house in Goa, he was on home territory and more ebullient. He is a distinguished man in his sixties, with fine silver hair swept back with a side parting, copper skin and elegant features. He wore a black tailored shirt and grey trousers that looked far too fancy for rural Goa. His house is classic Goan Portuguese architecture, a double-storey mansion set in coconut groves and shocking pink bougainvillea trailing blossoms along the high brick wall that encircles the property.

The house is white with wooden shutters and doors painted black, a stark foil to the vibrant tropical countryside. A pair of lime parakeets perched in the shade of the porch, chirruping their welcome. The porch is decorated with one of Mario's signature blue and white tile murals, depicting the great churches of Old Goa. In the main entrance hall is a grand staircase with sweeping banisters, flanked by wooden pillars and to the front of the house is the dining room which graced parties and balls in honour of US ambassadors, literary icons and the political greats of India. We settled in his salon, a large room with high ceilings and plastered walls the colour of soured cream. The furniture was antique rosewood, baroque designs carved with leaves and flowers and upholstered in sun-faded silks and cotton.

Piles of books on art, photography and Cuba—scene of his most recent adventure—jostled with trinkets on side tables and camphor wood trunks around the room; the walls were adorned with family portraits and informal photos juxtaposed with rare Persian miniatures. His boxer dogs scampered in and out during our meeting, long claws clattering like tap-dancer shoes on the mosaic tiled floors. The floor-to-ceiling shutters were partially closed, blocking out the harsh white light of a Goan winter's day and enveloping the salon in shadows suffused with the smell of jasmine.

A few years back, Mario was living in Mumbai. He intended to return to Goa to sell the house and thereby sever three hundred years of family history. But his wife, a Muslim from the former royal family of Hyderabad, took one look at the house and fell in love with it. She implored him to keep it and restore it to its former glory. He agreed and sank all his finances into the family home. It now houses Mario and his wife, their son and daughter-in-law, two grandchildren, three dogs, his art and a battalion of soft-slippered servants. It is living, breathing history rather than an atrophied relic of a bygone era.

Mario had that very Goan temperament of vivaciousness underscored with a melancholy brooding. It was very Latin and yet very Indian at the same time. The fusion reflected a history of Portuguese Catholic colonialism and the indigenous Hindu culture. This nature is reflected not just in the Goan temperament, but its architecture, its art, its food, its music: a fusion of East and West. It is particularly evident in the old Goan songs, sung in Konkani and sometimes Portuguese. As a child in London, my parents would drag me to the Goan AVC functions, AVC standing for the three villages of Assolna, Velim and Cuncolim. Here, the Goan reunions would feature bands with names like Black Shadow and lead singers called Rocky D'Silva would belt out cover-versions of Elvis and then move on to big band swing. Rhino-rumped Goan matrons swathed in purple satin would dance with diminutive husbands to the cha-cha-cha and tango.

By late evening, when too many glasses of feni and whisky had been downed, when the Goan buffet of samosas, pilau and sorportel had been devoured, the lights would dim, the disco ball would glitter above the dance-floor and Rocky D'Silva dropped the tempo with a medley of old Konkani ballads. It always ended the same way: old-timers gathered around the microphone singing Goan love songs, glass in one hand, a moist hanky in the other. One old man invariably began to weep, overwhelmed by a sense of loss in the ballroom of Battersea Town Hall. And that was all it took to unleash their lament for a lost Goa, the bitter-sweet melancholy of nostalgia.

As children, my sisters and I rolled our eyes as if to say, 'Here we go again,' as the adults swayed in their chairs by candlelight singing *Viva la Goa*. But as an adult sitting in Mario's living room twenty years on, sipping espresso and munching cashews, we found ourselves succumbing to that inevitable lip-quivering Goan sentimentality.

'We were Sardesais before we converted to Mirandas. Yet our family still retains parts of the old Hindu culture.

We still give donations of rice and coconut to the local temple,' he said. 'This is the Goan identity, a fusion of the Indian Hindu and the Portuguese Christian. But it's being destroyed. There's now a movement to bring an end to the Catholic influence in Goa. The RSS, the BJP, they want to rake up old history, the Inquisition, what happened under the Portuguese, as a way of undermining the Catholic part of our identity.'

Mario believed it was part of an effort to create a homogenized Hindu identity for India, just as the original Christian fundamentalists once sought to create a single Indian Christian identity in Goa.

'In what ways is change happening?'

'Socially you notice it most. Go to any party and there're more and more outsiders. There's been an influx of outsiders into Goa. Delhiites, foreigners, people from Bombay. They buy up old Goan properties but they're not interested in maintaining our way of life. Slowly they're eroding the traditions until Goa becomes just like any other Indian state, The Goans are responsible for their own demise, of course. They smelled money and sold their souls.

'Now we have chartered flights every day, bringing planeloads of riff-raff. And this external influence is bound to have its effect. In Goa, you see, we have this Latin touch that still exists. But for how long? I lived in Goa under the Portuguese regime and all that happened on Liberation Day is the Portuguese regime was replaced by the Delhi regime. For Goa to succeed it has to retain that Latin touch, that fusion of Indian-ness and Catholicism, otherwise Goa will become just another Bombay.'

The respect for that culture is already fading, he believed. Old chapels and churches, the architectural legacy of Catholic rule, are being razed to make way for temples to the new colonialists: the tourists. The old architecture is being torn down and replaced by hideous apartment blocks and tourist complexes. At its worst, the tourist industry is importing drugs and prostitution into the state. This was not a few trippy hippies smoking dope in the north, but organized crime rings from Eastern Europe and Russia who ran tours to India's coastal belt. Girls and Class A drugs are part of the package. In restaurants along the coast, Goan cuisine jostles with Kashmiri khaana, Chinese food and fish and chips on menus. As more youngsters are sucked into the tourist trade, they became enthused with all things Western. Even the hawkers along the beach are up to date with the latest Cockney lingo. You are more likely to hear trance music than ballads sung in Konkani these days, more likely to see arm-waving techno moves than the seductive sweep of the tango.

'I don't think the Goan identity will survive,' said Mario forlornly as he bent down to scratch his boxer pup's haunches. 'I see it changing. I've seen it since I came here from Bombay five years ago. Things are moving so fast after centuries of *no* change. Goa now has the film festival, more and more tourists, endless development. There're slums developing near the airport. Shanty towns. Then there's the communal question. The BJP is trying to raise Hindu awareness in Goa. When you say 'Goan' to any Indian, they think of a Catholic, not a Hindu. Catholics are no longer in majority here but their influence on Goan culture has been profound. For the Goan the Church is not just a religion. It's a way of life.'

The Catholic population tended to be along the coast, where the Portuguese had a clear path during their conversion campaigns centuries before. The Jesuits never really penetrated the interiors, the valleys, where Hinduism remained the dominant religion. But look along the palm-fringed strip of white coastline and every village boasts a beautiful white church which remains the centre of social life. Nestling amid coconut groves and tamarind trees, one can find examples of exquisite Italianate architecture, frothy, overblown wedding cake-like chapels, with ornate gold-plated altars and religious icons worthy of a cathedral.

Mass remains the focal point of village life in these Catholic villages. Parents parade their marriageable children at Sunday service. Church dances on saints' feast days double up as marriage scouting trips. In birth, marriage, family life and death, the church is the spiritual umbilical cord connecting every landmark, from cradle to grave.

'Take funerals,' Mario chuckled. 'In Goa funerals are a pastime. It's a rural place. There's not much to do. People get excited about a funeral. It means getting dressed up, seeing the community, getting the gossip, having a party. Funerals in Goa are great social events, places to see and be seen at.'

The other day my rickshaw was caught behind a Goan funeral procession. Under a canopy of palms, shafts of dust-filled sunbeams streaming through the fronds, I watched hundreds of people walk in line through the village to church, ladies shielded from the sun with parasols, girls with hair in white ribbons and best frocks, men in black three-piece suits, hair greased back with oil, each face wearing the mask of mourning. It was high drama. Mario's drawings captured the comedy and pathos of this everyday life, across all strata of society. For him it was easy, for he was drawing himself.

'When you sit down to draw the people, what comes to mind?' I asked Mario. 'What *is* Goa?'

'Goa *is* decadence,' he said, leaning forward in his chair, eyes lighting up, hands conjuring imaginary scenes in the air. 'My abiding image of the Goan is one of decadence, a comedic streak, a love of a good party, a passionate nature.'

'That's for sure. Always up for a party,' I laughed, raising my espresso in a toast.

'And yet... there is a melancholy that comes with the realisation that we're living in the past,' he added gently, as if speaking to himself; his earlier exuberance escaping from his voice, the spark of delight in his eyes usurped by sadness. 'If only we could do justice to this way of life. After centuries, these are our *last* days. What Goa needs is a Tennessee Williams to write it all down, about a centuries-old way of life that is collapsing in our very lifetime. Goans are a vanishing tribe. I tell you, in forty years, the old Goan identity will not exist.'

9

The God Squads

Today there are 24 million Christians in India, that's 2.3 per cent of the population. The Portuguese are documented as the first to bring Christianity to India. But there is a tradition of belief in south India that the first missionary was St Thomas the Apostle who came to India in 52 AD, landing on the palm-lined Malabar coastline in what is now Kerala. To the modern international traveller, Kerala is a haven of white beaches and cool backwaters overhung with wild orchids, a land christened 'God's own country'.

On December 31, 1952, Pope Pius XII issued a radio message to commemorate St Thomas's arrival in India: 'Nineteen hundred years have passed since the Apostle came to India...During the centuries that India was cut off from the West and despite many trying vicissitudes, the Christian communities formed by the Apostle conserved intact the legacy he left them.'

So, according to the Catholic Church, 1,500 years before St Francis Xavier set foot on the subcontinent, Thomas the Apostle brought the Word. He arrived in an India dominated by the ancient strictures of caste, presided over by the high priests of Hinduism, the Brahmins. St Thomas was a fisherman from Galilea 'and no match for the Brahmins in the subtleties of polemics,' noted P. Thomas, author of *Christians and Christianity in India and Pakistan*. But despite this, St Thomas is said to have won over converts by performing miracles. This earned him the name 'Apostle of the East'.

While the history books are far from certain about the veracity of the story of St Thomas's mission to India, the folklore of south India is alive with songs and dances about this foreign sadhu. It ended, as is often the case with missionary stories, in violent death and martyrdom. In July 72, the Apostle passed by the Mount in Mylapore where there stood a temple to Kali, the Hindu goddess of destruction. The priests of the shrine asked St Thomas to worship the goddess and they would feed him delicacies.

'What? Am I to sell my soul for a morsel of rice and worship the devil?' he is reported to have said. He said if he approached, Kali would run from her shrine and the temple would be consumed by fire. As the priests guided him towards the shrine, a light shone forth and Kali ran from the temple which was enveloped in flames. The furious priests fell upon the Apostle and a spear was plunged into his heart. A shrine marking what is believed to be his burial spot is visited by Indian Christians to this day.

But the real business of Christian conversion arrived with the Portuguese some 1,500 years later. St Francis Xavier and his Jesuits was the first proper God squad to visit India, a band of warrior priests determined to stamp out corrupt and immoral behaviour in this fledgling Portuguese colony.

While some of these early Jesuits relied on coercion, iconoclasm and in the final resort the violence of the Inquisition, to force Goans onto the righteous path, there were other Jesuits who decided subtle persuasion and understanding was a better route to God. Father Robert de

Nobili was one such man. Nobili arrived in Goa in 1605 and operated down the coast towards Cochin before leaving for Madhura where he studied Tamil. He was also a scholar of Sanskrit and his knowledge of Hindu culture led him to believe that if he could persuade the Brahmins to convert, the process of converting whole Hindu communities would be quicker and less bloody. He studied and admired the Hindu sacred texts, learned the local language and adopted the ways of the Brahmin. He is reported to have appeared in Madhura in saffron robes, sandalwood paste smeared on his forehead. An Italian, he distanced himself from the licentious Portuguese colonizers who were despised by the Brahmins, calling himself the Brahmin from Rome. He ate pure vegetarian food, conducted ritual ablutions and believed that caste was not necessarily a barrier to conversion, it being more a mechanism of social control.

This attempt to spread the Christian word through tolerance and understanding of the local believers, rather than violent means, was successful—just as the Sufis were successful in recruiting new believers to Islam, most spectacularly in Kashmir, through a message suffused with love. By the time of his death in 1656, aged eighty, he was credited with having converted 100,000 Christians through a sheer love of India and true understanding. Only this achievement can explain how Father Robert de Nobili escaped the judgement of the Inquisition despite his sympathies with local Hindu customs.

At this time in India's history, the Christian faith had a toehold in the south. But the Jesuits of Goa were ambitious and eyed the prize of the north of India under the rule of the Mughal King Akbar. There are detailed accounts of Akbar's court hosting debates between the learned priests of the different faiths to further understanding. The Jesuits were invited to Akbar's court—an invitation they grabbed as a possible opportunity to influence the highest power in the land. The first mission was led by Fr Julian Pereira in 1578.

Their hope of converting the king was ill conceived for while Akbar was open to debate, his faith was non-negotiable. During the debates the priests and mullahs would often become heated in argument so to cool their passions, travellers reported how Akbar would suggest the 'ordeal of fire'. Traveller accounts of the time say the king asked the mullahs to throw a Koran into a burning pit and the Jesuits to throw a Bible. Whichever book survived the flames would be the true book. The challenge was never taken up. The Jesuit fathers returned to Goa empty-handed in 1583.

My favourite story, however, is 'The Legend of the Sagacious Ape' during the reign of Jehangir, Akbar's son and successor, who was less drawn by intellectual and spiritual debate than by fancy. The story of the Sagacious Ape was relayed by the English diplomat Sir Thomas Roe and his chaplain. According to his account, a juggler from Bengal brought a monkey to Jehangir's court professing the beast had insight into spiritual truths.

To test the animal, Jehangir took twelve pieces of paper, each inscribed with the name of a prophet from every religion. The ape was instructed to take the name of the true prophet. After close examination of the choices, the ape chose the paper with the name of Jesus. Jehangir suspected the Bengali juggler had signalled to his animal and so the exercise was repeated but this time the names were written in a code known only to the king. Once again the ape chose the paper inscribed with the name of Jesus. A cunning courtier, wary of a Jesuit plot, then took the twelve pieces of paper and, withholding the name of Jesus, placed the remainder in a bag which was handed to the monkey. Confused, the monkey searched the bag and, failing to find the desired name, fell into a rage and attacked the courtier without mercy, wrenched the paper with the name of Jesus from his hand and in a display of piety, kissed it tenderly. With typical English sangfroid, Sir Thomas Roe remained unimpressed and caustically dismissed the episode as 'one of the many tricks of the Jesuits' in a bid for conversion.

While the Catholic powers in Europe used their Eastern conquests as missions to gather souls as well as spices, the Protestant powers of Europe were slower to turn their attentions to the potential for conversions in India and the East. The first Protestant mission to India came from Denmark, commissioned by King Frederick IV. The mission arrived in July 1706 at Tranquebar.

The English and Dutch powers were eying the Portuguese empire in India and moved to challenge its domination. The Dutch captured Portuguese strongholds in the south in 1663. England's East India Company, formed in London to prosecute trade, was established in 1600 and arrived on Indian shores within a couple of years. Through the Company, England eventually positioned itself to take control in the north once the Mughal Empire disintegrated. But the British government was not much interested in missionaries in the early days, leaving it to individual Churches to send out envoys on shoestring budgets. William Carey was one such envoy, a cobbler from Northamptonshire. A member of the Baptist Missionary Society, he boarded ship for Calcutta in November 1793. In the early years Carey and his family struggled until he had the lucky break of being offered a job as manager of a factory. With his salary and status secured, he began to build a mission which eventually spread as far as Burma and Bhutan. By 1818 his mission set up 126 schools, with 10,000 pupils and by his death in 1834, it was the richest of such missions in India. Many other missionaries landed in Bengal and that is why there is a large concentration of Christians in the north-east of India to this day.

But missions like Carey's were the efforts of the individual, not the state. While the Portuguese and Danish monarchies backed missionary works in India, the British initially viewed such missions as a potential hindrance to making money. In the Charter of 1793 the British Parliament gave the East India Company, a trading entity, powers to regulate migration to India and refuse missionary work which may cause problems to the firm and its profit-making activities. The British were mindful of how Portuguese missionary work had alienated many Hindus and bred a hatred of the colonizing powers.

But that edict was to change. By 1814 missionaries were given permission to spread Christianity. The change of tack followed years of criticism about the debauched nature of the British community in India. Reports home painted an English society in India which kept concubines and harems. The scandal of such a Godless society of Englishmen, even if it was in the colonies, was enough to tilt the balance in favour of the missionaries. The gates were opened to the English Protestants, who were followed by missionaries from America in the nineteenth century.

The missionaries used education and healthcare as a way of spreading their message through India. The establishment of schools, colleges and hospitals had a profound and positive impact amongst the poor. In Delhi, to this day, one of the best colleges is the Christian St Stephen's, seen as an academic hothouse for leaders and thinkers of tomorrow. But despite this contribution to Indian society, the missionary in India remains controversial. The Hindu fundamentalists have painted the missionary as an evil force, converting Hindus to Christianity by tempting them with books and free medicine and even money.

Christian leaders have reported that in recent years, especially under the last BJP government, persecution of Christians has been on the rise, with priests, nuns and missionaries targeted by violent Hindutva hardliners. Through 1998 and 1999, for instance, churches and Christian schools were attacked in the Dangs district of Gujarat. The issue of Christian persecution in India reached world headlines in 1999 when an Australian missionary Graham Staines was burnt to death with his two sons in their Jeep as they slept. The murder, in a remote region of the eastern state of Orissa, caused an outcry.

The Hindutva hardliners denied any role in the brutal murder, but exhibited no particular anguish. Instead, they explained such acts of violence as the manifestation of the pent-up anger of Hindus against forcible conversions. The missionaries were a destabilizing influence in India, they said, and pointed to their secessionist influence in the north-east of the country. While the British missionaries had dispersed all over India, the American Baptists were particularly strong in the north-east. Indeed, by the time of India's Independence in 1947, the American missions had succeeded in turning the far north-eastern state of Nagaland into a society with one of the highest percentages of Christians in the world. These former headhunter tribes embraced the American Baptist Church—today almost 98 per cent of Nagas are Christian and most are Baptist.

The success of the Christian missionaries in these areas is such that it has placed them in the target sights of the Hindutva movement. While Hindutva's militant elements have targeted churches and missionaries, its religious campaign and educational arms have set up schools across the tribal regions of India seeking to 'Hindu-ize' these locals who remain valuable voting banks.

There have also been moves to stop the successful

conversion campaigns of low caste Hindus to other religions like Christianity. Christian missionaries have targeted the Dalit community, promising equality before God and freedom from the constraints of the caste system which continues to dominate life. The Hindutva brigade has sought to prevent some of the mass conversion ceremonies taking place across India and in Tamil Nadu a law was passed to stop so-called 'forced' conversions from Hinduism to either Christianity or Buddhism.

In October 2002, Tamil Nadu's government introduced its anti-conversion law and a couple of months later police arrested people involved in a mass conversion ceremony involving thousands of Dalits.

This is not just a battle for God. In India, since the rise of Hindutva religion and politics have become interwined. A Christian may be more likely to vote for a secular Congress than the Hindu nationalist BJP, for instance. In turn, the BJP recognizes that if it can win over the tribal regions and keep the mass low-caste Hindus on side it has a powerful electoral base.

There is no doubt, the Christian influence is notable in certain areas of India: in Kerala and in Goa, for example. But the one place it remains positively dominant is in the north-east of India: a fragmented jigsaw puzzle of states which have been the target of Christian missionaries from the beginning and which is now the epicentre of a Christian separatist movement.

In Nagaland, India's far north-eastern state, such is the locals' zeal for Baptist Christianity that it forms the heart of their quest to secede from India and establish a 'Nagaland for Christ'. It is a hidden battle that continues until now. In Asia's longest running modern war, the Nagas are India's new crusaders, modern-day warriors for Christ.

10

Headhunters and Missionaries

'The golden fields, they lay unreaped and sere
As blood freely flowed
And mingled with the rains
And stained the virgin soil
Like a thousand scarlet sunsets
Streaking the evening sky
Back of the blue, blue hills,
The blue, blue hills...'

—From the poem *Kelhoukevira*
by Easterine Iralu

Kohima, Nagaland, March 2005

'There is a village, perhaps two hundred kilometers north of Kohima,' said Achiilie, eyes luminescent in the dark as we bumped along the ragged mountain pass leading to the Naga capital. 'I remember it clearly. I came across it after weeks of trekking. Inside the house of the tribal chief I saw a huge wooden bowl. It was placed in the centre of the room and inside I saw more than one hundred skulls.' He signified a slitting motion across the throat, sending the inevitable shiver down my spine.

'When were the heads taken?' I asked.

'During battle by Naga warriors. Not now. Long ago, maybe fifty years back. But all are saved. In Naga culture, a warrior is judged by the number of heads he takes. They say the more heads a man takes, the longer his life. When women married they looked not at wealth, but the number of heads in a man's house. *This* man must be from a tradition of great warriors.'

Achiilie leaned back in his car seat and we were silent as our minds conjured up the haunting vision of a pile of blackened skulls; the only sound to penetrate the evening gloom were the low rattle of the engine and the wind rushing through towering teak and bamboo forests. I had read somewhere that the Nagas believed the human spirit resided in the nape of the neck and in battle when they decapitated their enemy the spirit was freed and released into the skies. It was now complete darkness, the rain clouds had dispersed and the sun had set behind the blue-black mountains. Suspended over the jagged landscape was the first of the new moon, a sliver of silver engulfed by nightfall's bruised skies.

Headhunting has ended but war continues to plague this isolated territory in the far north-east of India. These one-time headhunters were famed through south-east Asia and beyond for fearlessness in battle. Through the last two hundred years, the Nagas have taken on armies of some of the world's mightiest empires in a bid to preserve their distinct cultural identity, one untouched for almost 2,000 years until the British settled in the tea plantations of neighbouring Assam. The Nagas took on the British and were never fully subjugated; although they helped repel the Japanese in the Second World War, arresting their designs to invade India in the Battle of Kohima which was a turning point in the war. Now the Nagas were fighting India, a country which absorbed their mountainous terrain after

Independence from the British Empire in 1947. For the Naga sees India as the latest foreign invader in its battle for sovereignty in south Asia's longest-running war.

In the eyes of the Naga people, it is not just a war for cultural identity, distinct from Hindu-dominated India: it is a war of faith. When the British first established contact with the Nagas in 1826, the Christian missionaries swiftly followed, bringing schools as part of their evangelizing mission. While the Nagas never took to the foreign powers, they succumbed to the teachings of these latter-day crusaders. Today, more than 95 per cent of them are Christian, with the majority following the American Baptist Church.

In the dark forests which provide sanctuary to separatist guerrillas, the battle cry of the various factions is united in a pledge to create 'Nagaland for Christ'. In the name of Jesus, militants are fighting for a Naga Christian homeland to preserve their millennia-old culture and act as a spiritual beacon for Christianity throughout the region. In bunkers with Biblical names such as Zion, camouflage-clad guerillas begin the day with a morning prayer, heads bowed in spiritual contemplation. Despite the official ceasefire with the Indian government which began in 1997, the main militant factions—the National Socialist Council of Nagaland (IM) which is run by Isaac Muivah and the National Socialist Council of Nagaland (K) run by a man called Khaplang—continue to battle for domination of territory.

The Indian jawan may no longer be in the firing line, but civilians are still game in this factional violence. From their jungle hideouts, designated territories unofficially recognized by the authorities, the insurgents practise military exercises carrying kits comprising a rifle and a Bible. They extort funds from the local community, a kind of 'terrorist tax' which they describe as a contribution to fighting for the Promised Land. Those who refuse to pay face kidnappings, beatings and executions.

Hell on earth takes place under the omnipresent sign of the cross, evident everywhere from the towns to tiny hilltop villages shielded from the outside world by dense woodland and near-impassable roads which bear placards proclaiming: 'Jesus Died, So You May Live'. It's a reminder of the duty to continue the evangelizing mission into the rest of the region. The influence of American evangelist missionaries is inescapable—the cross dangling from rear-view car mirrors, kids playing basketball in pot holed alleys, the taped voice of Billy Graham's fiery fundamentalist rhetoric blazing from car stereos, puritanical posters proscribing pre-marital sex. The choice of music of my driver, a hip young man with a shaved head and earring, is Kenny Rogers and Dolly Parton. The British and Indians may have controlled these tribal lands but it was the American Evangelists who conquered the people.

*

When I told friends in Delhi I was going to Nagaland, invariably I received one of two responses: 'Why go there? They're a bunch of dog-eaters' and 'Be careful. They're not like Indians.'

Both statements have a point. Nagas *do* eat dogs. Achiilie, my sometime guide during the visit cheerfully explained that dog meat is something of a delicacy in Nagaland. It costs eighty rupees a kilo from the butcher shop and is a particular favourite during the wrestling season when fighters want to bulk up quickly.

'The rest of India uses the fact that we eat dog as an insult to the Naga. But we don't eat strays,' said Achiilie. 'We rear the dog, fatten him and then kill him with a blow to the head. Many Nagas survived by eating dog meat during the worst of the '57 insurgency against India. It was dog meat or starvation.'

'What does it look like?' I asked.

'It has the colour of beef.'

'What does it taste like?'

'It tastes like chicken.'

Dog-eating is just one cultural characteristic which made the Nagas seem alien to the people of India's plains. Like other south-east Asian neighbours, the Nagas ate dogs, but the differences with the rest of India did not end there. Most Indians are of Aryan or Dravidian extraction, but the Nagas are of the Mongoloid race, with coppery red skin, slanted eyes and flat-sculpted features. They are a handsome people, and gentle in nature, despite their fearsome reputation as warriors. They have none of the typical Indian garrulousness, and a restrained dignity that reminded me a lot of the people I'd met during a visit to Mongolia ten years ago.

The Naga language is part of the Tibeto-Burman group of languages and is unrelated to the main languages of northern India: Hindi, Punjabi and Urdu. The culture is tribal, with each of the sixteen tribes retaining a distinct identity and dialect which differentiates people of one region from another in this small land of 16,579 square kilometers. Culturally, linguistically, genetically and in terms of their religion, the Nagas differ from other Indians who, despite their regional differences, often share other common characteristics.

For all these reasons, some Nagas felt they did not belong in India, just as some Indians did not believe the Nagas were really Indian. These thoughts resonated on my arrival at Dimapur airport, the only airport in the state of Nagaland. My welcome into Nagaland made it clear that this really was another country, even if it is part of India. A group of military police greeted me as I entered the departure lounge. They wanted to see the special permit issued by Nagaland House in New Delhi which allows foreigners to enter this restricted territory for a limited period. In order to get the permit I had to specify which areas I wished to visit and why. Failure to stick to the designated route could mean arrest and imprisonment. Even in Jammu and Kashmir, there were no such procedures.

I had to show my passport and visa, a requirement which is not necessary in India other than in the north-east, a jigsaw puzzle of territories afflicted by separatist insurgency movements.

The head of airport security was not satisfied with the visa and suggested the permit was a fake. After an aggressive questioning session flanked by four other officers, he finally took down my details in triplicate and said everything was in order; I was free to go. There were no taxis or buses at the airport and he suggested it was too late to travel to Kohima which was two hours on the highway that cut through the valley.

'It's getting dark. There're bandits. Not safe,' he concluded. Since there was no transport at the airport, he offered to drop me off at a hotel in the police bus which would be leaving shortly. 'Don't be offended,' he added in a softer tone. 'I have to be sure paperwork is correct—in case you go missing.' Welcome to Nagaland.

Nagaland is a semi-autonomous state within the Indian union. In a bid to appease the desire for self-determination among the Naga people and end the insurgency which afflicted the state, the Indian government in December 1963 inaugurated the state of Nagaland. Under the Constitution (Thirteenth Amendment) Act, 1962, it specified that Acts of Parliament in respect of Naga religion, customs, laws and procedure, ownership and transfer of lands shall not apply to the state unless the legislative assembly of Nagaland passes a resolution on it. By this, the Indian government hoped to protect the Naga identity within India, safeguard its resources and put a stop to secessionist sentiment.

The problem began when the British decided to withdraw from India in 1947. Despite having some Naga territories under British control, the Nagas had hoped that when the British departed they would allow Nagaland to become a sovereign state. The Nagas argued that theirs had always been a separate nation for thousands of years, with no connection to India. India was Hindu-dominated. Nagaland was a Christian state and did not wish to have its identity submerged within the Indian Union.

On August 14, 1947 the Naga National Council sent a letter to India, Britain and the international community declaring it was independent, one day before India won its Independence from Britain. Its declaration was ignored and Nagaland became part of India on the transfer of British Indian territories. Unbowed, in 1951 the Nagas held a plebiscite in which they said 99.9 per cent of the people voted using their thumbprint to declare they were independent and not part of India.

The leader of the nationalist movement was A.Z. Phizo and in 1953 underground secessionist activities began under his command. The Church remained a factor in all of this and after 1947 a flood of American missionaries came into the state. Indian Prime Minister Jawarhalal Nehru was mindful of their interference in the internal affairs of India and on April 3, 1953 during a visit to Nagaland, he blasted 'outsiders' whom he felt were leading the Nagas astray. He was angered when he found a letter circulating among pastors calling on them to celebrate April 5 as Independence Day. The Church was the invisible hand feeding the public appetite for independence.

In 1955 Phizo announced the formation of the Naga Federal Government and armed rebellion broke out. In 1956 the Indian army was called in. Phizo fled to what was then East Pakistan and then onwards to London in 1957, leaving his people to bear the brunt of the clash between Indian forces and the separatist guerrillas as open warfare ensued.

Since the insurgency began, Indian estimates put the number of deaths in the region at more than 20,000. But Naga separatist leaders say it is 200,000. Of those, they claim almost half the people died during the 1956/57 crackdown by Indian forces.

Kaka Iralu, a Naga nationalist, has written widely on the subject and his book, *Nagaland and India, the Blood and Tears*, is a catalogue of the alleged crimes perpetrated by Indian armed forces against the Naga people. Iralu's book accuses Indian forces of a policy of murder, rape and torture against the people on a mass scale in a bid to crush the nationalist movement—again, something the Indian government refutes.

His book compares the Naga struggle for a Christian homeland to the Jews' struggle for Israel. The theme of 'India's Israel' was something that came up again and again during my visit. Kaka Iralu urges Nagas to take heart and model themselves on the Jews who never lost faith in winning back their holy land. To India, he warned: 'Remember the Jews and learn from them: two thousand years of dispersion and oppression did not destroy them. Fifty-two years of your blood and my blood, your tears and my tears have not succeeded in destroying me or validating your lie.'

The formation of the state of Nagaland in 1963 did not bring the peace hoped for. India was determined not to give in to the Christian secessionists, fearing that an independent Christian Nagaland would trigger a rash of other secessionist movements across India in the name of religion and identity: in Muslim Kashmir or Sikh Punjab for example. Such a move could precipitate the eventual break-up of India. Just as Nehru was iron-willed against any threat to Indian unity, so his successors were equally determined to resist the Naga claim. But for the Nagas, a warrior race with Jesus on their side, the fight was far from over.

11

'Nagaland for Christ'

There are two things that dominate Kohima. One is the ever-present sign of the cross, whether Baptist or Catholic, rearing into the skies across the city's hilltop horizon of wooden buildings and shacks. The other is the police headquarters, a fortress-like structure on the city's highest point. It is the all-seeing, all-hearing embodiment of the nation state: India. Anywhere in the town, this bleak blue and white building with its slit windows draws one's fearful gaze; an architectural Big Brother.

Its positioning, making access without visibility an impossibility, is as clear an indication as any of the state of relations in Nagaland. The security forces and people have had to live with more than half a century of insurgency and guerrilla tactics. Before the ceasefire, the armed forces struck terror into the ordinary Naga. Even under the ceasefire, the militant battle for terrain continues, with the Naga caught in the crossfire.

The Nagas are friendly people, but sometimes I sensed a reticence in the faces I came across, a wariness of being watched, of uttering the wrong word, bowed by the burden of fear. The town was ripe with paranoia. Even if one asked an innocuous question such as 'Where is an interesting place to visit?' the answer was 'I don't know' with a poker-face.

Lt General V.K. Nayar, a retired Indian army chief who served in Nagaland at top level, gave a sobering description of the role that the militants played in the everyday lives of the Nagas, where anything was acceptable once cloaked under the mantle of a holy mission for a Christ-land. Nayar's book *Crossing the Frontiers of Conflict* described a world where the normal values of democracy and society do not apply:

> 'The nexus between the politicians, contractors, bureaucrats and the underground factions (militants) is well established, (it) apportions a major portion of development funds and people remain deprived and alienated... confrontation in the polluted environment has resulted in the last two decades in the carrot offered to the people being eaten by the nexus and the stick falling on the people.'

As far as he was concerned all parties were to blame for the Naga suffering. In Nagaland the militants were in control of state politics, the central government allowed suffering to continue through its 'inaction and tolerance'. It is a world where militants operate openly, extorting money and conducting kidnapping and hijackings. Like Kashmir and other areas torn by militant activity, there were parallel governments: the official state government and the counter-government run by the terrorists.

Naga militancy is a divided house and the only thing that unites it is Christian faith and devotion to a Nagaland for Christ. The NNC remains a minor faction under descendants of Phizo, with another faction, the NNC (K) under Khado Yanthan. These groups have limited influence in the Angami and Chakasang tribal regions. The two NSCN groups are the most powerful. The NSCN (K) is run by a Burmese Hemei Naga called Khaplang and has power in the Konyak and AO regions. The NSCN (IM), which is the most influential group of all, is run by the Isaac-Muivah leadership of the Thangkhul and Sema tribes. IM has influence on Semas, Lothas, Phoms and control over some Angami tribes in Kohima and Dimapur. IM's leadership has been in exile in Thailand but was in India that week for peace talks with the central government. Observers noted that given the divided tribal nature of Naga politics, a peace deal brokered by IM without the support of others could encounter difficulty when it came to delivering it on the ground. Their concerns never materialized as the talks ended in deadlock.

Muivah, the general secretary of the National Socialist Council of Nagaland (IM), said shortly after the talks that unless there was a breakthrough the ceasefire could crumble. Asked by a Reuters reporter in March 2005 whether he would take up arms again, he replied: 'That cannot be ruled out.'

Muivah's group wants the Indian government to unite all Naga territories in the north-east under a single Greater Nagaland. The Indian government, which carved off some Naga territories and reallocated them to its other north-eastern states, has refused to do so. While Muivah is seeking to reunite Naga territory, other more hardline militants groups want nothing less than sovereignty straightaway.

It is a horribly complex scenario and makes the Kashmir problem seem straightforward by comparison. Here is an explosive mix of tribal, cultural, religious and national politics, with a bit of outside interference from the missionaries, Chinese and Pakistanis to boot. To work my way through the moral quagmire that is Naga politics, I did what any good Catholic would do when confused—I went to see the local priest, keeper of confessions.

The Cathedral is set high up on the hills of Kohima. The

Bishop was away on business, so I spoke with one of his priests. The Catholic Church missed a trick in Nagaland, for although it is overwhelmingly Christian, it is predominately Baptist. Even though the Jesuits had penetrated these thick mountainous forests, they had not succeeded in establishing dominance like the Baptists. Out of a population of almost two million people in Nagaland, only 50,000 were Catholic. As a consequence, the Catholics are not part of the deadly nexus of militancy, evangelist Christianity and politics of the region. This makes them useful observers.

I met Fr Francis Cheerangan in the Bishop's house by the Cathedral overlooking the valley. It was a beautiful day with clear skies and a crisp mountain breeze that carried the smell of pine trees. The Cathedral can be seen from far and wide. It seats many thousands inside and the altar is overlooked by a huge statue of Christ on the Cross which is almost twenty feet high. The Bishop's house was a welcoming place, it smelled of incense that took me back to my childhood. The father and I sat over chai and biscuits served by a sweet old nun who periodically stood at the doorway, face wreathed in smiles.

Fr Francis was not like the dusty old priests I remember from Sunday Mass when growing up in London. Those were pickled old Irish padres beaten down by years of service and cynicism. In contrast, Fr Francis was like a man permanently plugged into an electricity socket, charged up and high on God's work. He was thirty-two years old, exceptionally bright, eccentric and possessed of a youthful handsomeness. His appearance betrayed his roots in Kerala, the coastal state on the southern tip of India: he had dark gold skin, wiry hair and intense black eyes. His slender frame was dressed in shirt and slacks, with a pashmina carelessly draped across his shoulders, giving him a slightly effete air. He was a restless character, constantly crossing and uncrossing his legs, leaning forward in conversation, arms waving—a complete contrast to the reserve of the Nagas. His speech was periodically peppered with a maniacal laugh—a series of wild, hyena-like yelps that bordered on craziness. Fr Francis had come as a boy, aged fifteen years, and completed his priesthood training in Nagaland during the worst years of trouble. During the last seventeen years, marking his graduation to manhood, this young priest had endured much.

'What was it like when you first arrived?' I asked.

'Challenging.' He issued a brief yelp of laughter. 'Initially, I was just a student and my dream was to bring the Church to Nagas. Somehow God gifted me this duty.'

'It must've been at the height of the troubles when you arrived. Did you feel in danger?'

'I was caught once, held in August 1997. I was in a vehicle and the militants stopped me. They said they needed it to learn to drive. I was unafraid. I argued for one-and-a-half hours that I could not hand over the car as it belonged to the church. They said they'd destroy the car. So I gave the keys. The next day they called me to a meeting.'

'What happened?'

'The commandant was angry that I challenged him. I sat on the ground and he sat opposite with six bodyguards behind him, all with guns pointed at my head. He said "You have a gun in your pocket. Surrender it." But I actually had a Bible in my pocket and I wanted to remove it and say "This is my gun" But I was afraid they might shoot.'

'What did they want?'

'He wanted to make a show. I had embarrassed him in front of some nuns in the car and he needed to scare me, show me who's boss. He took out his gun and his bodyguards steadied their guns to my head. He said he was going to kill me. I told him "Why six guns, one gun will do?"' He issued another yelping spasm of uncontrolled mirth.

'Then what?'

'Then he realized I could not be scared. He let me go. After three-and-a-half hours, I was allowed to go. If he killed a priest, it would be a big sin.'

'These people claim they're fighting in the name of Christ. For their identity as Naga Christians.'

'Religion has very little to do with it. It is murder and corruption in the *name* of religion. They use Christianity to win the support of the people. But they've hijacked Christianity in the name of terror.'

'Like al Qaeda has with Islam?'

'Yes. At first their ideas were good. The militants began by preventing drinking, patrolling neighbourhoods to protect the people, they were against drug trafficking—this area is a route for the heroin distribution chain. Now they're part of that drugs trade which helps finance their war.'

'Have you heard the groups use this phrase "Nagaland for Christ"?'

'They all use it. They say Nagas are the chosen people of God, chosen to have a Christian homeland, to spread it to the non-Christian lands that surround them.'

'They say it's the will of God to have a Nagaland for Christ,' I suggested.

'When they talk like this, it reminds me of the Jewish mentality in Israel.'

Yet again, the comparison with the Jews: the Nagas also saw themselves as a distinct tribe of people fighting larger and more powerful enemies to preserve their holy land. They too described their battle in religious terms, a holy mission to preserve this island of Christianity, rather than Judaism, amidst a sea of unbelievers. They took heart from the Jews, pointing out that they had never relinquished their hope for Israel and in the end, despite millennia of persecution, they succeeded. The Naga separatists wished to emulate the example of Israel.

'But surely they realise Israel survives because it has a powerful friend in the US? Politically, economically, strategically, it is protected and therefore survives. The Nagas have none of these advantages. How could an independent Nagaland ever be more than a dream?' I asked Fr Francis.

The father agreed. 'Let's be honest. If ever Nagaland won its freedom, there is a strong fear that China would invade.' The Catholic Church was supportive of greater autonomy, a solution within the Indian Constitution, he said.

'These people have an idea of Nagaland but they have no idea of what it means. The state cannot even manage now with the funds from central government. Why do we have this desire for independence?' he mused.

'Where do you think it comes from?' I asked. 'You know these people intimately after seventeen years of dealing with their problems.'

'It's true that cultural identity lies at the heart of it. The Nagas feel the differences with Indians is too vast. But also, there's very little development here. Money comes from the Centre and missionaries but much of it isn't well used. Backwardness leads to alienation. Any business is owned by outsiders and locals are kept low. They feel oppressed and they react. They have this idea of a separate state but I think many don't have any idea of what it means to be a separate state.'

'So they support the insurgency?'

'You have high unemployment. Alienation. The militants offer young men free food, free money, excitement, so they join. It's not so much ideological as practical.'

'The Baptists are often portrayed by some Indian security officials as a silent player in the insurgency drama. Do they encourage this movement?'

He paused to consider and answered carefully: 'The Baptist Church is identified with Naga identity. So what the church does, the people do and vice versa. If the church has a discussion on this matter, they begin with a prayer, so a subtle link is made.'

Despite the bleak scenario, Fr Francis agreed that things had improved since the ceasefire. Tension and violence had lessened. But the scars of almost six decades of war had left their mark.

'The people still live in fear,' he said, voice pregnant with gravity as he pushed the plate of biscuits away from him. 'The present generation is a tougher generation and a more fearful one. Just the sound of an oil tin dropping onto the road awakens the old fear, the memory of gunfire.'

The Catholics could afford to be frank. But I expected the Baptists to be an altogether more defensive group, given their dominance in the region. Evangelism was an integral part of Naga culture, as much as tribal life. The two had become entwined. Before the American missionaries came the Nagas were animists. At first there was resistance to the foreign preachers. No doubt a few lost their heads, but by 1872 the first tribals accepted the Word. In a tribal society where the leader made the decision on behalf of his people, once the Baptists had persuaded the tribal chief they invariably won the whole village. In that way conversion was swift once it got underway. Their evangelizing mission was assisted by funds that built schools, introducing the Nagas to reading and writing for the first time in their history. Church soon became an integral part of their identity. Lt General Nayar noted in his book, 'The spread of Christianity, while providing Nagas a sense of identity, also simultaneously promoted a sense of separateness from the rest of the country.'

The Baptist Church is the crux of Naga life now. Its affairs are overseen by the Nagaland Baptist Church Council which represents twenty associations across the state and 1,344 churches in the region. Its secretary general is the Reverend Zhabu Terhuja. The Reverend agreed to meet at eight in the morning at his residence. The building was watched over by a guard dog. Sitting on its haunches, it looked like a menacing white wolf. Nervously, I approached the door as the dog eyed my every step. Suddenly, it arose on abnormally short legs and scurried into the distance with a look of terror in its eyes. I had forgotten this was dog-eating country.

The Rev. was behind his desk which was spread with files. He had a holy calendar on the wall and a map depicting the region. He was a jolly-looking man, fair-complexioned, with almost Chinese features. But behind the smiles I sensed a built-in caution. He launched into a history lesson of how the missionaries had won over the people.

'The Gospel was first accepted in 1872. The British were trying to control the Nagas and they could not do that, so they hoped Christianization might help tame them. At that time American Baptists were on their way to Burma and while in Assam they first came into contact with the Nagas.'

'How were the missionaries received by these headhunting tribes?'

'At first they were not so friendly,' he chuckled. I imagined a group of sunburned priests being chased by naked Naga headhunters. 'But we made progress gradually, mainly through tribal leaders, education. When the missionaries went into the jungles they went alone, with a few converts. Eventually, Nagas came to believe that God had a special purpose for them—that He wished to reach out to this people in particular.'

'So Christianity became part of who the Nagas are.'

'When you read the 1929 memorandum to the British Simon Commission on the position of minorities in India, it spells out the Nagas' apprehension even then. They feared if we became part of India we would be trampled upon either by Hinduism or Islam. So in that sense Christianity has become a large part of our identity.'

'There's a suggestion that the Church is behind the separatist movement?' I ventured.

'The Church has no political agenda. But, the aspiration of the Nagas for self-determination is the right move. Unlike the Kashmiris or Punjabi Sikhs, the Nagas are truly different from other Indians. The Naga claim is a genuine one.'

I asked how Naga identity had been damaged, if at all, after almost six decades of being within the Indian family. He suggested its participation in the Indian political process was changing old tribal ways such as the village tradition of nominating leaders. That system is undermined by the election system, he said. He also accused party politics— whether Congress or BJP or regional parties—of playing a divide-and-rule game among Nagas in the fight for a vote bank, playing on old tribal loyalties.

'In this way, modern politics has factionalized religion and is weakening the Church,' he concluded.

'But the Church also plays its part in Naga politics,' I added. Before I came to Nagaland, I had been told by senior security sources within the Indian government that they suspected certain Baptist churches of channelling funds to Naga militants. 'Why are the Baptists suspected of encouraging insurgency?' I asked.

The Rev. sighed and spread his palms flat on the desk before looking at me full on, all smiles gone.

'Who is behind this campaign? We've heard it very often. Delhi suggests the Baptists are behind this. I don't think the Chinese or Americans are behind Naga separatism. To those who say the Church is supplying arms through its foreign aid, I say show me the proof.'

The Rev. seemed reluctant to put me in touch with the people running the evangelizing mission, or indeed any of his people on the ground. It made me wonder what message the Church imparted to its ordinary members. The Baptists clearly backed the Nagas in their claim for sovereignty. And in the end, insurgencies are not just fought with bullets, but words. An independent Nagaland for Christ seemed to fit in very neatly with the Baptists' own plans for the region—a spiritual nerve-centre which would export the Word into neighbouring countries.

I arranged to visit a typical Naga village. Konoma is set high in the mountains, more than an hour's drive from Kohima along snaking pot-holed roads which overlook heart-stopping sheer drops into valleys of orchards, trees with pink cherry blossom and neat cultivation terraces growing rice, the food staple. More than 82 per cent of the Naga population is rural, according to the 2001 census. Agriculture is the main livelihood of the Nagas, with 73 per cent of the population working in this sector, according to the 2004 State Human Development Report. These mist-filled valleys below were farmed still using old-fashioned methods which closely observed the needs of the environment. The tribes used rotating cultivation known as *jhum*.

Rain had fallen heavily just before we set out in the taxi, so the roads were waterlogged and somewhat difficult to manage. In the monsoon, these mountain roads become sliding slopes of mud, making travelling along these passes perilous. Mud slides could take whole sections of the hillside down into the valley. Soil erosion remained a major concern for farmers

The Naga landscape on the way to Konoma was unlike any I had seen in the rest of India. The vegetation ranged from pine forests, teak and the world's biggest species of bamboo to palm trees and cherry blossom. I even saw some tall cactus. It was a cross-section of nature's abundance, helped by a temperate climate, fertile soil and untouched landscape. The region was also rich in plants used in herbal or Indian ayurvedic medicine, making it a potential treasure trove for India's huge market for natural remedies.

But the Naga mountains and valleys contained riches far greater than these. Nagaland's largely untapped mineral wealth is no doubt a major reason why India cannot relinquish this territory—apart from the primary strategic reason, that is. It could also explain why 'outsiders', whether they are the Chinese who helped train some Naga militants or Americans whose churches champion the cause, could be interested in this backward and isolated bit of India. After all, centuries ago, the Catholic missionaries worked with their governments in a joint quest for Eastern 'souls and spices'. Their interests coincided. Today Nagaland is a place to save souls and prospect for oil.

Nagaland has proven oil reserves of 600 million tonnes. But the full extent of Naga oil and natural gas reserves is not yet known. It is believed there is oil along the Belt of Schuppen which is seen as a priority for oil exploration. Nagaland also has large reserves of limestone, marble, granite and coal. The locals also speak of diamond and gold mines. But war, lack of development and isolation continue to prevent the region from being tapped—so a vast source of resources remains untouched while the people continue to live in poverty. Despite a relatively high literacy rate of 72 per cent for men and 62 per cent for women in 2001 census figures, unemployment remains high.

We arrived in Konoma by late afternoon. The skies were

smudged with rain clouds and darkness was beginning to set in already. There was not much going on as we parked by the traditional wooden gateway to the village. A few chickens scratched in the dirt but most people were holed up in their houses from the rain. The houses were wonderful wooden pitch-roof buildings painted in rainbow colours that nestled into the embankments of the mountains. It was a fairly developed village, explained Achiilie, unlike his own one. 'My village is small. It has no proper road. The Church calls it heathen village.'

We chatted to a few locals. It turned out the pastor had gone up the mountain to attend a meeting with some elders. The road was only passable in a four-wheel drive, rather than the taxi we had travelled in. The rain threatened to break out again, so Achiilie took me to meet one the of the remaining village elders, a man who was related to the father of Naga nationalism, Phizo.

Sebi was in his eighties but looked remarkably good on it. His father and Phizo's father had been brothers and he claimed Phizo was born in this very house. Sebi's face was deeply lined, but he looked robust and in good health, although he initially did not wish to talk, explaining to Achiilie that he had not been well. After some persuasion he relented and we went through the shop selling foodstuffs and household items to the back of the house where he lived. It was a large house, obviously one of a well-to-do family, with walls painted a soft moss green and a whitewashed wooden ceiling. Chairs were set out in a square and his wife brought through some tea and biscuits. Out of the living room window behind us was a panoramic view of the valley.

He was a village elder from the Angami tribe and proudly wore his black and red tribal blanket, draped over a grey fleece and trousers. In his day he must have been an imposing figure, I thought, looking at his strong hands and muscular feet. He still had a fine head of steel-grey hair which stood up in a quiff, framing his square face. Achiilie acted as translator as we began our three-way conversation, observed by a chicken that had entered and flown up onto the opposite chair, head cocked as if listening to our talk.

'Do you feel Indian,' I asked Sebi.

'By my colour, creed, culture, appearance, religion, I disagree that we Nagas are Indians,' he said. 'I am a descendant of Phizo. The principles of the Naga movement go back to the 1940s. Those principles are close to the will of God—restoring an area of land given to us by God. But after the 1980s, separatists are fighting among themselves. It's a dirty game, the ugly side of Nagas.'

Phizo's father Krusietso was the second convert to Christianity in this village. As a punishment he was driven outside the village gates and lived in exile there. He slowly tried to convert others and gradually a Christian community grew here.

'Your ancestor began this movement. Today, the separatists claim to be fighting this war in the name of Christ, for a Christian homeland,' I said.

'At first, their actions were acceptable. But present things are against God's will and the sentiments of the people.'

Achiilie interjected with his own comment, looking visibly upset for the first time: 'These militants are shattering the dreams of the Nagas, shattering his family's dreams. This family is the seed of the Nagas.'

'Has this village experienced militancy?' I asked.

'I feel strongly about the IM and its mission. They tortured our youths in the village, they demand money from us. When villagers started a logging business they demanded taxes. When we refused they came to the village and started torturing.'

The IM was not alone in its brutal methods. Other groups also used violence. I asked him about the Church's role in encouraging separatism.

'Inside the Church, we cry to God to put his blessing on Nagaland and ask that this beautiful land that belongs to Nagas should be peaceful again. We pray for those leaders leading us into a pool of blood.'

'Does the Church use its services to call for Naga independence?'

'The Baptist Church says whoever has faith in God has patriotism in his heart. The strongest prayer of our church is do not allow anyone to disturb this beautiful state God has given us. Don't let any foreigners destroy this.'

'Who are the foreigners?'

'The Indians.'

Achillie and Sebi engaged in a long discussion and then the former turned to me and said that the old man wished to make a point about the British, since I was an Indian from Britain (in Nagaland the combination could not be worse).

'At the departure of the British,' said the old man, looking at me directly now instead of through the interpreter, 'they trampled on our rights and handed us to the Indians. In the Battle of Kohima in the Second World War, we fought against the Japanese invaders, alongside the British, even though the Japanese were ethnically closer to us than the British. We gave the best of our youth, our weapons. In that battle, Naga blood flowed with British blood. When it was over we trusted them to remember.'

In Kohima I had seen the war memorial, a moving tribute where Indian soldiers are buried alongside the British in gardens filled with English roses. Mountbatten, Supreme Commander of the Allies in Asia, had described the 1944 Battle of Kohima as 'one of the greatest in history'. It was seen as a turning point in the War, compared to Stalingrad in Europe, because it was here that the Japanese invasion was arrested after a battle of three months in which the Nagas were crucial in terms of intelligence-gathering and providing guides, as well as capturing the enemy. Out of 85,000 Japanese soldiers, only 20,000 were left standing. Almost 19,000 Allied troops were killed, wounded or missing.

But after victory came betrayal. On Independence, the Nagas expected freedom in return for their sacrifice. They were deeply shocked by the turn of events.

'With its betrayal, the British have done something very cruel to the Nagas. We are suffering to this day. That was the beginning of things. I have a question to ask the Britishers. Why do mighty nations forget smaller nations after they have used us?'

The room fell silent as we watched the speckled chicken which had now skipped onto the floor and was edging dangerously close to the cat, which was poised to pounce. In a flash, the cat moved forward and the chicken squawked in dismay, flying into the air, releasing a snowstorm of feathers. As we all jumped around the room trying to grab the hen before the cat did, it seemed a perfect metaphor for the Nagas' predicament. Through history it had been the weaker player falling prey to larger predatory neighbours. This time at least, the chicken was saved and lived to fight another day. Sulking, the cat retreated to the corner, furious at its loss.

'It's Easter this month,' said Sebi. 'You celebrate Easter?'

I did, although the highlight of my Easter was always the chocolate eggs. As a family we celebrated Lent by giving up chocolate until Easter Sunday. So, Easter was a time for making up for lost ground as well as remembering the Resurrection of Christ. As a child I had always been enthralled by Passion Week, especially the re-enactment of the Crucifixion during Good Friday Mass when the congregation was required to play the part of the crowd who urged Pontius Pilate to 'Crucify him!' It appealed to my Goan sense of drama. The Passion Week, commemorating the Last Supper, Crucifixion and Resurrection, was about Christ's sacrifice to save man from his sins. The message of Salvation had particular resonance here in Nagaland.

'What will you all pray for in Church?' I asked.

'We will pray for the drunks, the heroin addicts, the terrorists, the leaders who would destroy the real identity of Nagas,' said Sebi simply, plucking a stray white feather from his blanket.

As we got up to go I wished him well and a happy Easter. He was full of warmth and reminded me to send his message to 'the Britishers'.

'I didn't want to talk to you at first,' he said. 'I felt so tired. But speaking to you of these things, I don't feel tired anymore.'

12

Blood, Tears and Oil

Naga nationalism was born in that house, which clings to the rocky mountainside. But in death, Phizo could not have been further away from his beloved motherland. He died in exile in the gently undulating British countryside, his dream unrealized as India drew the Nagas closer into its iron embrace. The major powerbrokers in the region today are NSCN (IM) leaders Isaac-Muivah who have the ear of the political leadership in Delhi, while maintaining dominance of the Naga streets with their militant muscle.

Kaka Iralu, the Naga nationalist leader and writer, was no fan of the IM or others who espoused violence. His was a campaign of letters, lobbying and books. Where others chose bullets, he chose words to fight for an independent Nagaland. Yet for all his moderation he was an irrelevance in the peace talks that were underway in Delhi at the time of my visit. When I met him at his house in the Mission Compound, a picturesque blue chocolate-box house surrounded by flowers and set in the hillside of Kohima, he seemed a man all dressed up for the party, but still waiting for his invitation.

His teenaged son showed us into the living room, a prettily decorated haven with embroidered cushions, flower-patterned curtains and eggshell-blue walls. The windows on two sides of the room opened onto a vista of mountains, pine trees and flowers. Kaka was a stocky man with thick muscular arms, a barrel chest and wide neck. His salt and pepper hair was parted at the side and his face was a rich copper, with small slanted eyes and a ready smile. He looked like he may have been a pretty good wrestler in his day. In his late forties now, he had given up a life in business to become a campaigning journalist/writer/freedom fighter for Nagas.

Although a big man, Kaka was light on his feet and moved with great rapidity around the room when he needed his lighter, cigarettes or paper. He was friendly, open and passionate in his advocacy of the cause but he was also highly strung and edgy. He sat by the window and would glance across his shoulder to the public path that ran down the mountainside past his house. He smoked constantly and would eat little paan leaves filled with white powder which he chewed frenetically. On top of that he drank coffee. Kaka was so pumped he looked as if he'd bounce off the ceiling.

It was little wonder Kaka was addicted to stimulants: he could not afford to relax as he felt he was a marked man. He was no friend of the IM leadership which was the dominant militant and political group in Nagaland. This same group was in talks with the government and he feared that if they struck a deal, he would be a dead man.

We began by chatting about the ongoing peace talks in which he had no faith. It was one thing to draw up a blueprint in Delhi with IM leaders. It was quite another for IM to deliver it on the ground. He feared they would settle for less than a free and sovereign Nagaland in favour of a deal that would doom the separatist cause and enrich the IM leaders themselves. He said such a peace deal would lead to internal warfare as other militant groups resisted.

'India is trying to give the impression that by persuading IM, it has the mass-based Naga leadership. But there are rival groups. I can see the possibility of a bloody civil war between the Indian army allied with IM and the rest of the Naga factions. It would be a bloodbath. Therefore, I say to India, widen your peace talks if you truly want peace.'

As the sun went down, the son came in to turn the lights on. He was a typical teen, desperate to avoid a heavy discussion. When we'd arrived earlier he'd still been asleep, recovering from a night-time hunt with friends for partridge and small game. He looked like he was also nursing a bad hangover and smiled sheepishly as I asked if he'd caught up on his sleep. As he left the room, his father finished his cigarette, its red tip glowering as he sucked deep.

'Don't get me wrong,' said Kaka, blowing smoke out the window. 'The IM leaders are smart people. But they have very few taboos. They shoot and kill without compulsion.' He paused to light a new cigarette and drew the smoke deeply into his lungs. The nicotine hit pacified his nerves a little as he continued.

'I was abducted by this very group last September 14 and released on the 17th. I had been exploring their crimes on Nagas and I delved into their history. My conclusion was they perpetrated much the same violence as the Indian military. Despite the ceasefire, we have a territorial battle between militant groups for control of Nagas.

'They're all bad. But the IM is the worst. They were trained in China and inculcated in Marxist ideology. If a person is inculcated in Marxism, elimination of the individual becomes methodology.'

Some militants had trained in China in the past and been armed. Yet they retained the Christian part of their identity and claimed to be fighting for a religious homeland. I asked Kaka about that apparent contradiction.

'They are first and foremost Baptists. In the name of Christ, they kill. In the name of Christ they extort money. Well, there are two types of Christians in this world: the real Christian and the hypocritical Christian.'

'Why doesn't the Church condemn the violence, given its influence?'

'Many times the Church has spoken out against the killings. No church leader has been killed so far. But people like me are open targets. I've criticized India and I waited for a response from India. None came. Yet at all times I carry a loaded revolver,' he patted his pocket. 'Why? Not because I'm scared of the Indian army, but because my own people are out to get me.'

Kaka said he was writing a new book, one which would focus on the atrocities of the militant groups, following his last book that dealt with Indian security atrocities. He said he would not be able to remain in the country at the time of publication as he feared he may become a target. 'My children's passports are ready. We're ready to flee at any time,' he added.

The lights in the valley suddenly went out. I caught my breath. This place, Kaka's talk and the sudden darkness made me jumpy, even though it was just a routine power cut. There were no candles so we continued our conversation in inky blackness.

'I don't see how this problem can be resolved,' I said. 'I don't see India giving in on this one. After all, if it gave in to the Nagas it would open the floodgates of insurgency. It won't happen.'

'I can see India's problem,' his disembodied voice agreed. 'It fears, first Nagaland then what? The rest of the northeast? Kashmir, Punjab? India could disintegrate. It could mean the end of India.'

The words hung in the darkness as we contemplated their terrible implication.

'But the Nagas will not give up,' he said, voice steeled with determination. 'We have spilled too much blood. We have shed too many tears to give up now.'

It was late and I needed to get back to the sparing delights of the Hotel Japfu. We fumbled our way through the dark to the door and arranged to meet the next day when he would be less busy and less tired. His son came with a torch to guide me up the hillside path. He was sporting a camouflage bandanna and looked quite rakish, with the black tufts of hair sprouting over the top. I wondered where his allegiances lay. As we reached the car, he smiled broadly. 'I told you he'd bombard you with information,' he laughed. 'Until tomorrow.'

*

So, what is a Naga?

It sounds like the beginning of a mother-in-law joke. But it's a serious question.

The heart of the Naga cause is they are different. Within India they feel as alien as Martians. The next day I met up with Kaka at his house and we sat down to resume from where we had left off. Since his wife Easterine was away in Norway, giving a lecture, his son was standing in for his mother, providing coffee and snacks.

'What is the Naga?' I asked Kaka. His answer came without hesitation, a cascade of words, a rushing force of emotion that gushed forth as he perched on the edge of his chair. 'We are unique. We are a classless society. Our tribal structure is made up of clans or *khels*. There's no hereditary leader and the village is governed by a council of elders. We are Mongoloid by ancestry. We are warriors by tradition.

'Every *khel* has a duty to defend its clansmen. When you hurt one Naga, you don't hurt an individual but a whole village. In our culture it is shameful not to avenge a clansman's death. In our culture we have a word for honour. It is *mosho*. I am a man, therefore I act like a man. The Japanese were great warriors and they told us: "We thought we were the greatest warriors. But despite your smallness, you beat us". That is the Naga.'

'The people of India are so diverse, yet they're accommodated within the Indian family,' I said. 'Why not the Nagas?'

'We are *not* Indians. We are Mongoloid, our language is Tibeto-Burmese. Our faith was animism and is now Christian. Linguistically, culturally, historically, every–ically you can think of, we're *not* related to India.'

Kaka was angry that after two thousand years of separate living and distinction from its neighbours, the Nagas' identity had been absorbed into another nation. The people had gone from independence to dependence within a couple of generations.

'India pays our salaries, buys our goods, then we buy their goods. Indian produce and culture is swamping Nagaland,' he said.

'Isn't this the nature of society today? A series of interlocking trading regions. No country can live in isolation. If Nagaland was independent it would be in the same position in order to survive,' I suggested. It seemed to me that the Nagas were different from the rest of India and I think it is a point India fully appreciates. Geographically, the north-east hangs on to India by a territorial thread. Look at the map of the region and one will see that the north-east is connected to India by a slender corridor of territory which is surrounded by Bangladesh, Nepal, Bhutan and the other regional giant, China. So the gulf is evident.

But even if the Nagas were able to persuade India to give Nagaland sovereignty—which I thought could never happen because of the implications for the rest of India I believed that such a nation could not survive, economically or politically. India has long been locked into a territorial game with its neighbours China and Pakistan. In the north-east, China and India are like two chess masters playing out their moves over the decades, waiting for a chance to checkmate. Even if it were not for Nagaland's resources, it would still be too important a piece of the game to be allowed to remain independent.

Kaka pondered the issue for a moment as he brought a small tray of paan leaves containing white powder. He folded one into a neat parcel and popped it into his mouth, chewing as he was thinking.

'Economically, it is true, we are in a global village and we cannot insist on being separate. We are ready to be inter-dependent, to be members of SAARC or ASEAN, while retaining a national identity. As for our economic survival, I say this: our lands are fertile with forests of pine, teak, bamboo. As far as horticulture and agriculture is concerned, 80 per cent of the world's herbal medicines comes from the golden triangle of which Nagaland is part.

'Besides that, we have oil. In eastern Nagaland they say there are lakes of oil, bubbling to the surface. You can scoop it up. So far India has found one major oilfield which has 600 million tonnes of reserves. That could be one of hundreds. India cannot use our oil without our permission.

'Burma on the border is rich in diamonds, iron, nickel, copper and gold. The same veins run through our lands. If the political conflict was resolved, Nagaland would be transformed into a Singapore or Thailand. We don't need India to do that. We can use Japanese or US technology. The Americans are interested in exploring for oil in Nagaland. The question of us being helpless and dependent does not exist. Even if India cut us off, we would not care. We don't care if they build a Berlin Wall. We will align ourselves with our south-east Asian brothers.'

It was a pretty dream. But Nagaland was like the chicken in Sebi's house. Too tasty to be left alone. If it flew from the Indian coop, how long before someone else snapped it up? As one of the last few uncharted terrains with big oil reserves, it was too tempting. Kaka was envisioning a mountainous Singapore. But Nagaland was landlocked, surrounded by potentially predatory neighbours. It needed strong defences to survive and good relations with neighbours to secure its trade routes. But Kaka believed that this very issue of Nagaland being surrounded by potentially hostile neighbours was part of a divine plan.

'God indeed might have a plan for Nagas. We're surrounded by Muslims, Hindus, Buddhists, so God may have in mind for us to be a missionary centre. God forgive me if I'm wrong, but we could be like the Israel of India.'

He and other Nagas point out that a Greater Nagaland would be four times bigger than Israel. 'If we were independent, we would fight the invaders just as we've fought the Indians. With the help of our international friends we could be self-sufficient in defence within twenty years, just like Israel.'

'Twenty years is a long time,' I said quietly. One month was a long time in this part of the world if you were defenceless. And this particular 'Israel' would not have US coffers and arms at its disposal.

'In the meantime, Nagaland could adopt political alliances to protect us. Personally, I want good relations with India, especially as we have a fearsome neighbour to the east, China,' he replied.

But it all went back to the point he made yesterday. Despite the tragedy, the arguments, despite the unyielding determination, India was unequally unyielding when it came to protecting its territorial integrity. A mighty nation facing internal tugs-of-war with separatist groups could not afford to show magnanimity to the Nagas. Such a move would be interpreted as weakness and constitute a slow suicide. Would it not be better to accept greater autonomy within the Indian union, to start developing the economy now and allow the people to reap the benefits of their country? That would be a step along the road of progress. The missionaries had also been invaders, people who took their message into hostile headhunting terrain. Now the Christian faith was as much part of Naga identity as tribal tradition.

But for people like Kaka this was a ridiculous argument. He suggested that it was no more acceptable to Nagas than it would have been for the British to tell India it was in its long-term interests if it remained part of the Empire. That was doubly the case in regard to economic development. The Nagaland State Human Development report, an optimistic document which projected into the future, said by 2020 with proper development and peace, the economy could thrive on tourism, timber, spices, horticulture, medicinal plants, farming, oil and minerals. Its proximity to south-east Asia opened trading opportunities in the ASEAN region. There was just one big problem.

'There can be no economic development before a political solution,' said Kaka. 'Look. What foolish company would invest in oil pumps and pipeline when it could go up in flames in a terrorist attack? So, solution first, economic development next. Besides, we have our supporters overseas: US, Japan, Germany and Sweden are sympathetic.'

'India is a very powerful economic nation. I think many countries will not risk their economic relations with India for the Naga cause,' I suggested.

'India has many wooers but it also has many enemies,' he said softly. 'If not Japan, we have China. But then again,' he chuckled, his face collapsing into a rueful smile, 'China is a dangerous nation. It may help us and then try to swallow us.'

Humour was the refuge of the desperate. 'Do you sometimes feel it's hopeless?' I asked. 'It seems such an impossible task you have. I can't see how the Naga will win.'

The smiles evaporated as he nodded gravely. He looked out the window towards the horizon and then back at me. The features of his chubby face set hard. 'I am a small man. And the task is so gigantic I sometimes feel lost,' he conceded. 'But I *do* believe in God. As long as I'm faithful to my convictions, the solution belongs to God.'

Enveloped in night, it was time to leave. As we made for the door, Kaka pressed a bunch of speeches and articles into my hands: the campaigning never ended. He also kindly gave me a copy of his wife's new book, a fictional account of tribal life. Despite the scale of his task and the ever-present threat to his life, he remained cheerfully undeterred and relentlessly focused. I greatly admired his courage and it made me understand the ethos of the Nagas: that there was honour in risking one's life to protect your people. I wanted to tell him to be careful, but decided not to dwell on the evident dangers that plagued him. Instead, I told him I'd be in London shortly and he said he may also be visiting in connection with his wife's new book. Perhaps we would see each other again? He nodded enthusiastically as I suggested dinner with a mutual friend, a BBC journalist also in London. We shook hands on the doorstep; around us the Naga hills were studded with lights from houses across the valley. The sweet smell of wood fire filled the night skies as people prepared the evening meal. It was tranquil and beautiful.

'Thank you Edna,' his handshake was strong, like a tiger's paw. 'I'm glad to say it has not been a hardship to spend these hours with you. We may or *may not* meet again.'

PART 3

Land of the Pure

13

Land of the Pure

'Such are the blasphemers
Who set themselves up
As the leaders and rulers of the world;
They consume daily the forbidden fruit of falsehood,
And yet they preach to others,
What is right and what is wrong;
Themselves deluded, they delude others also
Who follow their path.'

—Guru Granth Sahib,
Majh, M1

Delhi, October 1984

The Tantric was from Varanasi, one of the seven most holy cities of Hinduism. It was here on the banks of the sacred Ganga that the old man drew up astrological charts predicting the future.

It was the autumn of 1984, and India's future seemed fraught with uncertainty and danger. Months had passed since Operation Blue Star, when Prime Minister Indira Gandhi ordered her stormtroopers to enter the Golden Temple of Amritsar to flush out the radical cleric Jarnail

Singh Bhindranwale and his band of Sikh militants fighting for a separate Sikh homeland. The siege ended after a firefight that left the holy of holies riddled with bullets, the seat of Sikh temporal power reduced to rubble and many hundreds of devotees killed in the crossfire. The martial nature of the Sikh religion meant the desecration would not go unpunished. A sense of foreboding descended over the political capital of New Delhi. Many sensed retribution was inevitable: Indira would have to pay. It was her karma.

The elderly Tantric in Varanasi was also fixated on the destiny of India's Prime Minister. In late September he took details of Mrs Gandhi's birth and devised an astrological chart of her future. He was shaken by his readings which showed that within one month she could be dead. Packing together some things, he left immediately for Delhi.

He had heard of Mrs Gandhi's yoga teacher Dhirendra Brahmachari, a kind of yogic Rasputin who had developed a deep influence on her over the years. The Tantric went to the house of the yogi carrying a letter setting out his prophesy. He was greeted at the door by a disciple of Brahmachari who had been a follower of the guru for many years. The Tantric explained he must urgently speak to the guru. But the guru refused to help. Undeterred, he delivered the letter to Mrs Gandhi's official residence at Safdarjung Marg and returned to his village, his duty completed.

She probably never saw the letter, but Mrs Gandhi already had a sense of destiny. On October 30 she gave an election address in Bhubaneswar in Orissa. Deviating from her prepared text, she spoke from the heart and alluded to a violent end: 'I am here today, I may not be here tomorrow... Nobody knows how many attempts have been made to shoot me... I do not care if I live or die.'

On October 31 Mrs Gandhi was back in Delhi, dressed and ready for the day by six in the morning. Her first meeting was an interview with the actor Peter Ustinov for a BBC documentary. She chose a saffron cotton sari with a black embroidered border. Just after nine, she left the house and made her way down the pathway connected to her office. It was a beautiful autumn day: the air was clear and the flowers were in bloom after the monsoon. Her political secretary R.K. Dhawan followed behind with a retinue of the PM's personal staff.

At the end of the pathway was her Sikh security guard Beant Singh, flanked by borders of bougainvillea. Standing nearby was another Sikh guard called Satwant Singh. As she approached, Mrs Gandhi gave the traditional namaste, lifting her hands together as if in prayer. Beant Singh lifted his revolver, took aim and after several seconds opened fire, hitting her in the chest, abdomen and armpit. Satwant Singh opened fire with a Sten automatic weapon, emptying a further twenty-five bullets into her frame. Her blood-drenched body was taken to the All-India Institute of Medical Sciences in a white Ambassador car. A team of surgeons tried to save her. By 2.23 pm Indira Gandhi was pronounced dead.

The assassination sucked the country into a vortex of chaos. Most of the violence took place in Delhi, although Sikhs across India were targeted. In those next few days, hordes of Hindus with torches, lathis and knives rampaged across the capital, targeting Sikh neighbourhoods. Sikh men, women and children were openly butchered. The police stood by and watched. In those terrible days, Indira's son and successor Rajiv Gandhi appeared to excuse the atrocities by declaring in public: 'When a big tree falls, the earth is bound to shake.' There is no evidence he personally directed the violence, but human rights observers said there was clear evidence of involvement by Congress Party members and workers and suggested the attacks bore the hallmarks of pre-planning, a charge the government denied.

Twenty years on, my old landlords in Sunder Nagar remembered. The Kochhars are a wealthy Punjabi Sikh family who migrated to Delhi after 1947. At the time they lived in a sprawling family house in another part of the colony. During those nights in early November 1984, palls of acrid smoke hung in the air like disturbed spirits waiting to be avenged. At night from the rooftops, one could see fires burning across the city's horizon, dancing flames pinpointing the presence of the marauders.

'For eight nights, while the violence raged, the men of the family would stand on the roof of the building with shotguns and rifles in case the mob came to our doors,' said Mr Kochhar over drinks and kebabs in his drawing room. 'We stayed awake all night, patrolling, watching, waiting.'

The women and children of the family remained inside, trying to take their minds off the danger with card games, book readings and so on. Elegant Punjabi memsahibs steeled themselves to fight to the death if necessary, keeping licensed pistols beneath the silken folds of their salwar-kameez.

'I kept a loaded pistol hidden beneath my clothes,' said Mrs Tara Kochhar. 'We were terrified they'd break into the house.'

'Would you have used the gun?' I asked.

Her soft face became hardened with the resolve of those days. 'I'd have used it to protect my family.'

I had no doubt she would.

The Kochhars were lucky. Their house was not targeted by the mobs. But many of their friends were not so fortunate. Entire houses were looted, gutted of every fixture and fitting and then burned to the ground. Families were killed without discrimination. Sikh men were 'necklaced'— rubber tyres filled with petrol were placed around their necks and set alight. Nearly 3,000 Sikhs were killed in Delhi during the days that followed Indira Gandhi's death. The killers were never brought to justice, melting back into society. Twenty years on they were still free.

The events of 1984 scarred the Sikh psyche as never before. In the years that followed, calls for a Sikh nation, Khalistan, grew louder and a more dangerous and virulent form of Sikh fundamentalism swept across the Punjab. Sikhs came under even greater pressure from the police and armed forces who viewed them as either terrorists or Khalistan sympathizers. By the Nineties, thousands of terrorists were operating in the Punjab and fears grew that the state could secede, thus risking the break-up of India. The stakes were high: Punjab was a frontier state, bordering India's estranged brother nation Pakistan. A police crackdown followed during which there were reports of widespread human rights abuses of Sikhs by Indian security forces. But by the late Nineties fundamentalism had been crushed.

India praised the police as heroes and patriots who had saved the country from the threat of fragmentation. But some who studied the terrorist phenomenon argued that the real heroes were the Sikhs who killed the Khalistan movement by cutting off the oxygen of public support. Such movements could only survive with the backing of the people. *With* the support of the people, no militant movement could be crushed by state might, no matter how onerous. One could see it in Israel and Iraq, where the Intifada and insurgency continued relentlessly. One had seen it in Northern Ireland and South Africa.

By the mid-Nineties sentiment had turned in the Punjab when the terrorists, self-styled religious warriors, began to wage war increasingly on ordinary Sikhs as well as the State. Far from being pure ideologues, they indulged in lootings, killings and rapes that repelled the Sikh community as much as the state oppression. Professor Harish Puri and his colleagues at the Guru Nanak Dev University in Amritsar interviewed hundreds of former terrorists who had surrendered and found many were motivated by a lust for adventure, power and status. It became clear these were no longer men with a holy mission of establishing Khalistan or Land of the Pure, but brutal opportunists. Grassroots' support disappeared and the movement imploded under the weight of its own licentiousness and religious hypocrisy.

India had won and Sikh fundamentalism had been defeated. But the sense of Sikh grievance endured. Blue Star, the 1984 anti-Sikh riots, the terror crackdown and human rights abuses made up a roll call of misery that left the ordinary Sikh feeling besieged in his own country.

In the anniversary month of Indira's death twenty years on, I walked around her house in Delhi that is now part museum, part shrine. Her blood-stained sari is on display in a glass cabinet, along with tiny leather sandals, drawing the biggest crowd in the museum. Large groups stared at the mawkish exhibit, reliving the terrible moment in India's history with wide-eyed fascination. In the gardens the pathway where she took her last steps is paved with crystal and the spot where she fell is adorned with flowers.

The Congress under her daughter-in-law Sonia Gandhi's leadership sought to draw this period to a close. By 2004, India had a Sikh Prime Minister, Punjab was run by a Congress minister and the party said the blood-letting was in the past and all wounds had healed. Khalistan by all accounts appeared to be a vanquished ideology. In Delhi, the well-to-do Sikh urbanites have moved on. India is developing into a potential economic superpower and the arguments for Khalistan seem even more outmoded. India remains the main market for Punjabi produce. And through India, Punjab has access to world markets for its export goods.

But the ideology of Khalistan was not born of economics. It was born of the desire for a distinct Sikh identity. The fundamentalists sought inspiration for their violent revolution from the martial nature of Sikhism. The Khalistani movement originated as a crusade for a Land of the Pure, a homeland rooted in the fundamentals of the Sikh faith.

Twenty years on, what had changed?

*

Anandpur Sahib, Punjab, September 2004

Gurmel Singh, my driver, is from the holy city of Anandpur, and he readily agreed to accompany me on the journey to his native place. For weeks he prepared his moustaches for the pilgrimage, experimenting with different styles and wash-in dyes for his beard. In the final days before we left, the beard went through at least three colour changes: jet black, Osama bin Laden-style. Too fierce. Then a soft wolverine grey. My personal favourite, but too old. He finally settled on grey/black tinged with henna. For me, he summed up the attributes of the Sikh: a fierce pride combined with a gentle compassion, plus a canny nose for saving money. A handsome man in his fifties, he had the looks of the frontier people, high cheekbones, aquiline nose, copper-coloured skin, light brown eyes fringed by long lashes. He also had a disarming charm that made him an agreeable travelling companion.

He had been in Amritsar just before Operation Blue Star and it scarred him deeply. 'I will never vote Congress. I cannot forgive,' he said. Not even a Sikh Congress Prime Minister was enough to sway him.

'What's Anandpur like?' I asked.

'Very good place, Ma'am. Not like Delhi. Not many rushes.'

For Mr Singh all places in India were judged in terms of traffic density. A bad city having 'many rushes'. A good city having 'not many rushes'. Anandpur must be pretty good, I thought.

Anandpur, the City of Bliss, is the place where the martial nature of the Sikh character was forged. In 1699 the Tenth Guru, Gobind Singh, stood on a hilltop and issued his call to arms, urging Sikhs to become warrior saints, to defend the faith with steel and blood against their Muslim conquerors.

Mr Singh and I were driving to Anandpur from his sister's house, located a few kilometres away. Hardeep Kaur is a widow with three children. She had studied in Delhi and now lived and worked in Nangal as a medical adviser. We stopped at her house for the night and over dinner, beneath the gaze of a portrait of Guru Nanak, founder of the Sikh religion, we talked about the events of twenty years ago. I asked her what she thought of Bhindranwale: was he hero or heretic? 'He was protecting Harmandir Sahib,' she said. 'He believed in a return to Khalsa ways.' Hardeep was hardly a radical, soft-spoken and apolitical, yet twenty years after his death, she, like many other ordinary Sikhs, saw Bhindranwale as a champion of Sikh rights, not a political monster.

Breakfast was a more lavish affair than I was used to. Punjabis eat heartily in the morning. In less than two hours I had been given tea and biscuits in bed, followed by fruit, an omelette, parathas dripping with homemade butter, a tall glass of milk, and more tea. As a bonus, Hardeep also gave me a bowl of her homemade pickle which I shamelessly wolfed down. After calling on Mr Singh's elderly mother with a gift of a shawl, we were on the road to Anandpur.

It was just a few hours from Delhi yet a world away from the dust-clogged arteries of the capital. Punjab's lush countryside and verdant agricultural plains opened up around us. Trees canopied the road to Anandpur, branches rustled in the wind that signalled the change of season was upon us. Mr Singh's tape of Punjabi classics jangled on the car stereo.

The Punjabi Sikh is famous for his enterprise and ability to turn a profit. A huge garment-manufacturing industry has sprung up in Ludhiana town, making woollens, shirts and fabrics for export. Leather and sports goods is another native industry. And I was always hearing stories of ingenuity, like small-scale paneer manufacturers in Amritsar who used washing machines for the process, finding this household utility perfectly suited to their production requirements. I tried to find this particular outfit but with no luck. Sadly, the vision of great white cheeses tumbling inside a Hotpoint would live on only in my mind, unverified.

For the most part Punjab is known for agriculture. The greatest success of India's Green Revolution of the Sixties and Seventies had been demonstrated here. The state still remains the breadbasket of India. Wheat, rice, pulses, sugarcane are just some of the crops grown. As we journeyed through the countryside in the Maruti Wagon R, Mr Singh was swept away by nostalgia. The years fell away and he was no longer a fifty-five-year-old man but a footloose teenager. 'Here, as a boy, I would go into the forests for picnic. For hours we would enjoy. Eat, drink and sleep in the grass with full stomachs. Then in the evening we would walk many kilometres to the gurdwara.'

We passed a field of sugar cane that awakened the sensuous tastes of childhood. 'I would take one kg milk and one kg sugar cane juice, mix with a stick and drink. Very good taste.' As we drove past a patchwork of fields growing different crops, he would explain helpfully: 'There we are seeing the sugar cane. Not ready for harvest. There we are seeing paddy fields. Soon ready. There we are seeing Kellogg's cornflakes growing.'

The journey went by quickly and we arrived in Anandpur by late morning. The city lies on the lower spurs of the Himalayas and barely four miles to the south-west is the Sutlej river. We parked the car at the Gurdwara Kesgarh Sahib, the Sikh temple that marks the historical spot. The white marble sparkled in the morning sun, dazzling our eyes, and the floor scorched our bare feet. We checked our shoes in at the cloakroom, Mr Singh smoothed his whiskers, I covered my head with a dupatta and we passed through the shallow pool of water at the entrance of the temple to cleanse our feet.

We entered the temple's inner sanctum where, on a small silk-draped palanquin, lay the Guru Granth Sahib, the Sikh holy book. Musicians flanked the holy book and a priest recited prayers. Men and women divided on either side to sit in prayer. Behind the holy book was a small glass enclosure that housed the original weapons of the Tenth Guru and his men.

Foremost among the exhibits was the Khanda, the double-edged sword used to swirl the Amrit at the baptism of the first members of the Khalsa. The Guru's short sword or Kirpan was also on display, together with his spear. There were discs of metal with sharpened edges. These lethal frisbees were spun through the air by the Guru's warriors, decapitating the enemy with a single blow.

My favourite exhibit was a spear cast in the form of a snake. The spear was used in the battle of Anandpur by a young Sikh warrior called Bachittar Singh. The Guru's enemies were seeking to break open the gates of the fortress. Their secret weapon was a mighty elephant wildly intoxicated by drink, with seven plates of armour on his forehead. The enemy's soldiers were lined up behind, ready to swarm into the fortress once the gates were breached. The young Sikh warrior was charged by the Guru to fight the beast. He went forth, armed only with the spear and a steel sword. Galloping on horseback, standing upright in the stirrups, Bachittar Singh thrust the spear into the elephant's forehead, driving through seven layers of steel plate. Then, in a follow-up move, he hacked off the elephant's trunk with the short sword. In a drunken frenzy of pain and fury, the elephant wheeled about and trampled the enemy's men underfoot.

Mr Singh also particularly enjoyed this story and chuckled with glee, patting his moustaches. We took prasad and went out onto the rooftop to look across the horizon. The sky was a pale blue, streaked with formless clouds, and the sun was white hot. From this vantage point at the crest of the hillside, you could see for miles. An endless vista of greens and browns that surrounded the town below.

It was here on this airy hilltop in the spring of 1699 that Guru Gobind Singh initiated the warrior saints of Sikhism known as the Khalsa. The pure ones. Just before the Hindu festival of Holi that marks the advent of spring, the Tenth Guru sent word to Sikhs across the land to gather at Anandpur for an important announcement. He urged the Sikhs to come with beards and hair unshorn.

His view of the religion had been irrevocably shaped at the age of nine when his father, the Ninth Guru Tegh Bahadur, was executed in Delhi by the Mughal Emperor Aurangzeb. Tegh Bahadur had gone to to plead the case of the Kashmiri Pandits who had asked for his intervention after facing threats to convert from Hinduism to Islam. In the Emperor's court, Tegh Bahadur was himself advised to renounce his faith or face death. He chose death. He was beheaded on November 11, 1675. The site of his death is marked by a gurdwara on Old Delhi's Chandni Chowk or Moonlight Junction. Before his body could be quartered, a devotee stole away the Guru's head and bore it on horseback to the Punjab where it was cremated at Anandpur Sahib.

The death of his father led the young Gobind Singh to form the view that Sikhs must be prepared to defend their faith to the death if necessary, as his father had done. To survive and retain its identity, the faith of the Gurus would have to combine the prayer book with the sword. 'When all avenues have been explored, all means tried, it is rightful to draw the sword out of the scabbard and wield it with your hand,' he wrote in one of his epistles.

I imagined the great crowd of tens of thousands that would have gathered on the day of the festival, eager to hear the word of the Guru. Guru Gobind Singh appeared before them in sombre mood, with his sword drawn and called for five men to come forward and offer themselves up for sacrifice. 'Let one of my true Sikhs come forward,' he began. 'My sword wants a head,' he said. None came forward and he issued his call once again. Finally, Daya Ram from Lahore stepped forward and said: 'My head is at thy service, my True Lord.' He was taken into a nearby tent and the Guru emerged with his blade dripping with blood.

He asked for another head. Another man volunteered and was taken to the tent. The Guru emerged once again with a bloodied sword. This was repeated a further three times until five had sacrificed themselves. Then the Guru went into the tent and emerged with the five men, still alive. He had killed goats instead, but those willing to sacrifice life for belief were named the Panj Piyare—the five beloved ones. They would form the core of a new group of Sikhs called the Khalsa.

The men were baptised. Guru Gobind Singh mixed sugar with water, churning it with his double-edged sword to form *amrit*. The five were of different castes but were made to drink from one bowl to show that all members of the Khalsa were equal. They were told to relinquish their

Hindu caste names and take up the single family name of Singh, meaning 'lion'.

He then set out the five symbols of the Khalsa faithful. They would serve as the basis of a Sikh identity that would endure through the centuries. Kes: they would keep their hair and beard uncut. Kangha: they would wear a comb in their hair. Kachha: they would wear an undergarment of shorts. Kara: they would wear a steel bracelet on their right wrist. Kirpan: they would be armed at all times with a short sword. Alcohol, tobacco and meat from animals bled to death were prohibited. The molestation of Muslim women was prohibited. The Guru then asked to be baptised, thereby becoming one of the Khalsa. He asked the followers to eschew other religions for Sikhism. Mass baptisms followed across the region.

Today, Guru Gobind Singh's picture graces every Sikh home; he is portrayed as the ultimate warrior saint: dashing, with handsome whiskers, and skilled in the martial arts of swordsmanship and archery. It was said his arrowheads were tipped with gold to provide a living for the families of his victims. He rode a stallion, with one hand adorned with a white hawk while the other brandished a drawn sword, poised for battle.

His formation of the Khalsa was not merely symbolic. He waged battle, built fortifications to protect his domain, developed arsenals of weapons for the holy cause and made clear in his writings that he meant to defend the faith of Sikhism with deed as well as word. In a missive to Emperor Aurangzeb he warned: 'I shall strike fire under the hoofs of your horses and I will not let you drink the water of my Punjab'.

They were the words of a true holy warrior that would shape the Sikh identity down the centuries that followed. If his religion or the land of his religion was under threat, the

Sikh had a duty to take up arms. The Sikhs would become the sword arm of India, fighting invaders through the ages. From Aurangzeb's hordes in the seventeenth century to Musharraf's troops during the Kargil War of 1999, the Sikhs were there, continuing Guru Gobind Singh's martial tradition of defending the homeland in the name of righteousness.

It was that martial nature, inherent in the religion itself, that was reawakened in the people during the events of the 1980s when a militant messiah emerged from the villages, preaching the gospel of a Sikh state or Khalistan and taking on the mighty Indira Gandhi herself. The Sikhs were a separate people in need of their own homeland that would free them from the shackles of Hindustan, he said.

Bhindranwale's mission set off a chain reaction of events that led to the storming of the holy of holies in Amritsar, Mrs Gandhi's assassination and the anti-Sikh riots which fuelled the Sikh sense of persecution, giving birth to a decade of fundamentalism that threatened India itself.

14

The Militant Messiah

Amritsar, 1984

Jarnail Singh Bhindranwale was born in 1947, the year of Independence and Partition, when the Punjab was carved in two, igniting communal violence and displacement for those who lost lands that became part of Pakistan. It sowed the seeds of discontent in the Sikh leadership that felt the Muslim got Pakistan, the Hindu got India, but the Sikh left the party empty-handed.

A child of Partition, Bhindranwale grew up in the village of Rode, near Moga. He was schooled at the Damdami Taksal which trained young Sikh preachers, and by the 1970s he had become a firebrand head priest who championed orthodoxy and developed a reputation as a compelling speaker. He sought to reassert the traditional Sikh identity through the five 'K's set out by the Tenth Guru at Anandpur Sahib. During his travels in Punjab's villages, he baptised hundreds of people and urged all Sikhs to bear weapons and shun alcohol and tobacco.

On the face of it, Bhindranwale's message was simple: do not forget the ways of the Khalsa. But he was no ordinary priest. From early on, he was positioning himself as the champion of the martial values of Sikhism and even modelled himself on the beloved Guru Gobind Singh, bearing silver-tipped arrows. He began to call on Sikhs to take up rifles and shotguns as well as wearing the traditional kirpan. Within years he had enough of a following to be seen as a powerful Sikh leader, one whom the Congress-ruled central government viewed as a possible counterbalance to its regional political rivals in Punjab, the Akalis.

In his book *The End of India*, journalist and author Khushwant Singh writes that one main reason for Bhindranwale's popularity was 'the prosperity that came to Punjab with the Green Revolution. With prosperity came sudden changes, Western influences, a crisis of identity, and degeneration—alcoholism, drug addiction, gambling...The worst sufferers were women and children, the wives and offspring of peasants who could not digest their sudden prosperity.' Women and the young thus became Sant (saint) Bhindranwale's constituency. With his martial image and fiery speeches that appealed to Sikh pride, he also won followers among 'unemployed young men who passed out of college but could not be absorbed into the ancestral farming business'.

All these things meant the time had come for a man like Bhindranwale. These were unsettled times, times of a changing economic order, times when the comfort of old religious ways was being challenged. Bhindranwale tapped into these insecurities and adopted the mantle of a militant messiah and soon began preaching a gospel of Sikh independence, an end to Hindu domination and the need to take up arms in this holy struggle. He travelled everywhere with a band of armed disciples and he himself was always armed, cartridges of bullets strung about his waist. His striking appearance had a magnetic effect on followers. 'Bhindranwale was a lean, impressive six-footer, with a prophetic air about him,' wrote General K.S. Brar who masterminded the storming of the Golden Temple in 1984. With burning eyes and flowing black beard, he epitomized the religious warrior. He became an idol of the idle youth and imbued them with a sense of holy mission at a time when there were few jobs and a sense of marginalization was taking root in the Sikh psyche.

The central government had refused to give the Punjab the city of Chandigarh as its capital. A dispute over control of Punjab's river water rights continued to rankle and demands for greater autonomy for the Sikh people went unheard. The Sikhs used to rely on the army for jobs, but an order restricting the percentage of Sikhs in the forces cut their proportion in the army from around 35 per cent to around 2 per cent. This, coupled with land reforms that made small holdings economically less viable, resulted in increased unemployment.

In 1982 the Akalis launched a Dharam Yudh or the Battle of Faith, and threatened to take their complaint to Delhi, threatening to disrupt the Asian Games planned for the capital that year. The government reacted by sealing the capital and forcing all Sikhs to endure humiliating searches at the border, making them feel like suspects in their own country. Any concessions that the Centre did grant the Sikh leaders after this were, in their view, too little, too late.

Bhindranwale was not willing to wait for handouts. Like a Wild West outlaw, he called on each village to raise a team of three young men armed with a revolver and motorcycle and charged them with the task of wreaking vengeance in the name of Sikhs. These turbaned biker warriors terrorized the countryside, targeting opponents of Bhindranwale and those who defied his orthodox teachings. Violence against the Hindu community was an important part of their plan, the aim being to drive Hindus from the

Punjab in preparation for the creation of a Sikh nation, Khalistan. Autumn 1983 marked the advent of a killing spree against the Hindus. A bus was stopped in the middle of nowhere and Hindu passengers were identified, taken off the bus and executed. As news of this and other militant horrors spread, an exodus of Hindus began. Bhindranwale's firebrand rhetoric was disseminated across the Punjab via audio-cassettes, exhorting the Sikh to rise up against Hindu hegemony. A government white paper on the Punjab later quoted one of his typical statements to the Sikh masses:

> 'It should be clear to all Sikhs, whether living in urban or rural areas, that we are slaves and want liberation at any cost. To achieve this end, arm yourself and prepare for a war and wait for orders.'

Under the guise of religious orthodoxy, the Khalistan movement of the Eighties and Nineties unleashed a reign of terror not just on the Hindus in the state but also on ordinary Sikhs, dictating how they should live their lives. Even the simplest of things were subject to militant diktat. Barbers, butchers and wine merchants were driven out of business by the terrorists. Women were ordered to dress only in salwar-kameez, with a chunni to cover their heads at all times. Khushwant Singh remembers being present at a speech by Bhindranwale at the Golden Temple: '...He warmed to his theme. "If I had my way, you know what I would do to all these Sardars who drink whisky-shisky every evening? I would douse them in kerosene oil and set fire to the bloody lot." The announcement was greeted with prolonged cries of "Boley So Nihal, Sat Sri Akal".' Referring to Hindus in the same speech, Bhindranwale tried to justify his gospel of hate by twisting what Guru Gobind Singh is believed to have said to his warriors. The Guru had proclaimed that each Sikh was a *fauj* (an army) equal to *sava lakh* (one and a quarter million), Bhindranwale said, which 'comes to thirty-five, not even hundred: divide sixty-six crores, then each Sikh gets only thirty-five Hindus, not even the thirty-sixth.'

The danger of this turbulent priest was becoming more evident with each passing day. Yet the Congress central government continued to tolerate his explosive brand of orthodox Sikhism. Indira Gandhi's son Sanjay and party man Zail Singh (who would later become India's President) had first suggested that sponsoring a Sikh Sant could be a useful political device. He could be used to split the Sikh vote in the Punjab to the Congress's benefit. Even after Sanjay's death, his mother stayed on the course he had suggested. Khushwant Singh and Kuldip Nayar's *Tragedy of the Punjab* quotes Sanjay Gandhi's friend, the politician Kamal Nath, who became India's trade and commerce minister in 2004, as saying: 'We would give [Bhindranwale] money off and on. But we never thought he would turn into a terrorist.'

Indira Gandhi was playing with political dynamite.

General Brar later described Bhindranwale as 'the Frankenstein of Sikh politics' but it was a monster that the Congress helped create and in the end could not control. Such was his growing popularity that soon the Akalis had to concede, and even tried to woo him away from the Congress, thus boosting his influence in the Punjab. His name was linked with assassinations of politicians, journalists and policemen in the state. His men ran riot through the villages dealing out vigilante justice. His court became a kind of latter-day Inquisition where people would report their grievances asking for retribution and where those who were not faithful to the cause were sentenced to death.

In the early 1980s, Bhindranwale moved into one of the guesthouses of the Golden Temple with his band of men. His guestroom was the citadel of Sikh separatism, where assassinations were planned and assignments given to his motorcycle death squads. Inside some padlocked rooms were his arsenals of weapons. All this took place with government knowledge but little was done to restrain him, and the police felt powerless.

Bhindranwale had moved into Sikhism's seat of temporal power, the Akal Takht, that lay within the Golden Temple complex and opposite the holy of holies itself. His guards moved around the Temple wielding weapons, and the holy seat of the Sikh faith, where the Guru Granth Sahib was kept each night, played host to divisive anti-Hindu rhetoric. It went against the very essence of the tolerant nature of Sikhism.

On India's Republic Day, January 26, in 1984, the flag of Khalistan was raised above one of the Temple complex buildings. Weapons continued to be sent into the complex, smuggled inside trucks of food supplies. The showdown was coming. Mrs Gandhi made renewed attempts to head off confrontation but her efforts to conciliate failed. By this stage Bhindranwale was in control of the Temple, the high priests and politicians were not.

The final act of provocation came with the announcement that a state protest would be launched on June 3, 1984 to block the movement of grain from Punjab. The Punjab is the breadbasket of India. For Indira Gandhi this was the trigger-point for confrontation.

Facing head-on collision with India's Iron Lady and her stormtroopers, Bhindranwale prepared to tough it out. The Golden Temple was fortified in preparation for the showdown and the Sikh separatist leader issued an ominous threat to the nation: 'If the authorities enter this Temple, we will teach them such a lesson that the throne of Indira will crumble...'

In his final interviews to journalists, Bhindranwale said a major clash was looming, reporting that 100,000 troops were moving into the Punjab. He had his informants across the state and the information was good. He was betting that once the showdown started, news of the Temple being stormed would enrage Sikhs across India, mobilizing them to come to Amritsar and fight. Then, with chaos reigning, the time would be ripe to declare the state of Khalistan.

It was a miscalculation.

A curfew was imposed and a media blackout put into place. Telecommunications links were severed. The government was adamant that news of what was about to happen should not leak out. In addition to hundreds of possible militants, there were also many innocent pilgrims who had come to the temple for a holy festival. At 10.30 pm on June 5, 1984 the first phase of Operation Blue Star began. Commandos stormed the main entrance of the Temple, coming under fire from all sides. The casualties were heavy. The Akal Takht was heavily fortified, protected by light machine guns that were deployed at regular intervals. Brar described it as 'a bastion of automatic weapons'. The Indian army was under instructions to avoid hitting the Harmandir itself. But in the crossfire around the rectangle of water that surrounds the holy of holies, the marble and gold-domed temple was hit by bullets. The library caught fire and handwritten copies of holy texts were destroyed. Brar denied that tanks were used inside the Golden Temple, but other observers reported that tanks were indeed deployed. I was also told by one source that an armoured personnel carrier and a tank were used inside the complex.

After two days of combat, the Akal Takht was reduced to rubble. Bhindranwale was killed, together with his lieutenants. Many pilgrims died in the firefight, unable to escape. The news swept across the world, inflaming Sikh sentiment in India and abroad. In London, one Khalistan hardliner appeared on BBC news and called for the assassination of Mrs Gandhi.

To Sikhs worldwide, the storming of the Golden Temple was no less than sacrilege. It seemed their very religion was under attack: innocent pilgrims had been killed, their holy book defiled, their beloved shrine polluted by blood and bullets. It vindicated all those suppressed fears of a religious minority under siege and spawned a new breed of extremist that made Bhindranwale's men seem like choirboys in comparison.

Sikh fundamentalism had only just begun.

*

Amritsar, Autumn 2004

It was 5.45 in the morning and Mr Singh and I were sharing what you might call a spiritual moment. We were sitting on the edge of the Sarowar, feet dangling above the pool of holy water that surrounds the Golden Temple. It was just before dawn and the air was cool. The sky was a liquid blue-black, with the slightest tinge of grey at the edges. The birds were twittering even though it was not yet light and all I could see in the Sarowar was the burnished glow of the Harmandir, its golden reflection imperfectly mirrored in the still dark waters. The only sound apart from the birds was the recitation of the Sikh morning prayer over the loudspeakers. I looked at Mr Singh in a trance of utter peace, eyes closed, lips whispering in prayer, hands still tightly clasped around the lump of prasad he had received earlier after paying obeisance.

I had come to Amritsar twenty years after Blue Star. The Akal Takht had been rebuilt, the damage to the rest of the temple repaired. By the dying moonlight I walked around the Harmandir. Its exquisite marble walls inlaid with flower motifs were scarred with bullet holes filled with cement. I stood on the rooftop balcony of the shrine, looking out across the waters and beyond into the dark. My gaze was drawn back to the shimmering reflection in the black waters of the Sarowar. After Blue Star, the state was gripped by a renewed upsurge in terrorist violence that saw thousands of militants operating with the aid of foreign-backed money and sophisticated arms. For years it retained an iron grip over the state until the Khalistan insurgency was ground into dust by the late Nineties after a zero-tolerance policy was adopted by the central government.

Today, the city receives international flights as it tries to boost tourist revenues. In September 2004 it celebrated the 400th anniversary of Sikhism's holy book, the Guru Granth Sahib; a spectacular celebration presided over by India's first Sikh Prime Minister Dr Manmohan Singh—a Congress man. Dr Singh was born in Pakistan and after Partition moved with his family to Amritsar. It is his hometown. It was a fitting symbol of the full circle the Sikhs had come in these last twenty years. It showed the nature of India.

I had come to Amritsar to get a sense of how people felt about Blue Star, Khalistan and the Sikh's place in India, two decades on. Although the fundamentalists had been defeated, the damage to the Sikh psyche lingered. Sikhs had seen tanks and automatic gunfire desecrate their shrine; a campaign of killings of Sikhs in the wake of Indira Gandhi's assassination; they saw the Sikh branded a terrorist in the Punjabi insurgency that followed; they suffered human rights abuses on a grand scale, including summary executions and mass cremations. Many Sikhs wanted accountability and apology.

When it was announced that Sonia Gandhi would forsake the prime ministership in favour of her Sikh right-hand man, Sikhs celebrated with firecrackers and danced to bhangra in the streets. Her act of political sacrifice was welcomed as a token of peace to the Sikh community. Indira Gandhi was assassinated by a Sikh and the price was paid by that community. Now twenty years on, Indira's daughter-in-law handed the reins of a Congress government to a Sikh. It was political poetry, checkmating the Hindu nationalists who opposed her foreign birth while addressing historical Sikh grievances. But after the celebrations had ended and the hype had died down, was it enough?

My guide around town was a young Sikh journalist called Jagmohan Singh who worked for the Press Trust of India and the French news agency Agence France-Presse. Jagmohan was tall, thin and blessed with impeccable manners. It was like hanging out with a nineteenth-century chronicler. He would twirl his moustaches, open doors, no favour was too much for him, his patience during our sometimes-long days was admirable. He was a stickler when it came to food and hygiene. When I suggested lunch one day at a local dhaba, he looked horrified and delivered a lecture on the dangers of ghee and germs. Everyone in Amritsar knew him and seemed to like him. Yet my favourite thing about Jagmohan was his sly wit. 'There is no need to be thanking me, Madam Edna. When I come to Delhi and ask things of you, you can be sure there will be no thank-yous then,' he would say with a wicked flicker in his eyes.

I had asked Jagmohan to arrange a meeting with Mr Apar Singh Bajwa, the now-retired Deputy Superintendent of Police in Amritsar at the time of the Blue Star Operation. Mr Bajwa had tracked Bhindranwale for years and was asked to identify his dead body when the Temple fire-fight was over. The ID of the body was important as for years Bhindranwale's supporters claimed he had escaped and gone to Pakistan for training. One day he would return and take Khalistan, they said. There was no doubt Bhindranwale was dead, but as one Punjabi observer put it: 'I don't know which is more dangerous: a living legend or a dead one.'

The meeting place was the Ritz hotel, a typical business-class hotel on The Mall. Mr Bajwa arrived on time. He was a large man, with an elegant grey beard and curled moustaches. He was tall and immaculately dressed in khaki turban, slacks and shirt, with brightly polished shoes, as one would expect of a security sort. His handshake was firm and friendly. We ordered coffee and water as he told me about himself. He had been in the service for thirty-five years and in the 1980s he was charged with the duty of investigating Bhindranwale.

'I met him several times. He was well built, tall and slim, with hawkish eyes and a very good knowledge of religion. He was a good preacher. In fact, at the time, Sikhs felt heavily discriminated against, so someone had to raise their voice for the Sikhs.'

Before the showdown he remembered weapons were routinely being smuggled into the Golden Temple as the police did not have the manpower to stop it. 'Every day, fifty trucks loaded with devotees would come to the temple. Plus food supply trucks. It was impossible to stop, unload each vehicle and keep the city moving. The government policy was that police should not enter the Temple, which encouraged the militants further.'

'What type of weapons were found inside the Temple after Blue Star?'

'There was a mix of both licensed and unlicensed weapons. Some of the weapons clearly came from Pakistan, evident from our interrogations. They had Chinese or Russian markings. There were 303 rifles, AK47s, light machine guns, 12-bore shot guns, pistols, grenades.'

He said his team was not involved in the operation, nor were they taken into confidence. But Mr Bajwa was called to ID the body of Bhindranwale when it was all over and to clean up the mess.

'I knew him by face and I was called to ID the body on June 6, 1984. His body was lying beneath the clock tower, near the stairs. There were gunshot wounds to the face, the jaw and stomach.'

'Are you sure it was him?'

'As sure as we are sitting here.'

'How did you feel when you saw his body?'

'My feelings were injured on seeing the innocent bodies around. I was very much touched. He was not innocent. But I felt he was made a victim of circumstances, used and killed.' He meant used by politicians, both in India and Pakistan.

His body was taken to a local cemetery and burned according to Sikh rites. The cremation took place one kilometre from the Temple. He was cremated with 800 other persons, of which only three or four were identified.

Mr Bajwa was angry that innocent Sikh devotees had died in the siege, including women and children. It was the job of his men to clear the bodies after the siege was over. All bodies had been stripped of possessions by the time the police arrived to clear the area.

'I supervised the removal of 800 bodies. Most of the bodies did not have clothes. The men, their clothes were removed and their hands tied with their turbans and then they were killed, shot dead. The army became so vindictive when their own people were killed, they killed all survivors. This is clear. Men, women and children. They did not spare anybody.

'Do you know, of all the persons arrested or killed, nothing was recovered from the bodies. Not a single paise. As a person sitting here, I have a watch, a wallet, loose change. These people had nothing. No jewellery, money, personal effects. Even their clothes and shoes were missing. The army stole the clothes of the living and the dead.'

He was still upset about the anti-Sikh riots that erupted after Indira Gandhi's assassination. The events remained locked away in the darker recesses of the mind, sometimes forgotten, rarely forgiven. Mr Bajwa had seen the worst excesses of the Khalistan movement, yet he felt betrayed by the excesses of the Indian army against Indian Sikhs. Even now, it was difficult to erase the images.

'What about today? Today things have moved on, you

have a Sikh Prime Minister under a Congress-led government. Is the desire for Khalistan dead?' I asked.

'Some hidden fear remains in the mind of the Sikhs. The fear psychosis remains after 1984, after Sikhs were targeted. After all, when Mahatma Gandhi was assassinated by a Hindu, not a single Hindu was attacked in India.'

'What about Dr Manmohan Singh? It must give the community hope to see things have progressed to this point.'

'It makes no difference. We're proud of him because he is a most intelligent and honest man. But everyone thinks he will do no favours for anyone. As for the Khalistan movement, it is a dead movement. It never had widespread appeal among Sikhs. But that does not mean Pakistan will not try again. They're still trying. There're still infiltrations into India. There're still black sheep in the police force. So we have to be careful. Remember, Pakistan wants revenge for Bangladesh.'

He was referring to the 1971 war when Indira Gandhi acted as midwife to the secession of East Bengal from Pakistan and its rebirth as Bangladesh. In revenge, many Indians believed that Pakistan wanted Punjab to secede from India, diminishing its territory and sphere of influence.

Suddenly Mr Bajwa looked drained. At times during our interview I noticed he struggled with his speech and appeared distracted. His eyes had the misty quality of someone who drinks a lot. I suggested we drink our coffee, which was going cold. I said Amritsar was a wonderful city and that he was lucky to live beside the Harmandir. He smiled weakly and looked up from his still-full cup.

'You know, the holy pool was filled with bodies. It had started to smell as flesh turned putrid,' he said. 'I don't feel like taking *amrit* from there anymore. When people take *amrit* from the Golden Temple, I see dead bodies floating there.'

15

The Unforgiven

Amritsar, Autumn 2004

The Sixth Guru Hargobind Singh succeeded his father Arjun, who died in 1606 of terrible injuries sustained during torture by the forces of the Mughal Emperor Jehangir. It was a graphic illustration of the clash between religion and realpolitik. Hargobind wore two swords about his waist: one representing temporal power, the other the spiritual. They were known as the Miri Piri, the political and religious sides of Sikhism. They represented the duty to smite the oppressor and protect the innocent. In Amritsar, the Golden Temple is the sanctuary of the spiritual and the Akal Takht, a marble building situated opposite the Harmandir, is the seat of governance. The Akal Takht, throne of the Timeless God, is the highest seat of authority in Sikhism and its head is the Jathedar. The Sikh equivalent of the Pope.

I was due to meet the Akal Takht Jathedar during my stay. But the first stop was Mr Manjit Singh Calcutta, honorary secretary of the Shiromani Gurdwara Parbandhak Committee (SGPC) which controlled and managed the Sikh temples. Mr Calcutta was also a leader within the Akali party. Jagmohan and I went to his house in Amritsar. It was

a large house in one of the smarter colonies and in one of
the rooms on the ground floor was a nursery. Toddlers
scampered around us, kicking balls into Jagmohan's shins.

A servant eventually saved him from further humiliation
and took us through to the reception room. It was a white
room, with a marble floor and a table and sofas. This room
was clearly for business: there were no personal effects, no
trinkets on display. Mr Calcutta came in to greet us, dressed
in white kurta-pyjama and a royal blue turban, the traditional
colour of Sikh warriors. He was fair, with a white beard
and light brown eyes. Jagmohan was extremely deferential
and explained that our host was a great scholar of Sikh
history.

This was the cue for a long history lesson that he
delivered over forty-five minutes, only stopping to call for
rasmalai. Glass bowls of chilled rasmalai, a Punjabi favourite,
were placed before us. Spongy dumplings soaked in saffron
and pistachio-laced milk, washed down with chai.

'We Sikhs have always fought against tyranny. Before
Partition we fought against the vivisection of the country.
We wanted a united India. When Partition happened, we
opted for India on a promise from Nehru that he would
bear in mind our demands for a geographical area. We
never asked for a separate state, only more autonomy.'

Of course, Akali leaders did call for separatism. There
was a fear that in a Hindu-dominated India the Sikh
identity would be eventually subsumed into that of Hinduism.
Indeed, Hindu nationalists often argue that Sikhism is no
more than a branch of Hinduism—a claim Sikhs robustly
resist. Calcutta himself had warned of the dangers of the
RSS to India's minority religions like Sikhism. Yet, strangely,
the Akalis and BJP were sometime political bedfellows,
willing to forget differences for the sake of keeping the
Congress out of power.

'The Sikhs had a crisis of identity. Even then we feared that Hindu forces would take Sikhism into a killing embrace, like it had done with Buddhism and Jainism. Then came Blue Star. When the army invaded the Temple it ignited a fear among Sikhs that they were second-class citizens. We were not treated like Indians. We were made the villains. India blackened our face as separatists. We Sikhs had shed blood for our country then saw Sikh blood shed in the streets of New Delhi.'

'Twenty years have passed. The Punjab is peaceful again. You have a Sikh as Prime Minister. Surely the issue now is development?'

'All grievances remain,' he said, his brow knitted in a frown. 'Not a single key demand has been conceded. The anger, anguish, psychological hurt from those events are still uppermost in the Sikh mind. The Congress made a Himalayan blunder. I concede it's the first time that being a Sikh has *not* stood in the way of such a thing. But we must remember that even under the cloak of secularism, the rulers of India have done anything and everything.'

I asked him how this could be left in the past.

'Even now the Indian Parliament has offered no soothing words to the Sikh psyche for this Himalayan blunder. The country owes us an apology. If cows are butchered in one part of India, the Indian Parliament will condemn the slaughter. If a train derails, the Indian Parliament will profess its dismay. But thousands of Sikhs are killed, imprisoned, impaired for life and not a single word of sympathy.'

He believed until the sins of yesterday are formally atoned for, there could be no forgiveness. That was needed before the Punjabi Sikhs could have closure and move on. After Dr Singh's inauguration as Prime Minister, Calcutta along with many Sikh leaders had spoken warm words in the hope that the government would take swift action to issue a public apology to the Sikh community. He seemed disappointed.

But it was in the Akalis' interest to keep the feud between the Sikh community and the Congress festering. The Congress had made some effort to repair relations. Sonia Gandhi used her leadership to offer an olive branch to the Sikhs, visiting gurdwaras and making expressions of regret for the past sufferings. It was a low-key approach. And it was one that began to pay dividends back in 2002 when the Congress won state elections. Now it leads the central government coalition and Sonia Gandhi has endeared herself to the Sikh community by sacrificing power in favour of her close confidant, Dr Singh. I asked Mr Calcutta why old spectres should be raised now when Punjab faced the challenge of development rather than insurgency, and the Khalistan movement was no more than a bad dream from the past. He sipped his tea slowly, drained it and carefully placed the cup and saucer back on the table. Things were better, that was for sure. But the ghost of Punjab's past had not yet been exorcised from the Sikh psyche.

'Political ideas always have chance of opening up again. Sikhs are a separate people, with a separate identity but we want to live in India. However, we'll fight any hegemonious design. That fight continues. Sometimes on the mental plane. Sometimes through the pen. Sometimes down the barrel of a gun.'

Later that afternoon we received a call from the Akal Takht. Jathedar Joginder Singh Vedanti would see us at six. In 2003, on the nineteenth anniversary of Blue Star, the Jathedar had presided over a ceremony to declare Bhindranwale a martyr. His son Isher Singh was presented a robe of honour. Some thought this was a gesture destined to lay his ghost to rest by declaring that Bhindranwale was dead. Others saw it as a signal to honour him, giving him his place alongside other heroes of Sikh history.

My driver Mr Singh was like a meerkat on hearing the news of our meeting: erect and alert, highly jumpy. He wanted to come too. I asked Jagmohan if he could arrange for Mr Singh to join us during the interview, since Gurmel Singh was a devout Sikh. Jagmohan came up trumps. At six the three of us were escorted past the armed Sikh guards outside the Jathedar's quarters within the Golden Temple complex. A striking young man, armed with a large dagger, took us up the stairs into a reception room on the first floor. From the balcony behind one could see a magnificent view of the Harmandir Sahib as the sun was setting.

The room had white shuttered balconies on either side, open to the breeze. In the centre was a plywood table surrounded by plastic chairs. It was the day before the election of the new SGPC president, a position that Mr Calcutta was also in the running for.

We were told to address the Jathedar as Singh Sahib. I was grateful for an audience as he had only returned from London the previous night where he attended an event in connection with the 400th anniversary of the Sikh holy book. Mr Singh twisted his moustaches in anticipation, eyes soaking up every detail to be relayed to his household in Sujan Singh Park, New Delhi.

The Jathedar entered, flanked by his guards. He was dressed in white, with a royal blue turban folded in tiers. He had a golden complexion and white whiskers. But what struck me was his air of serenity. It reminded me of the time I had met the Dalai Lama at Westminster in London. The Jathedar had the same God-given glow. He spoke no English so his translator Sadar Dalbir Singh would do the necessary. The translator was ex-army and as a result felt compelled to control everything, even if it meant superimposing his own opinions on the proceedings. As the interview began it quickly became apparent that the retired army officer was trying to stage a coup. The Jathedar looked at Jagmohan, giving him the signal to take over.

I asked him what the greatest challenge to Sikhism was today. He said the biggest threat was a decline in traditional Sikh values among the young, whether due to Western influences, media, Bollywood or lack of education. The old ways were slipping away.

'Sister, it is our first duty that our present generation has to be more aware of the duties of Sikhism. The new Sikh generation is going away from the Sikh tenets more than those before them. If this generation can be controlled then the whole community will be set on the right course again.'

'Do you feel there has been a dilution to the Sikh identity?'

'Gone are the days when children would learn from parents. Now children spend time with the TV. But we face other threats to our identity. The Punjabi language of Sikhs overseas. They speak English. Every Punjabi should speak their language wherever they are in the world. It brings them closer to their religion and keeps their identity alive.

'Under Sikh religion we must not cut our hair, avoid intoxication, not look towards a woman other than our wife. So many Sikh children are moving away from this. So many Sikh men are now clean-shaven. The Sikh identity is under threat as never before.'

He was particularly concerned about two developments abroad. One, since September 11 many in the US had wrongly mistaken Sikhs for Muslims. Sikhs had suffered abuse and violence as a result. Second, the turban ban in France in the name of secularism had threatened to create a new generation of Sikhs who could abandon the traditional Khalsa ways altogether.

'The answer is every Sikh must wear a turban and flowing beard. Every Sikh must educate the rest of the world about our religion, our differences with Islam. We can do this through the media. But we must also do it through education.'

Behind the scenes he was also mobilizing Sikhs to defend their identity. In France Sikhs who had traditionally been a quiescent religious grouping were now taking to the streets, brandishing placards proclaiming their right to assert their identity. Here was an example where the rigid imposition of secularism had succeeded in radicalizing, making religious identity more of an issue in society. But there were threats to Sikh identity closer to home than Europe. The Hindutva movement itself.

'This is a direct threat, I admit. We are ready to face it through media, through education. We are sending our preachers across the state to deal with the issue. Most of the time, Sikhs prefer to remain defensive than offensive. But we are vigilant against this Hindu fundamentalism,' he said.

I asked him about the comment of Mr Calcutta: did Sikhs feel aggrieved even now? The Jathedar agreed the 'injuries received are still deep and unhealed'. Contrition by the Centre would be a way forward, a way to rehabilitate the Sikh community in the heart of the nation. Only then could both sides move forward. He thought a government led by a Sikh was a perfect opportunity to turn the page on Punjab's painful history.

'For twenty years governments have come and gone. None has adopted a resolution in Parliament to heal the wound of the Sikhs. Now one can only hope with a Sikh as PM, Dr Singh can help us recover from those wounds and raise the Sikh identity around the world,' he said.

The Jathedar had another meeting, so we took our leave. The sun had set and the Golden Temple was glowing in the dusk under arc lights. Pilgrims milled on the marble concourse beneath, some gingerly dipping into the holy waters. We stood on the balcony and watched for a while and then walked downstairs and through the gates into the heart of the old city.

The night markets were buzzing: open-fronted shops swathed with jewel-bright fabric and salwar-kameez suits modelled on pink plastic mannequins with ill-fitting wigs. Glass bangles twinkling like rainbows in silk boxes, shoe-wallahs selling sequinned slippers with curling toes, turban material shops offering all colours under the sun, sweet shops with trays of laddoos decorated with beaten silver, young men sipping lassi at roadside stalls, wiping white froth from their moustaches. The smell of hot parathas and incense mingled beneath a cold night sky studded with stars. Everywhere, the cacophony of car horns and bartering between gesticulating shopkeepers and customers. When it came to bartering nobody could beat the Punjabis of Amritsar. Except perhaps my mother.

Amritsar was at its best at this time of night. And looking at it now, it was hard to imagine the dark days of 1984 and the years that followed. Those events sent the country into shock and resulted in a religious intensity that radicalized many Sikhs. The terrorist threat post-1984 was far worse than anything that preceded Blue Star. Blue Star acted like a recruitment campaign for hardliners wishing to exploit the sense of Sikh injury.

It seemed strange to me that no previous Indian government sought to mend bridges with the Sikh community after Blue Star. For long, that chapter in Indian politics and the pain of the assassination were too much to bear. It was a classic Indian reaction. When a terrible disgrace befalls an

Indian family, the first instinct is to close ranks and go into denial. Let's not talk about it. Let's pretend it didn't happen. The source of disgrace is never mentioned at the dinner table, sent to conversational Siberia. Of course, such an approach rarely yields progress in families or nations. There is evidence to suggest that some form of national introspection can be cathartic. The South Africans' Truth and Reconciliation Commission examined the horrors of apartheid in forensic detail. It proved to be a healing process in itself.

All the Sikh leaders I spoke to in Punjab welcomed Dr Manmohan Singh's inauguration as India's Prime Minister and expressed great pride in him. But in the next breath they complained of India's failure to officially acknowledge the abuses against the Sikhs. Not all Sikhs were terrorists during those dark days, they pointed out. Yet monumental human rights abuses took place in the name of anti-terrorism. The Sikhs were punished for Indira Gandhi's death, but nobody punished the murderers of the thousands of Sikhs killed in the 1984 riots. These issues tainted the Sikh sense of self, their place in India, twenty years on. It had happened once. It could happen again. In short, they wanted apology and redress: that would be a *real* and lasting healing touch.

*

After a long day I took Jagmohan out to dinner. I suggested the Crystal Chinese restaurant in Amritsar city centre. He looked agitated. 'I will check to see if the food is suitably prepared,' he said. He made a phone call on his cell and then told me. 'The preparation is good. But sometimes there is music.'

It was late, I was hungry and I thought Jagmohan

should live a little. So the Crystal it was. I had another reason for wanting to go there. This was the local hangout for a group of American children who had converted to Sikhism, leaving the Promised Land of Consumerism to come to India to study at the Sikh Miri Piri Academy, a temple to Khalsa asceticism.

As we entered the ornate chandeliered dining room, full of couples and families, I remembered my first sight of the Miri Piri students a year ago. It had been Saturday lunchtime and a group of American teenagers had walked into the restaurant, grabbed the largest table and dropped their bags on the floor. They wore long blue robes, the colour of the Sikh warrior, and white turbans. A group of girls eyed the young man holding court at the centre of the table. He was the oldest, in his late teens. A white American with a long beard, wild and unkempt, and robes tied at the waist with a sash. He wore a sparkling white turban above blue eyes blazing with militant pride, the curve of a Sikh dagger resting on teenage hips.

The Miri Piri Academy was set up by a man known as Yogi Bhajan, or Siri Singh Sahib to his followers. He was a former Indian customs officer who left for the US in 1969. At the fag end of the Sixties he set up the Healthy, Happy, Holy Organisation or '3HO Foundation' which taught yoga and brought the tenets of Sikhism to students in New Mexico.

Yogi Bhajan's follower base grew and it now has 300 centres in thirty-five countries. His crest bears a lion and the symbol of Sikhism, crossed swords, with the motto 'In God I dwell'. He set up the Miri Piri Academy just outside Amritsar to instruct the children of his original disciples who were no longer hippies, but now quite wealthy middle-class parents. The offspring of the flower power children were now in India, learning the ancient arts of the Khalsa in a gruelling schedule that involved waking before dawn every day for lessons that included martial arts, sword-fighting, yoga, Punjabi and the study of Sikh holy scriptures. The aim of Yogi Bhajan was to create an academy of Warrior Saints.

Of course, not everyone was a true believer in this leader of white-turbaned American Khalsa warriors. I asked Jagmohan about their reputation over dinner. He pulled a face.

'They are *not* real Sikhs,' he said, hand touching his turban. His large nose quivered with distaste. 'I have heard *stories*.'

'What stories?'

'Stories of un-Sikhlike behaviour. Drinking of alcohol, hashish, sexual practices in the dorms. It is only to be expected when you mix the girls and the boys in the same school,' he sniffed, taking a sip of Coke.

'All teenagers have their wild side.'

'Do you drink alcohol?' he asked.

'Yes.'

'What does it taste like?'

'I drink wine which tastes quite nice. But I doubt you'd like it, Jagmohan.'

'I doubt I would,' he said, examining the quality of the vegetables in the Veg Jalfrezi. 'The food here is okay.'

Jagmohan's look of scandalized prurience soon evaporated when a rather curvaceous young teenager walked in with her family. Her spray-on jeans sent my friend into a tizzy as he gazed at her reflection in the mirrored walls.

'I need to get married,' he said in relation to nothing in particular.

The sex scandals he spoke of had been splashed over Internet sites. Together with stories about the leader himself. There was much talk of his palatial home in New Mexico and a harem of female attendants who looked after his every need. Salacious talk of a round bedroom and so on. It was classic guru stuff. What I found curious was that American kids would want to come to India and live here for nine months of the year, steeped in quite an extreme religious regime. I had been to a Catholic convent girls' school but there was no way I was getting up at four in the morning for any nun. The next day I went to meet the headmistress Sadanand Kaur, a Californian woman who had just taken over the school.

I was taken through to the principal's office. Ms Kaur was a friendly woman in her early forties, wearing a white turban, kurta-pyjama and sandals. Her face glowed with good health and was pleasantly pink from the sun. She sat behind her desk and asked how she could help. I explained my interest and detected a slight defensiveness in her manner. I decided I would not bring up the alleged sex romps and the yogi's round bedroom.

'We've got 105 students here from the US, Germany, Mexico, Australia and South Africa. But most are American,' she said in a sing-song Californian accent. 'We don't push Sikhism but we do have Sikh studies: music, scriptures, the lives of the Gurus.'

'What do you hope to teach the kids about Sikh identity?'

'Discipline in oneself, working as a community. Pride. Daily meditation has helped them to see the truth. The Sikh is a searcher of truth.'

'Did the kids come of their own will? Did they choose to become Sikhs?'

'Some students here were forced to come and rejected it and went home. But there are some who returned to the US and then they decided something was missing and came back to India. We're at capacity now. But Singh Sahib says no child will be refused. If they want to come, the money will be found.'

I asked about the school fees, but she refused to disclose the costs. The fees are paid in rupees, not dollars. But the school looked expensive to maintain, with large grounds, dormitories, a vast staff of cleaners, cooks, administrators, teachers, workmen, gardeners and so on. This enterprise needed big money. The kids looked like they were from wealthy backgrounds. They would need to be—dispatched overseas for nine months of the year, with all the expenses that entailed. From the youngest to the oldest, they wore the blue robes tied with a sash and white turbans tied in a rounded, wraparound style, rather than the more angular Sikh way of tying the turban. A look of seriousness also marked them out from regular children.

The kids learned to fight with steel swords. Wielding weapons almost half their size, they put on warrior displays as part of the curriculum. They also learned gatka, fighting with long lathis. A typical day started at 2.30 am when some children performed voluntary worship or duties until 4 am. All children awake at 5.30 am. This is followed by the morning prayer, the Japji and then yoga or gatka. Room inspections were followed by breakfast, then lessons took place from 9 am to 3 pm. The rest of the afternoon is filled with sport, more yoga and an early dinner at 6 pm, followed by extra-curricular activities that may include playing the sitar or learning bhangra. Evening meditation was followed by bed at 9 pm. Each day, every day, the children submitted to this packed regime. Surely, it was a recipe for rebellion.

'Do they maintain these disciplines when they leave?'

'Some do, some don't. It depends on the kids. Ninety per cent remain on the path.'

I asked how she became involved.

'Through yoga. My yoga teacher, my mentor, is a student of Singh Sahib in Los Angeles. I was an educator in

LA for ten years. I was asked to do this. I had always known I'd come to India but I knew it would be for a specific reason. So the decision was already made and there was no way I could say no. It was karma.'

Yoga is a discipline of Hinduism and not usually associated with Sikhism. Also, the aim of yoga is to reach a state of non-attachment, which jarred somewhat with the martial disciplines of Sikhism. Even in this supposed bastion of Khalsa tradition, a hybrid version of Sikhism was being taught, diluting the Sikh identity with elements of Hinduism.

We passed through the sports ground to the car park. The kids were playing what looked like hockey, dressed in shorts and sports shirt and their white turbans. They looked happy and healthy and holy, as Singh Sahib's mantra goes. But I really wondered how they would fit in when they returned to the States. As it was Asian Sikhs found it difficult to blend into American society after September 11. These kids would find it difficult to act as ambassadors for their new religion in such a defensive political environment where anyone with a turban was seen as a threat.

It all linked back to what the Jathedar had said. Education. It seemed curious that it took a former Indian customs officer-yoga teacher in New Mexico to set up a school in Amritsar that sought to return to Khalsa traditions. The Jathedar had said that education was the only way to inform the world and stop the erosion of Sikh values and traditions, a return to the fundamentals of the faith. He was pinning his hopes on Sikh schools, perhaps not unlike this one, to do the job. The Miri Piri Academy's white turbans were meant to signify purity. The purity of the faith of the Khalsa, the essence of Sikh identity. Yet even in such a grand experiment, there were problems in this 'Made in America' nirvana.

Ironically, it was American values broadcast through

cable satellite channels like MTV, HBO and Star World that were slowly eroding and corrupting religion in India. A TV diet of *Baywatch* and *Zeena Warrior Princess* could distract anyone from their scriptures. The Jathedar recognized the corrosive effect of TV in many Punjabi households. A world had opened up to Sikh youth where hair was short, sex readily available outside of marriage, alcohol and cigarettes were emblems of the sophisticated man or woman. These were problems for all religions for sure, particularly so for one whose Gurus proscribed such things.

In Delhi the new generation of Punjabi Sikhs was more noted for knowing how to party than abstinence. If you wanted good whisky and kebabs, a Punjabi party was always the best bet for the discerning Delhi gadfly. For the Sikh leadership, it began with cut hair and whisky on the rocks and ended with the irrevocable erosion of the Sikh identity. It was this very threat that had fuelled the fanaticism of Bhindranwale, leading to his cry for a Land of the Pure, an orthodox quest that dragged Punjab into a decade-long spiral of destruction.

Sex, drugs and MTV were tempting the pure from the path of righteousness, whether they were Punjabi Sikh or American convert teenagers.

16

The Disappeared

'Does it really matter whether I die on my bed, in an accident or as a martyr to my cause?'

—Jaswant Singh Khalra answering his father
Kartar Singh's question as to why he risked his life by
investigating Punjab's secret cremations.
September 3 1995

Around 9.20 am on September 6, 1995, Jaswant Singh Khalra was outside his house at Kabir Park, washing his car. He was waiting for a journalist from the *Indian Express*. Khalra was the general secretary of the Akali Dal's human rights wing and had been investigating the 'disappearances' of Sikhs taken into police custody for questioning. The anti-terrorist crackdown was at its height. After Blue Star a new campaign of Sikh insurgency gripped Punjab in the decade that followed, leading to a tough crackdown first by Julio Ribeiro and followed by his successor, Director General of Police in Punjab K.P.S. Gill.

By this time, thousands of militants were operating in Punjab, with hundreds of terrorist cells aided by foreign funding and weaponry smuggled into the state from overseas. Terrorists no longer had pistols, but AK47s and rocket launchers. These were no longer local boys following one turbulent priest. The new breed of Sikh militant included professional, foreign-trained fighters. After Blue Star, some hardliner Sikh leaders fled to Pakistan where they received training to mount a counter-offensive.

It wasn't just hostile neighbours who kept the terrorists going. The largest funds came from the prosperous Sikh diaspora in Canada, UK and USA, many of whom had always been more reactionary and orthodox than the Sikhs in India.

The Indian government was iron-willed in its desire to destroy this network at any cost. No Sikh was above suspicion. Arrest, interrogation, torture and disappearances took place in the fight against insurgency that threatened to escalate into a secessionist movement that risked the integrity of India. The stakes were high. So was the price for ordinary Sikhs.

Against this backdrop, Khalra was trying to get to the bottom of what he believed was a covert campaign to cremate thousands of bodies of 'the disappeared'. He found evidence of police buying huge volumes of firewood at three crematoria in Amritsar. In one instance, police registered a purchase of 300 kilograms of firewood for the cremation of just one body. After gathering his case, he raised the issue with the Indian Supreme Court, held press conferences and was seeking to launch a movement to challenge the police head on. The campaign was gaining international as well as national momentum. On September 6 he planned to take the *Indian Express* journalist on a round of interviews on the secret cremations. He never made the meeting.

Around 9.20 am, neighbours saw a sky-blue Maruti van pull up outside the house. Armed commandos were inside. Behind the van was an official police jeep with officers in uniform. The officers were recognized by the locals as

Punjabi police. Khalra was beckoned to the blue van and then bundled into the back and driven away. His wife Paramjit Kaur Khalra, who worked as a librarian at Guru Nanak Dev University, was on her way to work when she noticed an unusual police presence at the top of her street. Later that morning she was informed her husband had been abducted.

That day marked the beginning of a long campaign to find out what happened to her husband. Three days later she filed a petition before the Supreme Court asking for the police to produce her husband in court. In November, the Supreme Court had ordered an inquiry by the Central Bureau for Investigation, India's foremost investigative body. It also had a remit to examine claims by Mrs Khalra that thousands more had disappeared and been cremated in Amritsar. In July 1996 the CBI reported that nine police officers acting on orders from the senior superintendent of police were responsible for Khalra's abduction and disappearance.

But even after this notable admission by the Supreme Court, Mrs Khalra did not find out the fate of her husband for many years to come. A former special police officer, Kuldip Singh, eventually came forward to inform the CBI that Khalra was kept imprisoned and interrogated under torture after his abduction. Kuldip Singh said on the night of October 28, 1995, Khalra was interrogated one last time. He was shot dead, dismembered and dumped in a local canal at 10 pm.

*

I visited Mrs Khalra at her house in Amritsar one evening. She was still fighting for justice as general secretary of the Association of Families of the Disappeared in Punjab. A decade had passed and her husband's killers were still free.

Her modest house was not far from the university. It was filled with the usual homely touches, but one wall was dominated by a huge oil painting of her husband, bearing the legend Shaheed or Martyr. He had a handsome face and kind brown eyes. The portrait towered over us and was surrounded by smaller photographs of her husband. It was like a shrine.

We sat on the sofa and had tea and biscuits. Mrs Khalra looked very tired, her hair was scraped back haphazardly into a bun; she clearly had little time for herself. She was a small woman, yet I detected a steely resolve in her eyes. Not once had she faltered in her fight. Her teenage son Janmeet joined us. He was a tall young man, with full, chubby cheeks. Quiet and thoughtful, he spoke little, but listened intently. His small white fluffy dog abandoned its half-hearted attempt at aggression and settled down by the sofa, eyes avidly darting from face to face as if following the conversation.

I asked Mrs Khalra when the threats to her husband first began.

'The moment he started the work. They were open threats from the police and it began the moment he gave a statement to the media saying he believed 25,000 people had disappeared in Punjab.'

'How did the police convey the threats?'

'One threat came through a local politician. He came to the house to give the message that my husband should restrain his activities and not raise his voice. He said otherwise "one more person will disappear".'

The husband and wife decided that despite the risks they would continue with the campaign.

'I never imagined the police would go to the extent of eliminating him,' she said. 'I expected threats, not illegal abduction. On the day of the abduction, one witness, Ranjiv Randhawa, saw the two vehicles. Around forty police surrounded our house. The neighbour said no arrest was made and three came from the van and took him.'

'What colour was the van?'

'Sky-blue,' said Janmeet.

They later found out that this van was regularly hired from a taxi stand by the police force. Janmeet continued as his mother poured tea and the dog tentatively approached the plate of biscuits on the table.

'We realized in 1998 that he was dead when an eyewitness, Kuldip Singh, who was in the police, told us he had been killed in custody. He witnessed the killing. First they tortured him. Then that night some senior official came. After that he was killed and thrown into the river.'

'How old were you then?' I asked the boy.

'Ten or eleven.' His voice was deadpan.

'The police would tell us for years, withdraw the case about your father. He is alive. They were giving us false hope to send us in the wrong direction.'

'What are your feelings, knowing what happened to your father?' He paused before answering.

'I feel proud.'

There was a long silence.

'Do you blame the system for allowing this to happen?'

'If the system is not good it must be fixed. There is discrimination against Sikhs in Punjab. Actually in all of India. Discrimination against all minorities,' he said.

'When Indira Gandhi was assassinated the killer was hanged within six months. My husband was killed almost ten years ago by the police and the case is still lying in CBI. *Nothing*,' said Mrs Khalra, raising her voice for the first time. 'The police are still working in the same police station and have been promoted.'

'Will you continue with your fight, despite all the problems?'

'Yes.'

How did they keep faith in the law after everything that happened?

'The work *he* did was within the law. It is the same with us today,' she said. 'We want justice for all.'

'All 25,000,' her son added.

While the Khalras had no time for talk of militancy, they conceded that other victims and families were embittered.

'If there is no justice, is it possible some may feel India does not care for the rights of Sikhs?' I asked.

'Yes. The system is wrong. Man is not wrong. There are families who've lost kin and no one from the administration asks for their well-being. This is my job—to help them.'

She said the effects of the years of terrorism and counter-terrorism were still being felt in Punjab today. The terror may have stopped, but the shockwaves continued to be felt by many Sikh families still searching for lost loved ones. Listening to her, I did not see how people would be able to put the past to rest if they could not lay their dead to rest first. Here was law without justice. Power without accountability. It was a hollow peace for the families concerned. Until there was closure, the risk remained that a new fundamentalism could rise from the ashes of the disappeared.

Jagmohan and I got up to leave. The Khalras walked us to the gate, the dog skipping around their ankles. It was pitch black by the time we left and we could barely see the path. The smell of wood smoke filled the air. I loved the smell of wood smoke. It transported me back to happy childhood visits to India, walking through the village in Goa as people lit evening fires to heat water in great black pots and cook the evening meal. For me it was the smell of India. But tonight it had less happy associations.

'You know, we'd only lived in this house one year when it happened,' she said. 'It happened where you're standing. Right there.'

She gave me a hug and they stood at the gate, mother and son, as they waved goodbye.

*

As I left the two of them in the drive, I wondered about all the others out there. While the Association of the Families of the Disappeared of Punjab says 25,000 people have 'disappeared', there are no official figures to confirm this. Their figures are collated by volunteers who have interviewed those victims who came forward. Perhaps it is the most definitive record of the disappeared.

In 1996 the Supreme Court said the CBI's final report showed 2,097 illegal cremations were carried out by security agencies in Amritsar. Of those, the CBI identified 582 bodies, partially ID-ed 278 and was unable to identify the the remainder. The Supreme Court decided to keep details of that report secret, but noted: 'The report discloses flagrant violation of human rights on a mass scale'. These same details were set out in another report on the disappearances called 'Reduced to Ashes' by Ram Narayan Kumar and other human rights workers. Its contents followed years of data collection and analysis that was described by Harvard's Human Rights Program as based on 'careful methodology' that was 'impossible to dismiss out of hand'.

But by the twentieth anniversary of the 1984 anti-Sikh riots, which led to the cycle of violence in the Punjab, there was still no sign of redress for the community. Groups ranging from Amnesty and Human Rights Watch voiced their dismay at the lack of action to punish use of torture, abductions, extra-judicial killings of the Sikh community by police and military. Amnesty warned on October 29, 2004, that 'until justice is delivered to victims and their families, the wounds left by this period remain open'. It called for an end to impunity for perpetrators of these abuses. Its 2003 report referred to 'thousands of families' waiting to hear of the fate of loved ones who had disappeared and accused the police of 'extra-judicial executions and illegal cremations'.

The Sikh Federation also gave written evidence to the UK Parliament in 2004 saying Sikhs still waited for justice. Its statement alleged torture, illegal detention and disappearances of Sikhs.

As a Sikh, Prime Minister Manmohan Singh had to address the issue. In August 2005 when Justice G.T. Nanavati's Commission of Inquiry published his report on the 1984 riots, citing witnesses who claimed that Congress leaders and workers had incited violence against Sikhs in Delhi, the Prime Minister made a statement. In it he said he would look into taking action against those police named in Nanavati's report and apologized: 'The past is with us. But as human beings we have the willpower and we have the ability to write a better future for all us,' he promised.

Finally, the Prime Minister of India had said the words that Sikhs waited twenty years to hear. Now they are waiting for action.

17

The Face of Judgement

Autumn 2004. Delhi

K.P.S. Gill, former Director General of Police of the Punjab, is credited with crushing the Khalistan terrorist movement and remains one of India's top experts in counter- insurgency. He served as head of the Central Reserve Police Force (CRPF) and Inspector General of the Border Security Force (BSF) in Jammu, another frontier-state racked by terror. Today he lives in semi-retirement in Delhi, writing and consulting on anti-terrorism. His expertise is sought from Sri Lanka to the US.

Gill suggested we meet for drinks on my return from Punjab. Taking down my home address, he informed me two of his securitymen would come to the building to carry out checks—he remains a target for his anti-terrorist activities in Punjab, Kashmir and Assam. That afternoon, while I was working at home, two men arrived in an armoured car and spoke to my driver Mr Singh. As soon as they left he rushed upstairs to tell me the news.

'Ma'am, Gill men come. They ask many questions. "Who is Madam? Show us where Madam lives. What is Madam doing?" They tell me, do not tell Madam we have come. So I am telling you.'

Mr Singh was very excited and for the rest of the day provided a running commentary. 'Mr Gill very big man, very powerful man.' I asked what he thought of him. 'Gill Sahib saved our Punjab,' he said simply.

The interview took place on a Sunday evening over whisky at Mr Gill's house on Talkatora Road, in one of Lutyens's grand imperial bungalows set in the environs of the Indian Parliament. He has lived in this house for eight years. One of his neighbours is the defence minister of India. Although now retired, he continues to face the threat of assassination. A swarm of armed black-uniformed commandos shadow him wherever he goes. To some he is the 'Butcher of Punjab' for his ruthless tactics and the widespread human rights abuses that took place during his command. Everyone knows the story of how he kicked a man to death during his years in Assam. But to others he remains the ultimate Indian strongman, a national hero for ending the secessionist terror in Punjab that risked the very Balkanization of India.

It was an ironic twist that a Sikh Punjabi should become the face of judgement during the era of Khalistani insurgency. Gill was the face of the nation state charged with straitjacketing the nascent separatist Sikh identity within a secular India. In the name of Indian unity he carried out and justified all actions against fellow Sikhs, not just terrorist suspects, but civilians caught in the crossfire. His tactics still divided the Sikh community, such was their brutality. Ten years on, many families were waiting to learn the fate of loved ones taken into state custody, never to return. The legacy of Gill's suppression in the name of India represented the unfinished business of that troubled era.

I waited for him in a drawing room at the front of his whitewashed bungalow. It was simply yet elegantly furnished with antique furniture, low glass-topped tables adorned with burnished brass figurines. A vase of pink and yellow roses lent a splash of colour. Side tables displayed fine blue crystal from Europe. On the walls were exquisite Persian miniature paintings in carved teakwood frames, and a beautiful old etching of the Golden Temple. In the centre of the room was a red carpet, which appeared to be Afghani, surrounded by comfortable chairs with plumped brocade cushions. It was the home of a superior aesthete.

A fan whirred overhead, suspended from double height ceilings that are a feature of central Delhi's gracious bungalows designed by British architects to be cool during the burning summers.

Gill entered the room. He lived up to his image as India's Super Cop: the man who cowed the most brutal of Punjab's terrorists. He is well over six feet four inches tall, even with a slight stoop. In his prime he must have stood over six feet five. Despite his age, sixty-nine, he has powerful shoulders and torso, and remains the ultimate warrior Sikh in appearance. The only sign of the march of time is a paunch, betraying a fondness for whisky and fine Punjabi food. He was dressed in cream shirt and slacks. He wore black leather loafers, buckled at the side with fancy fastenings, and dark blue socks. His elegantly tied turban was off-white and his cheeks covered with magnificent white whiskers, moustaches curled at the tips. His eyes were striking, dark and malevolent: a penetrating gaze that appeared to discern the secrets of your soul. As my driver put it: 'Gill Sahib is having danger in his eyes.'

I had read some of his writings before our meeting and from these he came across as a man of utter conviction, unshakeable in his belief that the ends justified the means. There were no regrets. Quickly we got down to business. The servant brought a large tumbler of whisky. Without preliminary small talk we began. His voice was rich and resonant, like an aged actor in a Shakespearian tragedy, each word weighed for content, measured for effect. There was no loose talk, no impassioned monologues. Just cold logic.

I asked how it all began.

'I joined the police in 1957 and after that I went to Assam. When this thing was happening I was not in Punjab. But during visits to Punjab, in 1981 or 1982, I remember getting a peculiar feeling, the way people were talking in the drawing rooms. Frankly, I was upset. I could see that the Hindus and the Sikhs would segregate themselves. There was no communication. So I spoke to people in authority that what is happening in the Punjab is going to be very, very serious.'

'Did Indira Gandhi ask for your intervention?'

'No. If you look at the pre-1984 terrorism before Blue Star, the number of killings, crimes committed under the cover of terrorism, was negligible compared to what happened later on. Very, very negligible. But at that time it appeared to be worrying, especially because it was happening in Punjab.'

Punjab is a border state with Pakistan. At the time of Partition in 1947, the state was carved in two, with a large chunk of territory going to the new Islamic nation. River and canal water networks were divided, leaving behind a bitter legacy. The state witnessed terrible communal violence at Partition that killed many Sikhs, Muslims and Hindus and led to massive displacement.

Until the close of 1983 Gill was stationed in Assam, charged with the job of seeing through the elections against the bloody backdrop of militant insurrection in the state. After the job was completed he left for a new post in another troubled frontier state, Jammu and Kashmir.

'(Assam) was a total success. Then I was moved out and

I went to the Border Security Force in Jammu. I went in January 1984. I spent eight to nine months there and then I got the summons to come to Punjab. By that time Blue Star was over.' The Blue Star operation was run by the army, under another Sikh, General K.S. Brar. Gill came to help clear up the mess that followed.

'When Blue Star happened, I imagine there were a lot of mixed emotions.'

'There were two things. Everyone was upset. All Sikhs were upset but then people like me thought you cannot use a place of worship as a shelter for terrorism. And I thought terrorism is something the Sikh religion doesn't sanction in any way. There's no chapter or verse one can quote from Sikhism. From the Koran you can quote many things which justify violence, the killing of the heathen, the killing of the kafir.'

'Some Sikhs have quoted to me the Tenth Guru saying that if you have tried all other means to defend religion and failed, then it is time to take up the sword,' I said.

'Obviously, any religion can have its words twisted by zealots.'

'Isn't it true Bhindranwale saw himself as taking on the legacy of the Tenth Guru, encouraging Sikhs to lay down life and defend the faith, melding it into the wider ideology of Khalistan?'

'First of all, the Tenth Guru said you should fight against injustice. Right? You tell the person who is unjust, "Do not be unjust". And you request, argue with him and when he does not stop being unjust then you take up the sword. By no stretch of the imagination could you say that not giving Chandigarh to Punjab, or not giving some water rights was injustice which would justify what happened. So, I thought the Bhindranwale thing was a total negation of Sikhism. I heard Bhindranwale's tape played to me...'

'These were his speeches?'

'Yes. He talked absolute muck. He was a bloody madcap. This Bhindranwale doctrine can be summed up in two or three things. He borrowed quite a few things, whether consciously or subconsciously, from Hitler's fascist doctrine. One was that the Sikh is superior to others, to the Hindu. Second was space, living space.'

'They wanted a homeland?'

'And the third was that by force of arms we'll compel the Indian state to give it. I remember talking to another stupid ass... who was one of the army people who joined this movement in large numbers. I said to him, "Do you not know the modern nation state? You are a handful of people, don't get into this. You'll get a beating." I didn't know at that stage I would be asked to do it. I was still in Assam.'

When Blue Star happened, Gill was in Jammu. He heard about the operation through his sources. Details of the storming were subject to a complete new blackout to prevent a Sikh backlash. While not directly involved in the operation, he saw preparations for it in the days before.

'I'd been to the Golden Temple before Blue Star took place. I was very unhappy with the way the deployment was made, eight to ten days before Blue Star. It was absolutely unprofessional and just a waste of manpower. They were supposed to surround the Golden Temple and stop weapons going in.'

'But that had been going on already for a period of months.'

'Yes, I went to see how things were still going in. You could see it was supposed to be a cordon but it was not a cordon. There were a number of openings.'

'There has been the suggestion that it was encouraged, because the central government effectively wanted a showdown to send a wider message across the country that it was tough on Sikh separatism. It does seem bizarre in retrospect that they allowed a situation to occur where this holy of holies was turned into a fortress.'

He smiled and turned his head away for a second before answering, 'Mrs Gandhi had to act through people available to her. I don't think in Punjab she had anybody. She didn't want an army operation. BSF was asked to undertake, we said we can't do it, we don't have the expertise. CRPF couldn't do it and then the army was called in and they said it would be a question of two hours.'

The problem became much greater in the aftermath of Blue Star. The storming of the temple radicalized many angry young men and Pakistan began playing a hand in stoking the secessionist movement. Several young Sikhs crossed into Pakistan and began training at terrorist camps. Ordinary, non-militant Sikhs, too, felt their religious identity was under attack. Gill was in Amritsar at the time as a senior police chief and began to tackle the fallout, taking over control of the Golden Temple from the army, removing the barbed wire and so on. He was there until 1985 when elections were held. The Akalis won.

'The first thing they did was dismantle the anti-terrorism measures I had set up in the year I was there—record keeping, making of lists, investigation of crimes, of terrorism. In 1986 when the situation was going out of control, the chief minister removed the handpicked DGP.'

Julio Ribeiro was appointed as the replacement. 'Ribeiro said within six months he'd finish it. He went in March or April and in June I was brought in with a restricted mandate to look after Amritsar and Gurdaspur. By 1987 we had control of the situation. Again, the terrorists were on the run. Then started a peace process.'

Gill says he was not in favour of the peace process as

part of this the controls over the Golden Temple complex were relaxed. According to Gill, this was when the 're-weaponization, fortification of temple' began. Terrorism was on the rise. 'President's rule was imposed and I was made DGP. Immediately afterwards, we started the Black Thunder II operation.

'We had a meeting in Rajiv Gandhi's house. There was a map. So what do we do? I as the junior-most officer waited for others to speak. They came out with nothing, so I told Rajiv, "Look, with your permission may I say something?" He said yes. I said there are three rectangular areas. One is the sarai. Then we have the langar building [community kitchen] and the last is the holy of holies. I said we should take over the first and second, third we should assess the mood, make limited forays at night, kill as many terrorists as we can and withdraw.'

'With snipers?'

'Snipers. Eight or ten officers going in for a quick raid. So, Rajiv said yes.'

'How many were under your jurisdiction for that operation?'

'It was not a very large force.'

The surrender was quick. Operation Black Thunder II took place from May 12 to 18, 1988. The plan which utilized anti-terrorism National Security Guards or commandos known as the Black Cats, used precision explosions and sniper fire to secure a victory over the terrorists occupying the complex. There was no repetition of the horrendous deathcount of Blue Star, injuries were minimal and it was deemed a success. Gill subsequently wrote that the loss of the Golden Temple complex and the gurdwaras was a loss from which the Khalistan movement never recovered.

'In 1989 we had reduced terrorism, confined it in

thirteen police districts out of 220-230. The terrorists were
sending us messages by March 1989—"Please give us a way
out and we will lay down our arms". I sent that message to
the director of the Intelligence Bureau in March 1989.
There was no response. It was a political decision, I think,
that this residual terrorism should be allowed to remain
until the election. If you see the 1989 campaign [for
national elections], if you go through the newspapers and
images, this was the crux of the Congress campaign. As the
elections approached they said, right, *now* talk to the
terrorists.'

At the time, the terrorists wanted an exit strategy
without appearing to be defeated by the government, he
said. The terrorists wanted a formula which allowed them
to lay down weapons without conceding defeat. In turn, the
government wanted to make security and peace in Punjab
an election issue.

Despite his efforts, Rajiv Gandhi was defeated in the
1989 national elections and succeeded as Prime Minister by
Vishwanath Pratap Singh. A turbulent period in national
politics followed. It was during the next prime ministership
of Chandra Shekhar, who came to power in November
1990, that Gill was transferred back to Delhi just weeks
after the new government was formed

Gill bided his time in Delhi. Then in May 1991, the
political order was overturned again by the assassination of
Rajiv Gandhi, now Opposition leader, during the election
campaign by a Tamil Tiger suicide bomber. In June,
Narasimha Rao was swept to office on a tide of sympathy
after the assassination. By November 1991 Gill was back in
Punjab as Director General of Police once again.

Suddenly, our conversation was broken by the ringing
of his red telephone. He answered, spoke briefly and shortly
afterwards his servant came bearing a tray containing five

mobile phones. None were ringing. He had one fixed line, two cordless phones, making a total of eight phone lines in one room. A lot of phones for one retired police chief. Was someone listening in, I wondered? It was easy to feel paranoid in his company, after all this was a man who lived to control.

'When I went back,' he continued, 'we had 500 hardcore terrorists, 5,000 terrorists of lesser grade.'

'How do you grade the hardcore?'

'Hardcore is the one who leads a little gang or cell. And we had 15,000 supporters.'

'How did you classify supporters?'

'Those who gave them shelter, food.'

A Sikh I knew told me the story of his sister and her husband who lived in a village in Punjab at the height of the terrorism. One night a gang of four terrorists armed with rifles and shotguns appeared on their doorstep. They demanded food and shelter. The woman and her husband were not sympathizers, nor were they in favour of Khalistan. But they feared for their safety. The woman prepared dinner, beds and then breakfast the next morning. That night they barely slept. When the men left their house, they were too terrified to report it to the police, knowing informers would be shot. This family was lucky. I had heard during my visit to Punjab that many such families, innocent bystanders, had been either killed by terrorists or hauled in for police questioning. Many were beaten for information during interrogation. Some did not return.

I asked him about abuses in custody. How far should a state be willing to go to protect the integrity of the country? There had been many reports of human rights abuses in custody, disappearances, reports about deaths in custody, use of torture, mass graves. I suspected that as long as these abuses remained buried, it would be hard for Punjab to leave the horror of these years behind. Gill didn't see it that way.

'First of all, there are no mass graves. There are no mass graves in Punjab at all.'

'What about the cremation grounds?'

'The cremation grounds are municipal cremation grounds. Somebody is killed, his post mortem is done, inquest is done by magistrate and his body is handed over to be cremated. If they were secret cremations then no record would be there.'

Indeed, there were records. But they were partial records. Some records did not even specify who the persons were. The records sometimes showed there was a body. But the name was not always included. I asked about the human rights activists' claim of 25,000 people who disappeared— people they believe were killed and cremated, or dumped in rivers or canals.

'Nonsense. First of all, have you seen the canal system in Punjab? The body, they say, will float down to Rajasthan. It'll never happen. Every few miles you have an obstruction in the canal. Then someone said they were thrown into the village ponds. The village ponds are situated in the village. The body will float after one day.'

'The rivers? Or these graves?'

'Where are these rivers? Where are the rivers where these bodies can be thrown?'

'Sutlej, Beas.'

'Beas is one river, right? I can't imagine 25,000 bodies being thrown in it. Sutlej is dammed and in the lower reaches is almost dry.'

'Why would the human rights groups say this?'

'Name one independent group.'

'Amnesty.'

As he veered off track, I asked him again about allegations

of illegal disposal of bodies. He shifted his weight forward in the chair, eyes blazing: 'These secret graves. Where are the secret graves?' he boomed. 'Not an inch of land in Punjab is uncultivated. There would be no peace in Punjab today...if it were true.'

'I've spoken to some people who have lost relatives in what they call abductions by police and subsequent disappearance. They're too scared to do anything as the killers continue to be in the police force.'

'Who are these people?' he asked. It was more a demand than a question.

'Not big people. Small people. They're not looking for Khalistan.' I didn't want to name names—as if they didn't have enough problems. Gill gave a broad answer to the general point, all the same, summing up:

'Fake names, fake villages, fake fathers... How's your glass?'

'I'll have a Coke.'

He rang the servant buzzer and ordered another whisky and a coke. He adroitly turned from the subject of the mass cremations to the global debate on human rights in a post 9/11 world. For men like Gill, who made the American Neo-Cons seem like limp-wristed liberals in comparison, today's terror-stricken world cannot always afford the luxury of human rights. Gill was not going to be lectured on the subject by foreign human rights watchdogs, or anyone else.

'The whole human rights movement was started by USA to allow them to intervene in the affairs of other countries. Now where has the debate gone to? What happened the other day [in Iraq]? Some vehicle of the Americans was attacked and one or two people were injured. The crowds were cheering. The Americans called for a helicopter strike and they killed fifteen-twenty people from the air. *That* is not human rights abuse. No one talks of *that*,' he replied sarcastically.

He scorned the double standards he saw in foreigners towards India's record on human rights. Taking another slug of whisky, he had a poser for his critics: 'I put this question to all human rightists. When a man takes up a gun, when there is another nation state which is arming, training, motivating and tasking him to come and commit acts of terror, not to destroy India, but to destroy the civilization— the ancient Hinduism, the glories of Hinduism—what should I do to that man when I find him and catch him?'

There was a long silence. I wanted him to answer his own question.

'Come on. You give me the answer,' he said. 'He's not after your nation. He's after your civilisation. What is Osama bin Laden saying?'

'What's *your* answer?' I replied.

'My answer is to answer them in kind.'

'A bullet for bullet?'

'Bullet for bullet.'

'Equal response?'

'Equal response.'

'No holds barred?'

'No holds barred.'

'Then how does that differentiate the state from the terrorist?'

'You have got into a bind here. What was our fight about? What was the message I sent to them? The message was, "You confront us. Either we kill you or you kill us. Either you get arrested and lie in jail or you remain a fugitive. But there's a fourth way. You come, surrender to us and we assure you, you will undergo trial if your case is heinous offences." Thousands surrendered with weapons. If 1,800 policemen die, I tell you, 5,000 terrorists will die.'

Political scientists at Guru Nanak Dev University in Amritsar published a study in 1999 that showed the average terrorist died within two years of taking up arms. Looking at Gill I was surprised it was that long. As he shifted in his chair, eyes burning with intensity as the alcohol took effect on his formidable frame, his great paw-like hand gripping the half-full whisky glass, his voice dropped a notch:

'There was a train going from Ludhiana, distance fifty km to its destination. Terrorists enter this train. Fifty-six people are killed. Bodies are loaded onto trucks. Then, in the mortuary their bodies are laid on the ground as there is not enough space. When I went to see them, on the floor there was blood semi-caked, thicker than this carpet. You can't reach the mortuary without walking through it. A layer of blood which sort of *springs* beneath your feet.'

He paused for dramatic effect, glass still nursed in his clenched fist before continuing in that rich baritone, breath redolent with the whiff of whisky: 'So what have these people done? And those who kill them—by what logic of humanity or politics, or what Musharraf calls 'root causes', by what logic did they kill them?'

There was no answer, of course.

Instead, I asked whether he wondered how history would judge him. The floors of Indian police interrogation rooms had also been covered with the blood of innocents. I understood his point, but equally found it impossible to forget the faces of Mrs Khalra and her son, who despite everything continued to work within the law, despite the officers of law working outside the law. Mr Khalra had been a victim not of terrorism, but his own country. Civilians had not just died by the terrorist gun, but at the hands of the Indian police. India sanctioned such tactics against its own. During this era, no Sikh was above suspicion of being the enemy within. Alienation fostered a sense of victimhood. It fuelled fundamentalism. Many Indians called Mr Gill a hero of India for saving the state from secession and the country from possible disintegration. They did not exaggerate. Others simply called him the Butcher of Punjab.

'I don't care about the Sikhs who call me Butcher of Punjab,' he said, lifting the tumbler to his lips and polishing off the last of its contents. 'They tried to destroy me. They tried to build up a case against me. It collapsed around them.'

He looked tired and it was late. I got up to leave and Mr Gill walked me to the door. He walked slowly, now an old man. He would be seventy in December. As I was about to drive from his gates a guard came running towards me through the gloom of the night. Sahib wanted to speak with me. I went back into the gated grounds, past the armed checkpoint and walked towards the house. Mr Gill's tall frame loomed at the doorway, silhouetted by the light behind him. He came up the car drive and offered me a copy of his book, *The Knights of Falsehood*, an account of the Khalistan movement and how he destroyed its false prophets.

'It's now in its third edition,' he said. He offered to speak to me again the next day. Then he would be away for two months but would be available to meet again in December. We shook hands and said goodnight.

The next morning we spoke again. I asked whether he feared Sikh fundamentalism could rise from the ashes. His book suggested this was a possibility. 'Khalistan remains their ideological platform,' he wrote. His book said a residual threat of terrorism remained in Punjab. More than 200 listed terrorists, including thirty hardcore members, were unaccounted for. Some were believed to be in India. Mercenaries were always on hand to be bought into any political cause.

Caches of weapons and military hardware were still buried across the Punjab countryside and could be recovered quickly if the need arose. He said Pakistan continued to run terror training camps which included members of the key Khalistan terrorist groups: Babbar Khalsa, the Bhindranwale Tiger Force for Khalistan, Dal Khalsa, the Khalistan Commando Force and the International Sikh Youth Federation. This was supported by a report from the home ministry in August 2004. That document warned of continued Pakistani intelligence efforts to revive Khalistan.

Fund-raising for these terror groups continued in Canada, the US, the UK and Germany. In each of these countries there is a sizeable and wealthy Sikh population, said Mr Gill. Another senior security source from the Indian Cabinet secretariat had also told me he had raised the issue of Khalistan-funding with the Canadian government.

Mr Gill felt that it was crucial for India to remain vigilant. He said issues of religious identity were being used to foster a sense of alienation for dangerous political ends in India and around the world. 'As religions become a tool for political mobilization, there is a skewed emphasis on conformity and religious identity, on the isolation of and loyalty to the community, to the exclusion of the spiritual and moral content of religion,' he wrote. I asked him whether he still believed all the above was valid.

'All these things remain and recently a gang was arrested in Gurdaspur, less then three weeks ago. It included two Paks, some Punjabi Sikhs and some Sikhs from J&K. The Sikhs from Jammu and Kashmir are now seeking a Muslim-Sikh alliance. It has not worked.' Both Punjab and J&K border Pakistan and both have suffered insurgency.

'You have to keep an eye on these elements. Unchecked, they're capable of causing considerable harm. They don't need many men, and if a few bomb attacks happen with sufficient frequency it will awaken fear that the movement is alive. But India has learned from past mistakes.'

We chatted about a few other points and the conversation turned to how he started policing, given that his educational background was an MA in English literature. It was an unlikely path. He came from a well-to-do Punjabi family. His father was an engineer with a fondness for poetry. Some evenings he would gather the family around and recite poems.

'My father was a great collector of books. In our house he would read poetry aloud. I remember, as a student in Mussoorie, there was a very good library. Also, books were cheap. You could buy Penguin books for sixpence. I kept up my interest in literature until very recently when my eyesight began to go. I now have an entire recorded version of Shakespeare with Sir John Gielgud. As a youth I had studied *Othello*, *Merchant of Venice* and *Julius Caesar*.'

He combined his early passion for Shakespeare with acting, treading the boards of the Gaeity Theatre in Shimla, a pretty Himalayan hill station that once was the summer capital of the British Raj and is now a retreat for wealthy Indians. I asked him what role he was remembered for the most.

'I played Shylock. You know the court scene? 'The quality of mercy is not strained'.'

I felt he rather liked the idea of playing one of literature's greatest villains, one who did not care for the judgement of others and revelled in his reputation for having no pity.

'To think, you could've been an actor, not a police chief, if things had turned out differently,' I suggested. He laughed heartily.

'I don't know if I could've been an actor. Those were different days. In those days I used to write poetry,' he said, voice dropping to a husky whisper. What had happened? What had turned this one-time poetry-writing romantic into India's most ruthless police chief, a moustache-twirling villain worthy of his own immortalization in prose? Sensing this was one place nobody dared go, I did not ask. Instead I blandly requested the names of other people I could speak to.

'Do you want to hear the absolute opposite point of view?' he boomed. 'People who will absolutely trash me?'

'Yes.'

'Call ***** and ******. But it's better you don't tell them I told you their names or that you spoke to me.'

After our chat, later that evening, I dug out my copy of *Merchant of Venice*. The line he quoted was from the speech by Portia asking Shylock for clemency, to show compassion to his victim by renouncing his claim for a pound of flesh in exchange for a reneged debt:

> *'The quality of mercy is not strain'd,*
> *It droppeth as the gentle rain from heaven*
> *Upon the place beneath: it is twice blest,*
> *It blesseth him that gives and him that takes,*
> *'Tis mightiest in the mightiest, it becomes*
> *The throned monarch better than his crown...'*

Of course, Shylock chose not to show mercy:

> *'The pound of flesh which I demand of him*
> *Is dearly bought, 'tis mine and I will have it:*
> *If you deny me, fie upon your law!*
> *There is no force in the decrees of Venice:*
> *I stand for Judgement: answer, shall I have it?'*

(*Merchant of Venice*, Act IV,
Scene I, Shakespeare)

PART 4

Saffron Warriors

18

The Godfather

'I am like a tiger who is wounded but will definitely retaliate one day. I may have been confined to a cage but don't dare tease me.'

—An elderly Bal Thackeray, leader of the Shiv Sena,
warning enemies and rivals not
to underestimate him, 2004

Bombay, March 2003

On March 12, 1993 Bombay awoke to another working day. Roads were solid with traffic as beggars weaved in and out courting death for a few rupees. Paan-sellers squatted by the road spewing blood-red arcs of betel juice into grey dust; hawkers stalked the well-to-do with frantic sales pitches. The air smelled of salt and diesel. Gulls skimmed the seafront, broken sunlight glittered on the bay like a million diamonds. Everything was normal.

The metropolis had slipped into a semblance of calm following riots just months before, triggered by the destruction of the Babri Masjid in Ayodhya. It was a rather nondescript-looking mosque. But like much else in India, its importance lay in its symbolism. To the Hindu right, it was the emblem of a past slavery by Muslim invader kings, since they believed Emperor Babur had built it over an ancient temple to Lord Ram. In December 1992, tens of thousands of Hindu extremists smeared with the holy colour of saffron and armed with iron rods and pickaxes stormed the masjid, and in a matter of hours reduced it to rubble. For Hindutva's holy warriors, it marked the dawn of a new Hindu age. For India's Muslims, it threatened religious warfare.

Thousands of kilometers away, high on this 'victory', gangs from the hardline Hindu nationalist Shiv Sena spilled onto Bombay's streets to celebrate, tearing through the financial capital in riots that butchered and burned Muslims in ruthless raids. The Shiv Sena goons answered to one man: Bal Thackeray. To followers, he was a leader worthy of veneration and the epithet 'Emperor of the Hindu Heart'. To opponents he was a religious gangster. He boasted that his 'boys' had taught the Muslims a lesson they would not forget. He was right. They didn't.

Three months later, on March 12, a series of bomb blasts ripped through the city in what was the single largest terrorist attack on Indian soil in recent history, killing more than 250 people and injuring hundreds more. The attack was blamed on Muslim terrorists avenging the Babri Masjid's destruction and the Bombay riots. It raised the spectre of Islamic terrorism in the heart of the Indian nation. For militant Muslims, it was payback time.

*

Ten years had passed and I was in Bombay to meet the man at the centre of that communal storm, the seventy-something Bal Thackeray, an open admirer of Hitler. A one-time cartoonist-turned-political-power-broker, he had founded the Shiv Sena in 1966. The Shiv Sena or 'Shivaji's Army' was named after the seventeenth-century Maratha king who waged battle against the mighty Mughal Aurangzeb. Thus he remains a hero of Hindu history—a warrior ruler who dared to defy the Mughal Empire at the height of its powers in northern India. The Marathi leader is a talismanic figure for Maharashtra Hindus, described by historians as a man who combined strategic intellect with formidable bravery, a man who went to battle brandishing a dagger in one hand and a tiger's claw in the other.

Thackeray unashamedly appropriated this iconic imagery as his own. His Shiv Sena stood for the iron fist of Hindutva, not the noble defiance of the non-violent Hindu embodied by Gandhi. In 2002 Thackeray urged the Indian government to attack Pakistan for sponsoring terrorism in Kashmir and in the same year urged Hindu youths to form their own suicide squads to wage a counter-jihad. Months after his call to arms, police raided a camp just outside Bombay with young men in commando training with rifles, explosives and other weapons. The camp was run by a former army general with links to the Shiv Sena. The Sena denied it had any connection with the project, but few believed it. It was clear Thackeray was one pensioner who did not intend to spend his twilight years tending the roses.

In 2003, *India Today* magazine had published a poll of the fifty most powerful people in India and ranked Thackeray at number four. By then, the Shiv Sena was no longer the party of power in Maharashtra, having lost the state elections after failing to deliver on electoral promises such as providing new housing. But the party remained a coalition ally in the central government led by the BJP until May 2004. At the Centre, the Shiv Sena's extremism was curbed by the constraints of high office and by its coalition partners. Yet in Maharashtra, Thackeray continued to wield a base type of power: the power of the street that crowned him overlord of Bombay, a seething metropolis of Bollywood and *badmaashes*, of economic and religious divide. He had tapped into the bitter insecurities of the urban youth—young Hindu men aged fifteen to thirty with no education, no prospects and no stake in India's boom city. Thackeray learned to harness their unspoken rage and they became his sainiks, soldiers. These men were his eyes and ears, his campaigners and boot boys, all enthralled by the big beast of Hindu nationalism—known to friends by the affectionate nickname Tiger.

For decades, Bombay remained within the tiger's grip and when he felt the sainiks' interests were threatened, like Shivaji, he roared and bared his claws. It was brute power, but tightly controlled, remote control anarchy being his weapon of choice. By 2004 his health and political fortunes were waning. A battle for succession began between his son and nephew and he struggled to keep the party together. Many said once Thackeray died, the Shiv Sena would be just like any other party, no longer the political showcase for one man's monstrous charisma and ego. But as long as he is alive, his incendiary brand of mob politics remains a force, even if a weakened one. His signal still controls thousands. Armani-clad, Wharton-educated business barons acknowledge that they needed him onside. 'He's the mafia king of Mumbai,' said one, over lunch at the Taj. 'Sure, he has no official power, but with one word he can still bring the city to a standstill. And we know it.'

His power manifested in different ways. Perhaps the most obvious example was the decision in 1995 for Bombay to ditch its name, dating back to colonial times, changing it to Mumbai—a name free of the taint of invasion and foreign rule. Over the years, his influence was evident in everything from the name of the city to who did business in *his* town. Whether it was the boss of Enron seeking clearance for a deal or Michael Jackson down for a concert in Mumbai, the great and the famous knew of the power that resided in a certain rose-lined avenue in the suburbs. If ever there was a Godfather in Indian politics, Bal Thackeray was it.

I took a taxi to Bandra East, a sedate middle-class enclave forty-five minutes' drive from the city centre. My elderly driver, Mohammed, was originally from Lahore. His was the old story of an erased existence that is still heard in much of India. Like many millions he too had believed for years that after Partition, once things settled down, he could return to his ancestral home that was now part of another country. It didn't happen. So here he was fifty years on, adrift in the seaside city of Mumbai. He wore a spotless white kurta, his silver head encased in an immaculate skullcap. The white Ambassador taxi was his living by day and a place to sleep at night. A strand of festive red tinsel brightened the dashboard to give it a homely touch. We drove past the slum and skyscraper skyline to Hindi love songs. He strummed his fingertips on the steering wheel to the beat of the tabla. As we approached the all-important neighbourhood, he swivelled his head away from the road to look at me, eyes wide with drama. 'Thackeray Sahib lives here.'

'We're going to his house.'

'But Madam is in need of appointment! Much securities. Many jawans stationed here.'

Armed guards, road blocks, checkpoints on the street where he lived. Mohammed wasn't kidding. After passing a security checkpoint, our car swung into Thackeray's road, lined with plush mansions surrounded by manicured gardens. Rows of trees cast a dappled shade. The thin sunlight bathed the streets in a honey-coloured glow and a faint breeze stirred overhead, swaying great bunches of fuchsia bougainvillea in the gardens of Mumbai's moneyed classes. Each walled garden was ablaze with colour—terracotta pots of pansies, candy-coloured dahlias and roses tended by sun-blackened malis.

Thackeray's residence was recognizable by an armed police roadblock, with the entrance to his large sandstone-coloured house guarded by another policeman wearing khaki uniform and a bullet-proof vest. His cap was tilted at a rakish angle and he nursed a rifle across his chest as he picked at his teeth with a grubby forefinger.

'I'll see you later.'

'I am waiting there only, Madam,' Mohammed pointed to a spot of shade up the road, away from the gaze of the security detail.

At the gate, I met my go-between, a businessman, who had arranged the meeting and we were ushered towards the garden. To the right was a security hut filled with high-tech audio-visual equipment. A guard monitored tape from TV surveillance cameras showing live footage from the road and various positions inside the house and garden. We entered through a side door, past an armed guard covering the stairwell, and took the lift to the first floor. On the landing was a heavy teak door which opened into Thackeray's reception. At the door the go-between removed his shoes, so did I, and together we entered the tiger's marble-floored lair.

The drawing room, with walls painted a pleasant cream, was filled with personal photos, memorabilia and bouquets from well-wishers. A small two-seater sofa was up against the wall and armchairs were placed opposite, all upholstered in dark orange velvet. Flower arrangements filled the room, scenting it with the pungent aroma of jasmine and roses. To my left was a large black leather massage chair, covered in ill-fitting red towelling. A flat white remote control panel for the chair sat on a small side table, with buttons denoting different positions.

It was an ordinary middle-class living room, except perhaps for the massage chair, and the huge soft focus photo of Thackeray with his arm around Michael Jackson. On the wall facing it were family portraits: an austere black and white photograph of his father draped with a single garland of yellow and white flowers and a painting of his mother adorned with white and red carnations.

Without fanfare, Thackeray entered. He was small and frail but instantly recognizable in his trademark deep orange kurta and lungi as the iconic figure of Hindutva. His small, pale feet were bare, the toes neatly manicured. Brown and white beads hung around his neck and his hair was swept back in a quiff: unnaturally black, silky and luxuriant. He looked like an Elvis Man. Large square Elvis-in-Las-Vegas-style sunglasses engulfed his thin, sharp-featured face, screening his reactions. My mind flicked to a basement club in the city: A tribute night to The King. A piano tinkling in the corner, blue cigarette smoke suspended in the air like question marks, lithe-hipped Sena boys sipping whisky by the bar. In the spotlight, Thackeray in a white tuxedo, with legs slightly akimbo, chin dipped into his chest, thin-lipped mouth crooked into a sneer, croons into the microphone to whistles and applause. 'Thankyouverymuch gennelmen, you've been beautiful!'

Back in the drawing room, Mr Thackeray greeted us with a quick namaskar and sat on the massage chair. The businessman bowed low, his face pressed close to Thackeray's feet. He touched the edge of his robe, then kissed it in a gesture of deference. Accepting the veneration, Thackeray lifted the remote control and pressed the 'on' switch. Red lights zipped across the panel. The massage chair hissed softly and the seat eased higher as it began to work on his body. Small balls within the chair gently pummelled his back and buttocks through the leather, issuing a sigh with each elevation and compression. To the rhythm of his mechanical masseur, he was ready to begin.

It was the tenth anniversary of the Bombay bomb blasts. What were his memories of that day? He closed his eyes, palms together in concentration, and spoke in a voice so quiet I had to lean in, like prey drawn by its predator. 'The day of the blasts is imprinted on the mind of every Indian. It was the biggest single terror attack in India and marked a new form of militancy in the heart of India. There were thirteen blasts and more than 300 people died. I felt there had to be strong, cruel, cruel steps to crush it so it was not repeated again.'

For Thackeray the only response to Islamic militancy was Hindutva militancy and for that he needed money. 'Today it's a mess. These extremists have the money power and the arms dealers who supply them. Against that kind of thing an ordinary man cannot fight back. So pelting with stones is not an answer to this. It should be tit-for-tat.'

These were not idle words, as the recent discovery of camps to train Hindutva's suicide squads had proved. Thackeray believed the country was swamped with Muslims, whom he viewed as the infiltrators of old, invaders who threatened India's security and its Hindu community. Muslims account for almost 140 million of India's 1.1 billion population. But the Hindu right muttered darkly of over-breeding Muslims and the day the Hindus would be a minority and India an Islamic state.

It was an old fascist ploy—propaganda about the over-breeding, murderous minority instilling fear in the majority. During the wave of colonial migration to Britain in the Fifties, Sixties and Seventies that brought my parents to those shores, the standard-bearer of the anti-immigration right, Enoch Powell, warned with relish that 'rivers of blood' would flow if the tide of foreigners was not stemmed. The rivers of blood never came. But bottles of Cobra beer and chicken tikka masala did. Middle England did not revolt. John Bull did not emerge from his terrace brandishing the Sunday roast carving knife to slice up the Pakis. Instead, he developed a penchant for Friday night curry over fish and chips. By 2003, ladies from Teeside to Thames Valley arranged nights out to London to watch *Bombay Dreams* at the West End theatre wearing stick-on bindis and snacking on samosas.

It was a slow seduction. Britain, a mongrel nation that assimilated invaders and refugees and emerged stronger for it, lived up to its tradition of absorbing newcomers, going through the phases of suspicion and insecurity to something approaching tolerance and accommodation. In the metropolis, the synergy of different cultures had created dynamism not just in culture, but in society itself. It showed Britain another side of India, a version updated from the days of Empire. India was no longer the place of the Raj and Kiplingesque elephant rides through jungle morning mist. It had melded with British identity to create a distinct Indo-British character—Punjabi, Gujarati, Konkani with a British accent.

The July 2005 terror attacks in London by Islamic extremists had reawakened the debate about the true nature of British identity and the place of the Muslim community within the country. It was a difficult conversation for Britons to have among themselves and Muslims felt under pressure to prove their loyalty to their adopted country. But nobody seriously suggested the answer was to fight Muslims head-on and drive them into the sea, reversing the history of immigration that had made Britain what it is today. The painful transition was far from perfect but it offered a lesson: you can't reverse the tides of history but you can learn to live with what it brings to your shores. It was a lesson that India itself had learned centuries ago, through its turbulent history of conquest by a series of invaders. Rather than fight the enemy head-on, the Hindus lived alongside their conquerors, co-existing, surviving and eventually it was the conquerors who were absorbed into Mother India as religious minorities. The Hindus remained in a majority to this day and India was a richer culture for its turbulent history.

But Thackeray was not interested in the politics of integration. Instead, his focus remained fixed on the hidden motive of the Mussalman in India—a community that had now been part of the nation for the best part of a thousand years but which he still viewed as the outsider. And now there was the new problem of illegal immigration from the poorer neighbours, Pakistan and Bangladesh. 'They're here in the country. Throw them out. Without passport, without visa, without anything. If there were a conflict, these Muslims would stand by Pakistan. Not by my country. Bodily they live here, heart is with Pakistan. This is dangerous to India,' he told me.

In the past, Thackeray had openly warned that only civil war could exorcise India of its historical ghosts and it seemed more a wish than a prophesy: 'I'm not an astrologer, call it intuition. Civil war will be there between Hindus and Muslims,' he said. In the background, we heard the gentle pop of a wine bottle and the tinkle of crystal. The servant hovered in the background, head bent in submission, eyes cast to the floor, waiting for the signal to serve. Thackeray took a break from cheerfully predicting apocalypse to fulfil his duties as host: 'Ms Fernandes, what will you have? I have an Indian white wine, a Chantilly. It's rather good.' The servant held a silver tray of crystal glasses, lace doilies and a bottle of chilled white for Thackeray to inspect. He nodded his approval and the servant poured his master's glass to taste.

Thackeray continued his theme, pointing out that India had more right than America to take pre-emptive action against its enemies. India's enemies were enemies within, he said, enemies who had long subjected Hindus to a reign of terror. 'America was attacked and it was shaken. Then you came to know there is terrorism? And we've been facing this Muslim terrorism in Kashmir for the last fifty-four years. Who are the mischief-mongers? In Kashmir it was the Pakistan Muslims right from the beginning. Who are the people in Nagaland who incited separatism? The Christian missionaries. We must know our identity is only Hindu and nothing else. Americans say we are proud to be Americans and Britishers say we are proud to be British. Why can't we say we're proud to be Hindu?'

'Why not say we're proud to be Indian?'

'Why should we say Indian? If we live in India, we are Indians, but I say if we live in Hindustan, we are Hindus. I WANT that term,' he leaned forward, forefinger stabbing at the air before collapsing back into the chair. For Thackeray, 'India' was another country, one of Nehruvian secularism and tolerance, a homeland for Muslims and Hindus alike. It was not his Hindustan, a land for Hindus, ruled by Hindus, where the Muslim must know his place.

Exhausted by the effort, he lifted the glass and took another swig. He succumbed again to the rhythmic embrace of the massage chair, closed his eyes as if in a trance and then uttered one word: 'Thatcher.' He was off on another flight of fancy.

For him, Thatcher was a heroine. Not for her free market philosophy but her attitude towards immigrants. He told a story—I had no idea if it was true—of how a Muslim delegation once tried to pressure the Thatcher government only to be rebuffed. A dish of nibbles in the colours of India's tricolour was served: steamed green ladies fingers, white radish and orange-red carrot. He continued talking, a ladies finger suspended between his thumb and forefinger, like a smoking cigarillo: 'The minister said: "If you want to live in Britain you have to follow the law of this land. If you don't, please quit Britain." Such a clear term. The delegation went to Thatcher who said, "My minister is right and I tell you the same thing." *This* is the key to protect the nation. *This* is missing in our government. If Muslims want more, go to Pakistan.'

The Shiv Sena was born in 1966, formed to stop south Indians coming into Maharashtra and taking jobs from the locals. In the beginning, before it was anti-Muslim and anti-Christian, it was anti-south Indian. It was against people like my mother who moved from neighbouring Goa to Bombay to live and work in the city in the early 1960s before she married and left for Kenya. Now the Shiv Sena had dusted off its prejudices and updated them to deal with a perceived political threat, rather than an economic one. As Maharashtra attracted more people from across India, it became a more cross-cultural society that drew those from northern India, south, east and west, people lured by the prospect of fast money. In order to survive as a political force, Shiv Sena had to appeal to a broader community: what better way to do that than upgrade his ideology to a pan-Hindu nationalism, where the enemy was no longer non-Marathi speakers but the Mussalman: 'When I started SS, that was a different time. Now my country is in danger and one cannot live as a Gujarati, one cannot live as a Bengali, one cannot live as a Maharashtrian. We alone cannot fight the ISLAM,' he boomed the word out loud, much as a father would shout the word monster or dragon to scare his children while telling bedtime stories. His delivery continued unabated: a breathless torrent of rhetoric now, streams of consciousness detached from reasoning.

'There was a house burning. I sat at home and thought it was not my house. But what about the flames? Are they going to touch my house? Today my country is in danger. It's my duty to see that my country is saved first. War will unite us. That is the Hindu war.' For him, the day of the tolerant and gentle Hindu was over. He wanted a replay of yesterday's wars between Hindus and Muslims. 'I see one man slapping another man. I tell the man: "Arre, he has slapped you." The man replies: "I did not notice." I tell him "*Get up. Fight*".'

These were festering wounds afflicting an ancient civilization, its national psyche still scarred by the memory of past wars and conquests. Men like Thackeray believed that in order to deal with the past, radical measures were needed, and quickly, to restore Hindu dignity. The slow evolutionary nature of democracy was not the answer. What was needed was revolution: swift and merciless. 'Dictatorship is one answer,' he suggested softly as if after much contemplation he had decided it was the most sensible policy of all. Generously, he was willing to take on that onerous task. 'I would be India's benevolent dictator. In the interests of my nation, not myself. My plan? It is locked up in my safe. If there's going to be a war, I'm not going to tell my enemy that from tomorrow my airplanes will attack from this direction. I will be exposed. So strategies must remain strategies, not to be exposed. Not even to your wife,' he giggled, forefinger on pouting lips as if to keep all secrets hushed. It was like watching Dr Evil in *Austin Powers*. All that was missing was a white cat being stroked in his lap. I couldn't help wondering how much of this stuff was real. How much was Thackeray the cartoonist using crude caricature to make his point, how much was playing to the gallery and how much was just plain craziness?

Our time was up. He rose to say goodbye and snapped his fingers. The servant came bearing a basket of fuchsia orchids. Thackeray presented them with a bow: 'Some flowers for you, Madam.' Click. The moment was recorded on camera. I left the house consumed with thoughts on the best way to dump the flowers. Standing at the car with the door open, Mohammed registered my 'blood bouquet' with sullen disapproval. Smarting with guilt, as I bundled into the backseat I was transported to my childhood in south London: shameful trips to the butcher as a child to collect the pig's head my mother had ordered to make the Goan delicacy of sorpotel. Swinging the carrier bag on my way home, decapitated hog's head in hand, I realized I was somehow complicit in the crime, horribly conscious of a snout pressed up against plastic, black eyes glittering their reproach, pink downy ears flapping in the wind.

After dinner at the hotel, I lay on the bed sipping Coke, listening to the tape of my interview as his disembodied voice filled the room with whispering menace. The flowers stood on the table at the foot of the bed, crimson under the pallid yellow light of the night lamp. The Catholic guilt had taken hold as I chastized myself for accepting his gift. Every time I looked at the flowers, a severed pig's head sprang to mind, sometimes mutating into Thackeray himself. For decades this courtly pensioner with a taste for jasmine and lace had been Bombay's conductor of chaos, picking up the telephone in his drawing room to dispatch 'the boys' into darkness to avenge ghosts buried centuries ago. The Sainiks were the foot soldiers and the General issued orders from his perfumed parlour beneath the gaze of Michael Jackson. In Thackeray's war, the history of invasion lived not in leather-bound volumes on library shelves but in the blood and sinews of India's Muslims. I got out of bed. The orchids had to go.

The next morning I was due to check out. It was early. In the dining room the first serving of breakfast was underway; staff in crisp uniforms served coffee, bringing out baskets of bread and plates of freshly cut papaya as fat black crows perched on windows left open to the morning breeze. I finished breakfast and went to the lobby to settle up. The sweeper woman was cleaning the floors, her head covered with a wisp of white muslin, the dark outline of her profile thrown into stark relief. A tiny cloud of dust danced around the hem of her sari as she swept into the corners and crevices. She paused by a display of orchids and stooped to pick up a flower that had fallen to the floor, and tucked the stem into the fold of her sari like a piece of pink treasure. She may have been Hindu. She may have been Muslim. Either way, it didn't matter.

19

Gujarat—The Ghost of Partition

Gujarat, February 27 2002

Just after six in the morning the Sabarmati Express pulled into Godhra station, packed with Hindu devotees on their way home from Ayodhya.

These were politically charged times: India and Pakistan were locked in a military standoff after a terrorist attack on the Indian Parliament in December 2001. India blamed Pak-backed Islamic terrorists for the assault and fears mounted of the risk of war between these nuclear powers. While their leaders indulged in sabre-rattling rhetoric, one million soldiers were squared off on the border. Through all this, the forces of Hindutva, represented by the hardline VHP, RSS and Bajrang Dal, were clamouring for action, issuing a cry for war on Pakistan while also calling on the BJP-led government at the centre to build a temple to Lord Ram in Ayodhya, on the site of the razed mosque. As a pressure tactic, bus and trainloads of kar sevaks—volunteers who would work to build the temple—were regularly taken to Ayodhya from across the country by the VHP and RSS.

The Sabarmati Express was bound for Ahmedabad, commercial capital of Gujarat, filled to capacity with families huddled tight onto single benches. Just before reaching its destination, the train stopped near Godhra, a town with a large Muslim population. Godhra had a history of communal violence and in preceding weeks tension had been rising as Hindu fundamentalists travelling to Ayodhya had clashed with local Muslims, trading insults and blows. There were reports of kar sevaks taunting Muslims on train journeys, tugging veils from the faces of Muslim women and urging their men to 'go back to Pakistan'. As the train stood waiting, a mob of Muslim locals gathered around the chai stands and a volley of abuse ensued. Twenty minutes later a carriage was on fire. Flames engulfed the compartment, filling it with acrid black smoke and toxic fumes as passengers struggled to escape. Fifty-eight Hindus, including twenty-six women and twelve children, were suffocated or burnt to death.

As the news hit national television, it evoked one of the most enduring and chilling images of Partition: a train pulling into the station, its silent carriages filled with the grisly cargo of passengers murdered in a frenzy of religious hatred. The ghost of Partition was resurrected.

Gujarat's hardline BJP chief minister Narendra Modi, who had built his reputation on anti-Muslim fervour, was quick to exploit the political capital. By the following morning he was quoted by the Press Trust of India as saying that the attack on the Sabarmati Express was a 'pre-planned violent act of terrorism'. The implication was clear: this was a Muslim act of provocation. His words became the match that lit a communal conflagration, the worst outbreak of religious violence since 1947, barring perhaps the anti-Sikh riots of 1984. On February 28, India awoke to newspaper headlines on the Godhra massacre and pictures of the charred remains of the train carriage on the front pages and in news bulletins. One Gujarati newspaper set the tone for what was to follow with a headline that read: 'Avenge blood for blood'.

The headline writers were taken at their word. February 28, 2002 marked the beginning of a killing spree that left at least 2,000 dead and up to 140,000 Muslims in refugee camps. Muslim businesses and homes were targeted in a synchronized assault that pointed to a pre-planned pogrom. Ahmedabad, which had a large Muslim community, proved to be the focal point.

'Between February 28 and March the attackers descended with militia-like precision on Ahmedabad by the thousands, arriving in trucks and clad in saffron scarves and khaki shorts, the signature uniform of the Hindu nationalist Hindutva groups,' said a Human Rights Watch report. 'Chanting slogans of incitement to kill, they came armed with swords, trishuls, sophisticated explosives and gas cylinders. They were guided by computer printouts listing the addresses of Muslims families and their properties... and embarked on a murderous rampage, confident that the police was with them.'

Their dress, weaponry and tactics bore all the hallmarks of the Hindutva movement's paramilitary organizations, including the RSS. The printouts showed detailed pre-planning. Even businesses with minority Muslim shareholders and Hindu names were gutted and burned to the ground.

The riots raged for more than two months and evidence mounted that the police were complicit. Mass graves began to fill up and gravediggers reported bodies with hacked-off limbs or heads. 'Gujarat Carnage 2002: A Report to the Nation' later spelled out the financial cost of the violence. In that report the Gujarat Chambers of Commerce put the economic cost of the violence at 2,000 crores of rupees. Retail outlets, textile mills, factories, showrooms, stalls, hotels, vehicles and homes were destroyed. According to police sources quoted in the report, 20,000 two-wheelers and 4,000 cars were burnt, 180 mosques and 240 dargahs were razed across the state, 25 temples were destroyed and more than 20 churches.

Gujarati business leaders found foreign investment scouts were cancelling their visits, the Confederation of Indian Industry's plan to launch Gujarat as a tourism destination could not have been timed worse as it tried to sell beach holidays against a backdrop bathed in blood. Hotel bookings collapsed, the state was branded a no-go zone by foreign governments. The stigma of shame was stamped on the state and those who did business there. One leading businessman spoke out when many would not. 'If government can't protect lives it should go,' said Deepak Parekh, chairman of India's leading housing finance firm HDFC in an interview with the *Indian Express*.

The chorus of condemnation from home and overseas grew louder by the day. This was the first communal riot in India's history to be relayed in 24-hour-news detail on primetime bulletins in India and across the world. It showed evidence of state and Hindutva paramilitaries acting hand in glove. The BJP was not just about economic liberalization. The RSS was not just men in shorts. What happened in those months was soon as the ultimate Hindutva experiment in BJP territory: an experiment to drive out the Muslim community.

The twist to this tragedy was that it happened in the state of Gujarat, birthplace of India's apostle of peace and Father of the Nation, Mahatma Gandhi. The images of sword-wielding Hindus baying for Muslim blood were wired around the world and left India under a cloud of shame and introspection about the kind of society it had become.

While the world called for action and reparation, in the

weeks and months that followed, the BJP did little. Families who lost everything and saw relatives killed were given compensation cheques for as little as 1,500 rupees, or twenty-one pounds. The BJP-led central government rejected calls to sack Modi for failing to serve all his people and save Muslim lives. One senior diplomat involved in the European Union's investigations told me their collated evidence showed the riots were not a spontaneous outburst to the Godhra incident, but 'genocide'.

I asked what he thought the ultimate motive was for the violence. 'The pattern of violence suggests the purpose was to purge Muslims from Hindu and mixed Hindu/Muslim areas. Gujarat marks a watershed in Indian politics,' he said, dropping all diplomatic niceties.

While the world levelled grave charges at the Indian government, the priority of the BJP was the ballot box. In April 2002 the party proposed early elections in Gujarat, having rejected calls for Modi to go. The party strategists sniffed opportunity in an early election.

The Election Commission of India thought otherwise. It opened its own investigation into whether the climate was right for elections to be held. The violence was still fresh in people's minds, the devastation had not been cleared, more than 100,000 Muslims remained in refugee camps and many on the election rolls were missing. The Commission's August 16 report into the riots reported with typical civil servant understatement that 'the situation in the state is far from normal'. Its conclusion was more direct, ruling out elections at that time: '...the full Commission has unanimously come to the view that it is presently not in a position to conduct a free and fair election in the state.'

Mr Modi and his BJP cadres would have to wait until December 2002 to fight that election. He fought on Hindutva and won. The BJP was re-elected in Gujarat and it was jubilant. Modi's victory secured him a place in the BJP pantheon. And in the weeks that followed he was heralded as a contender, feted by the Hindutva family as the man who had turned Muslim blood into Hindutva votes.

*

I visited Ahmedabad a few weeks after the riots began. The worst of the violence had passed, the curfews had been lifted but self-imposed curfews remained as shock and fear continued to permeate everyday life. It was the middle of the day, but on the drive from the airport to downtown Ahmedabad the streets were silent. The usual throng of people and traffic and eternal hum of horns was missing. Along certain stretches of road in the Muslim areas shop after shop was burnt out, blackened husks that had been firebombed and looted. Those businesses that escaped the arsonists were still closed, steel shutters pulled down and padlocked.

I had a meeting at the Holiday Inn. I stepped out of the taxi to be greeted by a small retinue of staff all desperate to assist, for the arrival of a guest had become a rarity. The hotel should have been bristling with businessmen and tourists, instead the grand marble lobby was a mausoleum. The general manager Joseph D'Couto invited me to lunch. 'The timing of this whole thing has been dreadful. Not just for business but also tourist travel. This week the Confederation of Indian Industry started an initiative to rebrand Gujarat as a tourism destination... It was to be a fresh attempt to put the state on the map. But now I'm worried. After this, we're at a standstill,' he paused to nibble on papad and pickle.

The heat of the chillies made him sweat. He mopped his brow with a napkin and clicked his fingers at a hovering waiter, calling for the air-conditioning to be switched on in the restaurant. With no guests they left it turned off most of the time to save on electricity bills. Faced with a collapse in his bookings and virtually zero occupancy, Mr D'Couto still had to keep the hotel running on full steam. While no money was coming in, the staff still had to be paid, the restaurants had to remain open, the hotel had to be cleaned. It was business as usual despite the lack of business. 'When the riots broke, the guests here were holed up inside. We were barricaded in and we could hear the trouble. We were terrified. Anybody who really needed to leave the hotel during those days had to be accompanied by minders,' he said.

'Whom do you hold responsible for what happened?'

'I cannot say.'

His evasion was understandable. Many other hotels had been burned down. His had survived, most likely because it was not Muslim-owned. Now it was simply a waiting game and Mr D'Couto feared that unless things picked up, some staff would have to go. One could see the uncertainty in the eyes of the waiters, ears straining to hear every word, seeking reassurance from the boss that things would improve. He was acutely aware of the weight of expectations.

'You don't want to be in my position,' he leaned across the table, voice dropping low. 'A boss smiling, telling everyone it will be okay, against this grim backdrop of trauma, fear and violence. How can I tell them everything will be okay when I myself don't know?'

Later I met up with local Muslim businessman Pahla Sureshwala. Pahla was a successful stockbroker and a member of Ahmedabad's affluent Muslim community that had built up businesses in finance, textiles and retail. He believed the riots aimed to target this business community in particular. We took a drive in his saloon car through the streets of the city. Brand-new apartment blocks earmarked for prosperous Muslims had been burned down, streets full of Muslim-owned businesses and shops razed to the ground. Pahla said the Hindu extremists had used economic targeting in these riots as a way of bringing the community to its knees. And the targeting was too precise to be anything other than pre-planned, the kind of planning that took months, not hours.

'Godhra was on the 27th of February. On the 28th Muslim businesses were targeted. Within twelve hours restaurants and hotels which were even 10-per-cent owned by Muslims, hotels with Hindu names, were targeted,' he said. 'These people did their homework.' He was angry. In Ahmedabad there was a large middle-class Muslim community. They had wealth, they were moving up from traditional slum areas into plush apartment blocks. Pahla believed this spawned resentment in some sections of the Hindu community who believed Muslims no longer knew their place. The riots were a chance to cut them down to size.

His comments were borne out by Hindu nationalist literature that had been distributed in the months leading up to the riots. 'Gujarat 2002', a compilation of evidence on the riots, reprinted text from VHP leaflets sent across the state. 'Wake up! Arise! Think! Enforce! Save the Country! Save the Religion!' it said. The leaflet urged Hindus not to buy from Muslim shopkeepers, to boycott their hotels, shun movies with Muslim actors, reject education from Muslim teachers and vote for those who promised to protect the Hindu nation. 'Did you read this leaflet? Then make ten copies and distribute it to our brothers. The curse of Hanumanji on he who does not implement this.'

Leaflets continued to be distributed throughout the riots and afterwards, aimed at keeping passions inflamed.

Pamphlets from the trident-wielding youth movement Bajrang Dal were the crudest, direct in their call for violence and plunder while betraying a rather curious anal fixation:

'Narendra Modi you have fucked the mother of miyas
The volcano which was inactive for years has erupted
It has burnt the arse of miyas and made them dance nude
We have untied the penises which were tied till now
Without castor oil in the arse we have made them cry.'

I had seen these Bajrang Dal boys at VHP rallies in Delhi. They were usually poor, low-caste, uneducated teenagers. On account of their caste, at least, they shouldn't have expected to find a place at the high table of Hindutva. But the new Hindutva that grew through the 1990s understood that it could make good use of aimless boys from a section of society that had been denied power and dignity for long. Of late, there were also young men from tribal communities among these foot soldiers of Hindutva—an indication of how successful the VHP and RSS had been, with NRI money, in what was traditionally the territory of Christian missionaries.

Wearing signature red bandannas, these boys swaggered through crowds on a drug-induced high, jaws grinding, eyes bloodshot, adrenalin pumping, aroused by the promise of violence. Economically impotent, sexually frustrated, they were looking for a way to matter in the world. Rape was as much a weapon against the Muslim community as violence or robbery. Sex was just another form of violent control and all part of the catharsis. The role of the Bajrang Dal was clear from its literature, it was the iron fist of Hindutva:

'With a Hindu government the Hindus have the power to annihilate miyas. Kick them in the arse to drive them out of not only villages and cities but also the country. Let the fuckers know that.'

Our car pulled in front of the refugee camp located several kilometres from the ashram where Mahatma Gandhi once prayed for Hindu-Muslim unity. This vast camp at Bapunagar was one of many that had sprung up in the wake of the violence, scarring the once bustling city and acting as a painful reminder of how religious hatred, a hangover from Partition, continued to traumatize India.

On the perimeters of the complex, there were orderly queues of people waiting to speak to those who ran the camp and I was struck by their forbearance. Despite everything, these people queued with patience and dignity. The camp organizers sat behind plywood desks dealing with new refugees, applications for compensation, medical concerns. It was endless work.

Arun, one of the aid workers, showed me a book of photocopied cheques given to victims of the riots. Some received as little as 1,500 rupees after losing everything: home, possessions, land, family. Many women and children were left without the breadwinner and their only recompense from the state was a cheque that would just about cover a dinner for two at a Delhi five-star hotel. The book of pasted photocopies with payout details neatly recorded next to losses was a catalogue of misery.

Sitting by the claims desk was Munir Bhai, a fifty-year-old ice vendor who lost his wife and two daughters. Despite the trauma associated with home, he hated the camp and wished to return to his village to rebuild his life. He tried to return days before only to be warned by his Hindu neighbours that things had changed. 'They told us to convert to Hinduism if we wanted to stay. I was born here. My grandfather was born here, yet we're told to leave.'

Fateh Mohommed, a forty-six-year-old pedlar whose head was swathed in bloodied bandages, was beaten with iron pipes by a Hindu gang when he tried to return home. 'I told them the police are coming. They said: "The police are ours. They'll do nothing for you".'

But they were among the luckier ones. An elderly Muslim gentleman sat cross-legged in the dust, rocking gently, his right hand on the crown of his head. His eyes were vacant. Arun told me the man had lost eighteen members of his family and could not come to grips with what happened.

But life went on. An open-air maternity ward bustled with activity as Red Cross workers prepared food in vast cooking pots over open fires. Tiny wicker cots holding newborns were rocked under the watchful gaze of their mothers. Born in the midst of some of the worst communal violence since Partition, these babies were the youngest and most innocent victims of the violence. Sixty heavily pregnant women waited to give birth in the burning 47-degree temperatures with no facilities, no privacy. Midwives checked over sleeping babies, protected from the ferocious heat by thin cotton sheets tied to poles to provide tent-like cover.

Birth, marriage and burial services had all been carried out inside the camp. Engaged couples, tired of waiting for peace, married inside the refuge. Whole generations of families lived cheek by jowl alongside strangers, their existence bundled into a single tied sheet. No beds, mattresses or chairs were available to rest on. Disease on the camp was common, with only one toilet for every 300 people. Food provided by the state was often rotten or insect-infested.

These people were mostly Muslim who, like Munir Bhai, had lived for generations in the same village next to Hindu neighbours, coexisting as fellow Indians. Their religions were different, yet they were the same. They liked the same Bollywood movies, spoke the same language and shared the same dreams and worries for their children. But in February 2002, everything changed. On the day the outsiders came for the Muslims, many Hindu neighbours stepped aside, closing their eyes to what was happening. In the worst cases, lifelong neighbours joined in the looting and killing, fired by private grievances and insecurities that had nothing to do with the broad sweep of history and everything to do with personal jealousies. The killers were not arrested and after the madness passed, they returned to normal life, melting back into the village routine. While the police progressed on arresting and bringing cases against those alleged to have been involved in the Godhra attack, there was no justice for the dead of Gujarat's riots. India's Supreme Court later ruled that these riot cases would have to be heard in the neighbouring state of Maharashtra, delivering a vote of no confidence in the ability of the Gujarat courts to impart impartial rulings. Like poison, the communal bias came from the very top, seeping into every section of civil life. On March 5, 2002, Modi made it clear he valued Hindu lives more than Muslims:

'The government has decided that families of those killed in the Godhra attack will be paid Rs 2 lakh (200,000) while relatives of those killed in the violence following Godhra will get Rs 1 lakh per victim,' he was quoted as saying in the *Indian Express*' Ahmedabad edition.

After the riots, the message from Gujarat's Muslims was clear: they no longer believed police would save them, they no longer trusted BJP justice.

20

Men in Khaki:
Goosestepping into the Sunrise

'If we worship in the temple, he would desecrate it. If we carry on bhajans and car festivals, that would irritate him. If we worship cow, he would like to eat it. If we glorify woman as a symbol of sacred motherhood, he would like to molest her. He was tooth and nail opposed to our way of life in all aspects—religious, cultural, social etc. He had imbibed that hostility to the very core. His number also was not small. Next to the Hindu's, his was the largest.'

—M.S. Golwalkar, writing about the Muslim
in India in his book *Bunch of Thoughts*,
which is widely seen as a mission
statement for Hindutva

Delhi, April 2003

Jawaharlal Nehru saw the dangers of Hindu nationalism long ago. To him the cult-like Association of National Volunteers or RSS was nothing less than 'an Indian form of fascism'. The Rastriya Swayamsevak Sangh (RSS) was born in 1925 in the city of Nagpur in the very heart of India. And at the heart of the RSS ideology was a vision to create a

Hindu Raj. By 1998 its political wing, the BJP, headed the national coalition government and Atal Behari Vajpayee, an RSS supporter, was Prime Minister.

This fleshy bon vivant was the acceptable face of Hindu nationalism. A moist-eyed bachelor with a penchant for saffron-laced biryani and poetry, he was possessed of a political finesse which could smooth over the less acceptable facets of Hindutva ideology. He portrayed himself as a man for all people despite a background steeped in the RSS movement. It was under Vajpayee that India conducted nuclear tests in 1998. It was under him that the country came to the brink of war and a nuclear standoff with Pakistan in spring 2002 following a terrorist attack on Parliament. It was his government that approved the rewriting of history: implementing changes in school text books to portray a saffronized version of India's past—one in which the Hindu was the eternal victim and the Muslim the wicked, barbarous invader. The new history books failed to mention that Gandhi, the Father of the Nation, was assassinated at a prayer meeting by an ex-RSS man.

It was Vajpayee's government that failed to act in February 2002 when Gujarat was engulfed by communal riots and the state administration was clearly complicit. While Gujarati Muslims burned and the eyes of the international community were transfixed by the horrors, Vajpayee played word games with the truth, quoted poetry and prevaricated. Those close to the Prime Minister spoke of a man tortured by the burden of those days, struggling to reconcile the voice of his conscience with the political necessity of holding the Hindutva family and his coalition together. Ever the skilful politician, his coalition held. But the events blackened India's image at home and abroad, depicting a land of medieval-ages-like religious intolerance. It was a stain on the conscience of the nation that would be difficult to erase. Vajpayee, mindful of his place in the annals of history, used the final months of his premiership to make amends, initiating peace talks with Pakistan.

In the months preceding the May 2004 national election, a flurry of confidence-building measures was implemented: transport links between India and Pakistan were reopened, diplomatic ties repaired, the first Indo-Pak cricket Test series was held with India winning the cup. But the feel-good factor never translated into enough votes to bring the BJP back to power. A rural backlash over lack of economic development in the villages as well as the mistrust of India's secular constituency and religious minorities led to an election rout that put a Congress-led coalition in power. The Italian-born Congress leader Sonia Gandhi, who married into the Nehru-Gandhi dynasty, checkmated her BJP opponents by announcing that she would not stand for Prime Minister, foiling their strategy to oppose a 'foreigner' heading the new government. Instead, the father of India's economic reform process and former Reserve Bank of India governor Dr Manmohan Singh was installed as the first ever Sikh Prime Minister. His integrity was seen as unimpeachable, his intellectual credentials world-class and his humble sense of duty a change from the showy self-serving verbosity of too many politicians.

Five years of Hindutva rule had been rewarded with a holy trinity of minorities presiding over India: a Muslim President (Abdul Kalam), a Sikh Prime Minister and a Catholic as the reputed power behind the throne.

The BJP leadership went into shock, plunged into a period of introspection as it struggled to come to terms with defeat and redefine itself. Vajpayee stepped aside as his hardliner deputy Lal Krishna Advani, the architect of the movement that culminated in the demolition of the Babri Masjid, took over the reins of the party. The Hindutva family began the painful process of analysing where it went wrong as insults and recriminations started to fly. Advani sought to appease the party grassroots by promising there could be no dilution in Hindutva's core values. But it was clear the movement was at a crucial crossroads in its ideological development.

By the close of 2004 the Hindutva family squabbles over future direction were out in the open as disagreement raged over how to take the political revolution forward. The 2004 election result was interpreted by the media and pundits as a rejection of the BJP's communal ideology as well as a stinging verdict on its economic record. While the RSS and VHP hardliners said success lay in yet more radical Hindu fundamentalism, the BJP moderates and political allies argued for a more consensus-driven approach. The jury remained out on who would prevail: the hawks or the doves. But one thing was clear, Hindu fundamentalism was a political factor that was here to stay.

Vajpayee's BJP-led coalition had succeeded in holding onto power for five years, evolved from an extreme political grouping into a force capable of holding together a diverse band of political allies and taking on the mighty Congress. It had built a slick party machine, legalized the RSS after decades of banishment under Congress rule. With the rise of the BJP and RSS, there was a surge in support for the Hindutva family's religious campaigns arm, the VHP, World Hindu Council. The VHP is now a mass movement that spearheads the quest to build a temple to Lord Ram on the site of the razed Babri Masjid. The Hindutva movement had also set up thousands of schools across India that aimed to inculcate the saffron message in the voters of tomorrow. The RSS and BJP had succeeded, in short, in placing Hindutva in the political centre-ground, making its language common currency in political debate, forcing Congress to debate the issue of secularism in India today.

*

Hindu nationalism began in earnest in the late nineteenth century and was founded as a backlash against British colonialism, Christian missionaries and growing Muslim influence. The root of Hindutva ideology remains the RSS. It was formed in the Twenties, taking on the features of a paramilitary group and split into cells known as shakhas that adhered to military discipline, wore uniform and learned to fight with five-foot bamboo sticks capable of cracking heads and breaking bodies.

Some shakhas held initiation ceremonies that swore allegiance to Kali, the blue-black goddess of destruction, with a copy of the holy Bhagavad Gita in one hand and a loaded revolver in the other. Contact between Hindutva leaders and the Nazis were frequent. Former RSS leader M.S. Golwalkar, a black-bearded yogi known simply as Guruji, said in his writings that Hitler was an inspiration:

'To keep up the purity of the Race and its culture, Germany shocked the world by her purging the country of the Semitic Races—the Jews. Race pride at its highest has been manifested here. Germany has shown how well nigh impossible it is for Races and cultures, having differences going to the root, to be assimilated into one whole, a good lesson for us in Hindusthan to learn and profit by.'

Today, RSS membership runs to millions and its influence is greater than Nehru could have feared. The founder of the RSS, Dr Keshav Baliram Hedgewar, believed Hindu submissiveness had been the root of all evil through history. 'It is no use blaming the strong. Who provokes the strong to be aggressive? The weak. To be weak is a great sin,' he once said. He wanted the RSS message to spread from person to person, spreading the light of the message 'from lamp to lamp'.

Now, millions of lamps are lit across the country. Secretive, sinister, cult-like, they meet at a dawn gathering called a shakha. I wanted to see it for myself, so I booked an appointment with the men in khaki.

Mr M.G. Vadiya was the RSS' national spokesman and based at the head office in Keekar Wala Chowk in north Delhi. Along the streets, copper vats bubbled with oil frying sticky orange swirls of sweet jalebis. There were stalls selling recycled plastic, vegetables, and white-feathered chickens with beady black eyes pressed up against wire pens and squawking their dismay. I was told to arrive at 4.30 pm sharp and as my Maruti Wagon R passed a huge bullock dressed in a khaki coat with painted yellow horns, I knew I must be close.

Inside the RSS offices, Dr Mishra was sitting behind a plywood desk spread with files and a copy of the *Pioneer* newspaper. He was an unlikely-looking fanatic. A neat man in his fifties, with salt and pepper hair that rose in spiky tufts. He had a kindly face and wore large brown glasses in the style of the British comedian Eric Morecombe, a maroon sweatshirt, salmon pink tank top and tan polyester trousers.

'Madam Edna. You are looking like an Indian,' he extended a hand. 'Are you Hindu?' I explained I was raised a Catholic but visited no church regularly. Dr Mishra smelled weakness. His mouth broke into a teddy bear grin: 'Once you're above the boundaries of religion, you're a Hindu. Indeed, a Hindu is anyone whose history, heroes, source of inspiration is India.'

Mr Vadiya was less cuddly: seventy-nine years old, with sharp features and a sharper mind. His skin was the colour of pickled walnuts and bulbous brown eyes glared from behind his specs. He looked like an angry koala. He sat behind his desk and wore the RSS black cap, a peach khadi shirt, brown woollen waistcoat with Nehru collar and high-riding khaki shorts exposing pale, hairless knobbly knees. He was fastidious in his speech and manner, speaking with hands together, fingertips pressed as if in prayer.

Spice-infused tea was served in small porcelain cups covered in roses and a dish of almond biscuits was laid on the table by one of the office youths. Mr Vadiya put the cup to his lips and sucked hot sweet chai through his teeth to cool it. Then, taking his biscuit and dunking it into the cup, he demanded to know what RSS literature I had gone through. Nibbling with furious concentration with eyes bulging behind specs, he was clearly unsatisfied with the choice of reading material and grabbed my notebook to jot down his own preferences.

'You must read all of these and then we'll discuss.' Then in an attempt at friendliness, he smiled. A stab of fear pricked my heart: Mr Vadiya wished to convert me. Or rather reconvert me. Back to Hinduism, the true faith. The faith of the ancestors before the Jesuits had their evil way with the natives.

'When did you join the RSS?'

'I've been an RSS member for the last seventy years. Seven zero. I am seventy-nine. I saw boys of my own age playing some games and so I joined. It was for the atmosphere, the camaraderie and eventually, the ideology.'

'Why would a boy who joined for the games still be a member seven decades on?'

He stiffened. His koala eyes bulged with indignation.

'How do you stick to your family? It's the same way,' he replied with brittle precision. 'The very structure of the RSS is based on the lines of a joint Hindu family. A single person is there, the leader, but he is not a dictator, not an autocrat, just as a father is not an autocrat. The RSS parades are for exercise and discipline. We congregate every day for one hour at 6.30 am. We play games, have exercises, recite prayers and disperse. It's not sinister. It is just like your Boy Scouts.'

The mission is to transform Indian society into a Hindu society by penetrating every facet of Indian life. While there is no central membership list, he put the number of shakhas at 41,000 across India and said membership could be as much as tens of millions.

'Had the roots been very weak, the RSS would not have spread so far or wide. We don't believe that political power alone can bring the desired transformation and we're confirmed in this by the Soviet State. They experimented for seventy years with the full might of state power and failed. We will not make that mistake.'

*

The next day Dr Mishra called on the mobile. Did I want to come to a shakha the next morning? Normally women were not permitted but they could make an exception, provided I was chaperoned.

The alarm rang at 5.20 in my Delhi apartment and I dragged myself out of bed. The RSS morning parade started every day at 6.30 a.m., across the country in all weathers. It was dark when I arrived at the office. The khaki-clad bullock was nowhere to be seen, being a sensible beast. I rang the bell three times and waited until a servant peered from the overhead window, eyes droopy with sleep. Yawning, he came downstairs to let me in and motioned me upstairs where the door to the office was wide open. There was Dr Mishra, watching the latest on the Iraq war build-up on *Star News* in what appeared to be his underpants. He was sitting on a chair, pulling on socks, pants riding up wizened thighs.

'Ah, Madam Edna. You have arrived. Come in.' It was

just past six in the morning. I had taken no coffee and was feeling rather raw. Nervously, I hovered by the door as Dr Mishra was clearly in a state of undress.

'Are you dressed, Dr Mishra?'

'Yes, yes, getting dressed. Come in.'

I entered, eyes cast to the floor, fearing another flash of RSS underwear before realizing he was wearing a particularly skimpy pair of khaki shorts. The paramilitary uniform of the RSS or Dr Mishra's version of it was a white pressed shirt, brown knitted tank top, khaki shorts scandalously above the knee, Dennis the Menace-style black and white striped socks, topped and tailed with a black topi and black loafers. Dr Mishra stood, smoothed the tank top over his stomach and ran through a commentary on the uniform:

'The full uniform of the RSS is worn by our troops. It is a black shoe, khaki socks, white shirt, black topi and khaki knicker.'

'Knicker?'

'Khaki knicker.'

'Khaki shorts?'

'No. Khaki knicker,' he slapped his thigh. 'Beneath the knicker we wear the langot. And then, the danda,' his eyes darted towards a door to the side. 'I show you the danda?'

'Not necessary.'

'Necessary.' Dr Mishra slapped his thigh once again.

The Hindi word for stick has a double entendre. He scuttled into the next room. I waited. Any moment now, he would emerge, goosestepping butt-naked from the doorway. Seconds passed and Dr Mishra emerged, not naked, but proudly brandishing his danda. A five-foot-high bamboo lathi. His very own lethal weapon.

'We use it for stick-fighting. If someone attacks us, our whole psyche must be ready to defend ourselves.'

I watched as Dr Mishra demonstrated a series of

marching steps coupled with deadly danda lunges. It was 6.15 am. There was no coffee in sight.

'Is the RSS a paramilitary outfit?'

'It's not pukka military but voluntary. We come every morning to do physical exercise, we meet, discuss in the shakha any subject between earth and sky. We march to keep fit. For us, the shakha is a physical, mental and spiritual experience. What is RSS? It's a factory that makes patriotic Hindus. It is a man-making machine.'

A man-making machine. But what kind of men did it seek to mould and what kind of India did these men wish to shape? Many feared the RSS aimed to create a Hindustan in which religious minorities would be marginalized as second-class citizens. The RSS aimed to reabsorb Pakistan into India and create a new Golden Age for Hindus. A new type of Hindu, not a mild and meek clone of Gandhi, but a Hindu who was strong and defiant, ready to fight to ensure Hindustan was never subjugated again.

It seemed strange to view this traditional tolerance of the Hindu as a weakness, when in reality it was its greatest strength. The ordinary Hindu struck me as being a pragmatist—life is hard, competition for survival is intense in a nation of 1.1 billion where roughly one third of the population lives below the poverty line, according to the World Bank definition of those who live on less than a dollar a day. India was never one homogenized society: it always had a composite character, with each state having its distinct identity, culture and language, making it more like a confederation of countries. Indeed, through their history, rather than wage a suicidal war against superior military powers such as the Mughal rulers or British, the Hindus sought to co-exist rather than indulge in a war which could destroy everything. Pavan Varma writes in his brilliantly insightful book *Being Indian*: "The Indian emphasis has always been on tenacious survival, not glorious martyrdom. Resilience rather than retribution, survival rather than conquest... has been their civilizational trait.' It is an equally perfect description of the Hindu mentality. Despite centuries of violent conversion campaigns by the invading powers, today more than 80 per cent of Indians remain Hindu. Yet the new militant Hindu nationalist movement seeks to recast the Hindu as the eternal victim, not the eternal survivor. He is painted as history's fall guy, kicked around by any new bully on the block. First, the Hindu was the victim of the Muslim invaders, then the British imperialists. Today he is a victim of the minorities, guests who have outstayed their welcome and demand special privileges. Today the Hindu is the victim of Muslim Pakistan, exporter of terror into India. The aim of the Hindutva right is to use history to provoke a desire for redress and a political will to create a Hindu Raj.

The time for the shakha was near. It was the shakha that mobilized Hindu nationalist sentiment across the country, instilling in Hindu men the feeling of patriotism that equated religion with nationalism. Dr Mishra and I drank down masala chai and headed to the car. Ten minutes later, we arrived at the local sports ground where sixty men were gathered on the pitch dressed in a version of the uniform, some in jumpers, some in shirtsleeves, some in flip-flops, some in Nike trainers, all in the khaki shorts and caps. They were from different communities and their skin colour ranged from the yellowish pallor of the northern Punjabis to darker complexions of the south. A ragtag army. The chief instructor called four men to the front. They marched out of sync as he barked 'Stand to attention' and the rest lined up behind. One cadre marched to a flagpole, legs swinging high as he held the flag of Hinduism. A flame-shaped saffron flag was raised on a pole positioned before the group and fluttered in the dawn breeze. The Bhagwa Dhwaj or saffron flag is symbolic of the 'yagna', or sacrificial flames. It also embodies the ideals of the movement and thus is revered. The RSS troops saluted. Their right arms swung out and their forearms snapped into a salute to the chest, elbows jutting at ninety degrees.

'Now the shakha begins.'

It opened with a prayer. They prayed to the gods, they prayed for Hinduism and India, ending with the cry 'Jai Bharat Mata'. The chief instructor barked at the group to form a circle and they ran to warm up, swinging their arms in sweeping arcs. Suitably charged up, the men turned to the main event. Wrestling. All the cadres stepped inside a white circle drawn onto the pitch, one man was 'it' and head-butted the others outside the circle. It was not sophisticated. The rule was there were no rules. The aim was to knock everyone flat. The point: perhaps it was useful in a riot. Perhaps these were the kind of tactics deployed in Gujarat? Flesh collided with flesh, bone jarred against bone, until it ended with the group collapsing to the ground, in a tangle of arms and legs, writhing in red dust and sweat. There was something vaguely homoerotic about it all: eyes and limbs locked in a semi-violent embrace. Dr Mishra chuckled appreciatively by my side, still hugely entertained after all these years: 'Just look at their faces!' I was looking. And it left me unmoved.

The sun rose through the orange haze of dust that obscured Delhi's skyline. The men formed a line in the direction of the sun and performed the yoga asana, Salutation to the Sun, to the sharp shrill blasts of the pracharak's whistle. The whistle punctuated every move. Six times they saluted the sunrise. One overweight cadre collapsed in an asthmatic fit, his large stomach moving up-down, like a set of outsized bellows. He reached into his pocket and pulled out a blue inhaler, sucking the puff of steroids deep into his lungs. Come the revolution, he would not be much good to the cause. The sun eased above the jagged horizon, washing the sports field in a warm glow that dispelled the dawn chill. The shakha ended with the men singing their prayer to nationalism before the flag. Dr Mishra translated:

'Oh Hindus awaken. Once you have awakened no one can do you harm.

'Hindus have destroyed that symbol of slavery: the Babri Masjid...

'Break Pakistan so all India is reunited. India is incomplete without Pakistan. Pakistan is part of India.'

Not quite the Boys Scouts then. Just as the Nazis dreamed of a Greater Germany, so this was the Hindu right's dream of a rebuilding a Greater India.

As the crowd dispersed, Raj Kumar Dhawan, a sixty-four-year-old shopkeeper and joint secretary of the local branch, asked Dr Mishra and me to join him for breakfast at his home. We walked through the streets of Karol Bagh, suffused with the smell of roti, past sleeping dogs to his house at the top of a steep narrow pathway. Mrs Dhawan greeted us at the gate. She was a beautiful woman: wide-set brown eyes rimmed in kohl and her mouth bearing a trace of pink lipstick, showing that she had expected guests for breakfast. She ushered us through the yard where chickens pecked at the stony ground and into the family living room that was decorated in flock wallpaper. Sofas covered in cotton printed fabric were pushed against the walls, with a coffee table already laid with plates, spoons and forks.

Against the back wall was a day bed, piled high with blankets and tasselled bolsters. Nestling amidst this cushioned comfort was Mr Dhawan's three-week-old grandchild, dressed in a pink knitted cardigan. Mr Dhawan sat down with a grave look and ordered his wife to bring the breakfast through tea, plates of parathas, laddoos, Bombay mix, black grapes and salted chipsticks.

Taking tea and paratha, he began to speak in a voice thickened by emotion: 'I am sixty-four years old and I've been a member for fifty-two years. The RSS is the only organisation which inculcates a feeling of love in our country. Reuniting with Pakistan is one of the motives of the RSS. Originally, my village was near to what is now the border with Pakistan. After Partition my family came to Delhi. We lost everything.' He put his paratha back on the plate and turned to look at the sleeping child.

Mr Dhawan's belief was shaped by first-hand experience of Partition in 1947 and the orgy of communal violence that followed. Millions became refugees. The trauma remains for many Indians of that age, especially Punjabis and Bengalis. Like Mr Dhawan, they lost everything in Partition and those who were fortunate enough to survive the holocaust had to start over once again. the painful process of finding a new way to make a living, another house to live, gathering together the scraps of a lost existence and weaving it into life again.

Delhi was the new beginning. And for people like him, the RSS provided a shelter of belonging and understanding. Mr Dhawan believed the RSS mission to destroy Muslim mosques, tear down the invader's history, was justified. It meant restoring the heritage of Hinduism that was lost during 1,000 years of conquest. It was not a matter of secularism or communalism. It was simply a matter of religious duty and pride.

'Muslims destroyed 30,000 temples during their invasion of India. Now Hindus say give us back only three sites of temples. The temples of Ram, Krishna and Shiva. They are most important to Hindus,' he said. 'We don't ask for the other sites and we say to the Muslims give us these three and the trouble ends. If not, they must be retrieved by force. If the Muslims resist and a situation of strife comes, then the number we demand will be not three, but 30,000.'

'Is the RSS willing to do this even if the price is India's unity and peace?'

'India will not fragment because Muslims and Christians must understand and accept this logic. They must understand this *will* happen. There is no choice.'

21

Turbulent Priests

New Delhi 2003

It was one of those white-hot days of summer. The kind I detested. Blanched skies and scorched air, dust dancing by the roadside as another Tata truck sped past, bumper bearing the legend 'Blow Horn Please'. The cacophony of honking was overlaid with the rasping whine of the paniwallah at Gandhi Market Maidan. Business was brisk as tens of thousands of Hindu nationalists converged on the marketplace named after India's apostle of peace. But this was no commemoration of Gandhian tolerance. Quite the opposite.

A maelstrom of VHP members dressed in saffron, flourishing tridents and chanting militant religious songs had gathered for the start of a seven-day agitation calling for Hindu rule. Peppered among the procession were bearded holy men, dressed in ochre robes, fingertips moving across the prayer beads around their necks. These were Hinduism's turbulent priests.

Most of the crowd was young men, saffron bandannas tied Rambo-style around their foreheads. All wore the colours of Hinduism, from pale ochre, bright orange to shades close to blood red. Women marched, segregated from the men. Some had babies, slung low on jutting hips with small hands pawing at the breast for milk. In their jewel-bright saris they painted the colours of India.

I had an appointment with the VHP general secretary Mr Champatrai, who helped organize the protest that showed Hindu nationalism was still a mass political force. It was 10.20 am, an hour before the rally was due to kick off. Small blue marquees were erected to the side of the lane leading to an open ground where the rally would take place. Inside the marquees were plastic chairs to provide shaded seating for the old, the important and the self-important.

Mr Champatrai's eyes were ablaze behind his thick 1950s horn-rimmed glasses. Dressed in a long white cotton dhoti and caramel kurta with a white handkerchief tied around his head and knotted under his chin like some diabolical housewife from that decade, he scuttled back and forth scanning the crowds, a manic smile playing beneath a thin grey moustache. A large orange tilak the size of a rupee coin was painted on his forehead. Occasionally he turned, hands on jutting hips: 'What's your estimate, Madamji? How many thousands? Ten, twenty, forty thousand? Tell me.'

Walking and talking at high speed, he took me to meet the VHP's most senior leader, Pravin Togadia, who agreed to a chat later that evening. I had expected a raven-haired firebrand, instead here was a man who looked like a provincial chartered accountant from Ghaziabad: nut-brown and balding, with a round face, bulging black eyes and a neatly trimmed moustache. It was the kind of forgettable face that one sits next to every day on the commuter train.

It was hot and dusty and Champatrai's manic mincing was fraying my nerves to shreds, so I escaped to sit in the shade of the VIP marquee next to Acharya Giriras Kishore, another VHP grandee. Mr Kishore was eighty-three years old and had devoted his life to the cause of Hindu power. A long white beard flecked with grey touched his chest and a mane of white wavy hair was swept back, emphasizing his domed forehead. Silver-framed glasses stood out in sharp relief against dark skin and a large red tilak was applied between bushy white eyebrows. He rested gnarled hands on a black and silver-tipped cane and on his right hand he wore two rings, one set with coral and another with a diamond that winked in the sunlight like a toad's eye.

In February 2002 Acharya Kishore was quoted by the Press Trust of India saying the Ram temple would be built at any cost. 'We are ready to face bullets.' He was at Ayodhya on the day the activists tore the mosque down.

'What was it like?' I asked, making conversation.

'It was a bad spot on the country. So it had to be pulled down,' he said, in the manner of a builder discussing a dry rot problem. 'The invader Babur constructed it after the destruction of the Ram Temple. Suppose we'd done that to a temple built in memory of Mohammed. Would they like it? Lord Ram is our God.'

'But you did do it.'

Feigning deafness, he gazed at the procession, periodically emitting grunts of approval like a grizzly patriarch watching children at play. He'd never married and like many Hindutva leaders had vowed a life of celibacy, making the cause his only passion and family. A succession of people entered the VIP tent and prostrated themselves before him, touching their foreheads to his feet in an act of veneration. A band of sadhus came in and more chairs were set in a square on the green and yellow carpet inside the marquee. All wore trademark saffron robes, long beards and fancy moustaches. The paniwallah was frantic, scurrying with tumblers of water to the waiting dignitaries, beads of sweat standing on his black brow like a string of pearls.

Rifle-toting police in berets and khaki-and-sky-blue camouflage jumpsuits stood guard over the VIPs. I counted ten armed police inside the marquee alone. The VHP leadership was top of the hit list of Indian Islamic terrorists, so security was tight. The procession ended with a rally where Togadia set out his vision. Speaking from a place named after the Great Soul of India, he envisioned an India that was at odds with the non-violent Hinduism that Gandhi had taught the world. The message was simple: the time had come for Hindus to rise up and fight.

*

Later that evening I arrived for my meeting with Praveen Togadia at the VHP headquarters in R.K. Puram, a vast ashram with families living and working on site. Four men sat at a reception desk with three phones set in a neat line, busy perfecting the timeless Indian art of doing nothing while looking extremely busy. They were engrossed in the celebrity section of the *Times of India*. The debate centred on the pneumatic merits of Bollywood starlets Kareena Kapoor and Bipasha Basu. After the steamy sex romp *Jism*, which involved a roll in the surf, the money was on Bipasha.

I was led through to Togadia's private office. The man who looked like the commuter accountant is in fact one of the most extreme Hindutva ideologues in India. His language lacks subtlety: the brutally simplistic voice of the Hindutva street. Togadia had publicly defended the Gujarat riots. He had called for civil war between Hindus and Muslims and once described Sonia Gandhi as 'that Italian bitch'. His verbal delivery was like a machine gun: a sharp, staccato rattle that echoed in the ear long after he finished speaking.

Togadia had made it his mission to pressure the BJP

government to build a temple to Lord Ram on the ruins of the mosque destroyed by Hindu extremists in 1992. 'Hindus believe the soul is important. Ram Temple is the soul of India and without the soul the body cannot survive. It is a holy mission to sustain Mother India. Ram is past, present and future.'

He compared the alleged destruction of the Ram Temple centuries ago to the destruction of the US World Trade Centre in 2001 and said the time had come for the West, India and Israel to unite against Islamic fundamentalism.

'Are you suggesting holy war?'

'Holy war? The concept of crusade and jihad is alien to India. It was never a part of our history. It's not part of our thinking. But destruction of Buddhas by the Taliban, WTC and the Ram Temple are manifestations of the same intolerant, violent, uncivilized ideology. One ideology builds Buddhas, WTC and Ram Temple or aeroplane. The other destroys it. India is facing onslaught of this barbaric, jihadi, fundamentalist ideology for one millennium. It has divided our motherland, ethnic-cleansed Kashmiri Hindus, attacked our Parliament and targeted our women and children. We *have* war in India.'

The Koran taught Muslims to wage jihad and jihad was already a fact of life in India, he said. The answer was to attack the root of the problem and that was Islamic Pakistan. Quite simply, nuke it. His answer was for India to take pre-emptive measures against its estranged brother nation. The US had shown that in the interests of the nation, pre-emptive action was acceptable: 'Iraq has not killed any civilian of the US. Pakistan has killed more than 40,000 civilians by supporting terrorist groups.

'We have two choices. Either we bleed and face slow death by terrorism or we face battle with the epicentre of terrorism. By one single strike of a nuclear weapon, India will not be destroyed. But by single nuclear attack by India, Pakistan will nowhere in the world remain. The patience of the public is wearing thin. People are becoming impatient and are ready to tolerate anything. Nuclear attack they are ready to suffer.'

I doubt he'd canvassed all of India's 1.1 billion people on this one. It was the BJP-led government that launched India's nuclear missile tests almost as soon as it came to power in 1998. Hindu nationalists had danced in the streets with jubilation, letting off firecrackers and chanting slogans saluting the might of the motherland. They saw it as a sign of India's military prowess, a coming of age. India had joined the big boys. The celebrations ended abruptly when Pakistan responded with its own nuclear tests. The enemies were matched once again and the showdown marked the start of the south Asian Cold War. Except this was more like a Hot War as in the 2002 standoff neither side had the parameters of constraint in place that had governed the rules of behaviour between the US and the Soviet empire. India had a no-first-strike policy. Pakistan did not. Nobody knew for sure where Pakistan drew its line in the sand. If India did not know where the line was there was always a danger it might be crossed, triggering a nuclear response in the event of war. This made for dangerous brinkmanship and brought India and Pakistan close to a nuclear standoff during the first half of 2002. Politicians on both sides of the border had openly talked of the nuclear option. It had been close. But for Togadia, not close enough.

'There is a fear psychosis in the Indian psyche, just as there is a fear psychosis in the US. We will not tolerate terrorism anymore. India demands a strong leader to defend this nation. Such a leader today should be willing to sacrifice. We should be ready to die for this cause. For the cause we should all be ready to lay down our lives.'

22

Lost Temple of Ram

'Theirs are exploits the world will keep alive in memory forever.'
— 'Ayodhya', 54.18, Valmiki's *Ramayana*

Ayodhya, April 2003

India is layered with reminders of its turbulent history, with emblems of past conquests woven into the fabric of the country. In Delhi you can take a rickshaw to one of the largest mosques in Asia and witness the awesome austerity of the Jama Masjid built by Emperor Shah Jahan in 1656. A short ride away is St James, a canary yellow and whitewashed church built in 1836 by Colonel James Skinner—the son of a Scotsman and a Rajput. The church was caught up in the Delhi battles of the Indian Mutiny of 1857 and yet to look at it today it would not be out of place in a village green in England, replete with brown sparrows chirruping in the bell-tower.

The religious imprint of India's history is not merely stamped on the landscape but on the national psyche. It is almost sixty years since Independence from the British and more than a century has passed since Muslim rule disintegrated, but for the saffron warriors the spectre of the invader remains. In the holy town of Ayodhya, a temple to Ram was razed to make way for a mosque, so they said. In vengeance, the mosque was razed to resurrect the temple. The temple came first, so the mosque never really existed. It was as simple as that. As easy to justify as that.

So where was the evidence of a Ram Temple? In February 2003 India's Supreme Court called on a team of archaeologists to answer this explosive question, to excavate for evidence of God, no less. The excavation site was on the ruins of the Babri Masjid in Ayodhya, a holy site desecrated by holy men in the name of another religion. The task facing the archaeologists: to find evidence of a lost Temple of Ram.

Sworn to secrecy, they began their work behind billowing pink silk marquees, watched by sharpshooter marksmen wielding rifles and AK-47s. Dusty men of science had crossed from the realms of history into contemporary politics. If they found evidence of a temple, it would be interpreted as the green light to resurrect it on the ruins of the mosque. If the archaeologists found no evidence of a Ram temple, what then?

Ayodhya sits 350 miles south-east of Delhi and the journey to the holy city cuts through India's Hindu heartland: flat brown vistas interspersed with lush irrigated paddy fields and pastureland. In ancient times it was one of India's most magnificent cities. Today little remains of those fabled riches but its glory lives on. I arrived the day after the festival of Lord Ram's birthday. More than ten years after the fall of the Babri Masjid the whiff of religious militancy hung in the air.

Small boys with heads shaved for the Ram festival played by the roadside. Pint-sized skinheads darted in and out of a jostle of cows, rickshaws and traffic, breaking off from playing to take a cooling drink from the water pump. A family of monkeys sat in the shade, their tiny nimble fingers weaving through one another's light brown fur to pluck out fleas, liquid brown eyes flicking upwards from time to time to survey the passing scene.

The pavements were lined with fruit and vegetable-wallahs calling out prices under a canvas canopy to protect their wares from the burning midday sun: neat rows of orange-red carrots, white turnips and gleaming dark purple aubergines lay next to feathery bunches of dhania. The smell of diesel, dust and jasmine mingled to form a sickly perfume.

Roadside stalls approaching the disputed site were full of religious paraphernalia—holy threads hanging in red bunches, aluminium platters with pyramids of red and saffron powder for putting markings on pilgrims' foreheads. Stalls selling pictures of Ram, from simple portraits to fabulously gilded mini-shrines with flashing lights dancing around the frame. Orange-robed sadhus squatted by the roadside and chatted. Others sat deep in contemplation, lips whispering in devotion. It reminded me of a childhood visit to the Catholic pilgrimage site of Lourdes: a town of holy kitsch and spiritual ardour, with the smell of self-righteousness suspended in the air like incense.

Ayodhya is to Hindus what Bethlehem is to Christians or what the Wailing Wall is to Jews. It is what Mecca is to the Muslims. For Hindutva's turbulent priests it is worth dying for and worth others dying for. The ancient Hindu sacred epic *Ramayana* tells the story of Lord Ram, a Hindu god who defeated Ravana, the demon king of Lanka, before returning triumphant to his kingdom to reclaim the crown of Ayodhya. He was the original warrior king and hero of the Hindutva right for banishing the barbarous invader. Around this religious epic, the Hindutva priests and political leaders wove their strategy to mobilize the Hindu vote into a single block which would provide the platform for national political power. The quest for a resurrected Temple to Lord Ram became no less than a spiritual quest designed to unite the fractured Hindu family from north to south, east to west. Ram's story, in which he roamed the forests of India for fourteen years until he returned to reclaim his throne, was one which could appeal across the nation to Hindus rich and poor. It was an inspiring tale of good vanquishing evil, of bravery, of sacrifice and eventual triumph. Lord Ram was a religious icon, portrayed in pictures and books of late as a muscle-bound warrior god who could inspire his people to unite against historical wrongs and defend their lands against modern-day threats.

At the local VHP headquarters, one could enter a darkened room and see a model of the proposed Ram Mandir, a two-storeyed building with 106 carved pillars. Intricately carved, the model was lit with strips of red neon lights that glowered in the gloom. The model itself was an object of reverence, where visiting pilgrims viewed it in solemn silence. It was the Hindu dharma to make the temple real, resurrect it from the rubble of history and create a spiritual beacon that would guide Hindus in the coming age. Efforts were already underway to make the building blocks for the actual temple at a vast work-yard just fifteen minutes' drive from the VHP offices.

As I got out of the car and entered the building site, it was like stepping into the set of a religious epic. Stacks of twenty-foot-high carved pillars and uncut stone in towering piles; at the entrance were two huge red sandstone pillars, surmounted by a carved header engraved with scriptures from Hindu sacred texts. The central yard hummed with activity as a large mechanical lift lifted pieces of uncut stone to masons who sat on stools and chipped away by hand.

The gentle tap-tapping of flint on stone filled the air as the men worked in burning heat, shirt backs slick with sweat, heads bent, absorbed in God's work and oblivious of the oppressive sun. To one side lay fifty completed carved pillars, resting on their sides like missiles waiting to be loaded.

The entrance to the disputed religious site is accessible through an armed checkpoint. Thirteen watchtowers ring the site of India's most sensitive religious shrine. On the day of my visit all had been peaceful. Hindu pilgrims lined up to pay respects to Ram Lalla, the infant Ram. I went down a narrow path, lined by stone walls topped with barbed wire. At the top was a clearing with a massive caged walkway for visitors to pass through. It is a militarised zone: sharp shooters surrounded the site and there were three checkpoints for body frisks.

The tiny statue of Ram Lalla appeared inside the old mosque in 1949 in the dead of night and the Hindu faithful saw it as a sign from God to liberate Ram's birthplace. The pilgrim cries of 'Jai Sri Ram' hushed as the devotees approached the excavation site behind a pink marquee. The wind had teased open gaps in the material to reveal men digging trenches of about ten feet by eight with trowels and pickaxes as supervising archaeologists viewed the dig from overhead. Small baskets of findings lay in rows to one side under twenty-four-hour armed guard and another part of the site had a covered area, where archaeologists washed and labelled findings. Hindu archaeologists were looking for evidence of a temple built for one of their most revered deities. I could feel the quickening pulse of exhilaration with each approaching step. The sense of anticipation was unbearable as I approached. The Lost Temple of Ram, where religion and politics, past and future, life and death were played out in one place.

The pilgrims in front pressed garlands against the barbed wire, murmuring prayers, but unable to stop for more than a few seconds before Ram Lalla himself, as nervous armed police waved them on with their rifle butts. In less than a minute it was over.

One man was charged with delivering the new temple that would house this impromptu shrine. Prahmans Ramchandra Das, a ninety-three-year-old devotee who had given his life to the struggle as head of the Ram Temple trust that aimed to resurrect the structure on the ruins of the mosque. I arrived at the trust's headquarters and walked through an arched gateway that opened into an inner courtyard. Ramchandra Das sat cross-legged on a teak-framed day bed covered in sun-faded cotton fabric. A matted white beard rested on his bare chest, a tangle of grey hair fanned out from his crown, framing a wizened face: he looked like a sinister marmoset.

His minions clustered like groupies and when he raised his finger for silence, they dropped to the floor and sat cross-legged ready for the lesson of the day, chins tilted upwards as they gazed adoringly at their master. Tea was ordered and a servant came with stainless steel cups of chai and an armful of tangerines. Ramchandra Das took one, offered it to me and began to peel another.

'Are you confident the archaeologists will find evidence of a temple?' I began.

'It's not a matter of confidence. It's a matter of faith. But I'm confident the decision of the court order will approve the solution,' he said, head wobbling in certainty as he sucked on a tangerine slice. 'I've agreed to accept the court order.'

'But what would happen if the court rules against you?' I asked. The question was clearly impertinent. His eyelids lowered a fraction, his limbs stiffened. A pause, then, the answer came like an angered serpent's venom, spittle flying. 'I do not accept any decision of court against this holy matter. I'm not going to build the temple in Mecca. So why should it hurt the Muslims? I am an *Indian* and I wish to do this in *India*. No power can stop the temple. I would lay down my life for it. The stones and pillars are already there. But I'm not interested to disclose the timing,' he said leaning forward slightly, adding in a whisper: 'The enemy will not be alerted.'

The enemy will not be alerted. Like Thackeray he spoke of 'the enemy'. Who was the enemy?

'Anyone who opposes the temple. Ayodhya is everything.'

'What about the destroyed mosque? This was also a place of worship.'

'It was not a masjid. It has always been the birthplace of Ram. So how could there be a mosque?' The logic was irrefutable to the priest and his followers. With a wave of the hand he dismissed further questions, reclined on his side and stretched his spindly legs on the daybed like some latter-day Caesar, dropping tangerine slices into his mouth. He was an old man now and had worked his entire life for the mission. For him, the building of the temple would be a final act of devotion. 'The life of a priest is such. It must be finished.'

I left the court of Ramchandra Das and went to the car. It was one of his last interviews as he died shortly afterwards, failing to see his life mission completed.

As the evening drew in, the wind lifted spiralling clouds of dust in the road. Herds of cows carefully picked their way through the traffic, fly-ridden rumps sashaying between carts like portly matrons on their way home from the shops. Through the haze the car passed the religious stalls busily plying their trade. In the doorway of one was a life-size statue of Ram, painted in rich technicolor, in warrior pose as if ready to fight the demon king all over again. In the half-light he looked alive, eyes gleaming, poised to spring forth any moment, thrusting a trident towards the invisible enemy. After that glorious victory Ram returned to his kingdom as conquering hero and king. His inheritors would not rest until they too had restored him to the Kingdom of the Righteous.

*

The argument over whether to build the temple continued to rage even after the BJP was voted out of office in May 2004. Hindutva hardliners blamed the loss of the election on the party's failure to keep its promise to build the Ram Temple during its period in power. Then, on July 5, 2005, Ayodhya exploded back into national consciousness once again as a group of suspected Islamist terrorists infiltrated the high-security cordon in a planned suicide attack on India's most politically sensitive religious shrine. The site is protected by thirteen watchtowers and around 1,500 police and paramilitary. Such was the security, the state chief minister Mulayam Singh Yadav once commented, '*Jahan parinda bhi par nahin maar sakta hai* (Even birds can't fly there).' Yet, the ring of steel was breached by a group of suicide bombers who aimed to destroy one of the most holy sites for Hindus. They did not succeed, thank God. If they had, India could have been plunged into a fresh bloodbath. All the terrorist suspects were killed in a fire-fight with police who later retrieved fifteen hand grenades, four AK47s, two nine-millimeter pistols and a rocket-launcher. The men were believed to be members of either Lakshar-e-Toiba or Jaish-e-Mohammed, two Islamic militant groups active in the fight in Kashmir. But no group claimed responsibility for the attack.

The attack sparked the inevitable row, with the BJP claiming that the ruling Congress was soft on terror, seizing upon it as an issue that could help revive its political fortunes. It showed Islamist terrorism had struck in the heart of the nation, at Hinduism's holy of holies. But the Congress argued that intense security arrangements had saved the Hindu shrine from destruction; the terrorists had been defeated. Aware of the possible consequences, the government was determined to keep a lid on the genie of communal tension. This was not a Muslim versus Hindu issue. The country was shaken, but the terrorists had failed in their attempted act of sacrilege and India was spared a replay of the Hindu-Muslim rioting of 1992. Even so, it acted as a chilling reminder to everyone: Ayodhya still had the potential power to divide India.

23

Weapon of Mass Distraction: BJP Babe on the Election Trail

April 2004, Meridian Hotel, New Delhi

It was Saturday night and I had a date with Miss World. Yukta Mookhey, in true beauty queen fashion, was late. In a city rife with sexual harassment or what Delhi-ites elegantly term 'eve-teasing', Yukta wisely never went anywhere without Daddy. A five-foot-eleven goddess in a city bristling with moustachioed perverts was always a risky combination.

Yukta had flown into town for a job: compering a Punjabi awards ceremony. On Sunday she would fly to Rajasthan to begin a rather different line of work as political campaigner for the BJP. In a country where 50 per cent of the population is under twenty-five, the celebrity factor was the BJP's last throw of the dice to gain support in the 2004 national elections. Projections on GDP growth, BPO jobs and a booming stock market may stir the hearts of the middle-aged middle classes checking out their share portfolios, but when it came to the economically disenfranchised urban and rural youth, the only figures of interest were the pneumatic charms of Bollywood babes and beauty queens—or so the BJP thought.

Yukta, along with a bevy of lovelies, was the latest addition to the BJP's electioneering armoury. Dubbed the Glamour Gang by withering Indian press hacks, they were what I liked to term the BJP's Weapons of Mass Distraction, designed to deflect tricky issues like communal violence and rural poverty and bring a bit of old-fashioned razzle-dazzle to the dry business of politics.

Yukta first hit the headlines in 1999 when she became the latest in a line of Miss Indias to win the Miss World crown. India hailed it as a victory for the nation. India may have 35 per cent of its population living on less than a dollar a day, swathes of the country afflicted by water and power shortages, ingrained corruption and medieval-style communal riots, but its girls could still bring home the crown. India has more Miss Worlds than any other country and a whole industry had developed around grooming girls to vie for the prize of becoming the ultimate princess. After her victory, Yukta returned to a heroine's welcome. She handed back her tiara in 2000 and teetered down the familiar path of her peers to the doors of Bollywood producers. Aishwarya Rai, a former Miss World, and Sushmita Sen, a former Miss Universe, had both hit big time in the film industry. But Yukta proved to be no Ash or Sush and sank without trace into the life of an Indian B-list celebrity. At the grand age of twenty-five she was stale news. Until, that is, the BJP came calling.

She signed up to the party, flashed her BJP membership card and smile for the cameras, and appeared on primetime news espousing the virtues of Atalji and his crew like a born-again convert. The lights were on; the best saris were removed from their tissue wrapping and jewels the size of gobstoppers glinted under the stage lights. Yukta was back on the front pages once again.

For these few days, everyone was talking about Yukta

and I wanted to meet the woman with the job of injecting glamour into Hindutva. In many ways she represented a section of ordinary voters who might be persuaded to buy the BJP ideological package. It included some attractive things like economic reform, the retail boom, telecom modernization. But the package also came with less pretty policies on communal harmony and the place of religious minorities, plus an economic growth that failed to generate much benefit to Indians outside the urban Hindu middle class. Yukta's job was to do a bit of a makeover on the BJP's image, highlight its best features while playing down the uglier ones that might scare off potential voters. I thought that by understanding where Yukta was coming from I could understand the appeal of Hindutva to the voter banks she represented. After several days of phone negotiations with her parents, it was agreed that I should meet up on her next assignment in Delhi. I went to some trouble for our date. For once my hair was blow-dried and tidy, makeup was applied and I put on a dress. If you have to spend the evening with one of the world's most beautiful women, it's wise to make an effort.

The lift doors opened and as she stepped into the polished marble-floored Meridian Hotel lobby, all eyes swivelled and rested on her statuesque figure. She personified a man's idea of a woman's figure: voluptuous, sashaying curves sensuously draped in chiffon silk. Almost six feet tall, with golden skin, flowing dark hair that fell around her shoulders and an exquisitely made-up face, she glided through throngs of admirers in a pale orange sari embroidered in silver, her ears and throat adorned by drop diamond jewels. With her Amazonian figure, she was the modern-day incarnation of Bharat Mata, Mother India.

Trailing in her wake was her father, a tall and distinguished looking man with thinning hair and an air of weary resignation to his role as minder. He seemed hot in a brown suit and tie and his eyes scanned the room for would-be stalkers with the meticulous efficiency of a professional bodyguard.

Yukta greeted me warmly and we walked to the car waiting to whisk us to the awards ceremony at a nearby venue. Bystanders parted like the Red Sea for us to walk through. I got in the back with Yukta and her father got in the front of the car. 'So sorry I was late, darling. It takes a little while to get ready and I'm sharing a room with Dad.'

'It's not good enough,' her father added testily as the car pulled into Delhi's rush hour. 'They've promised to shift us.'

On the way to the awards venue, she described her Punjabi Hindu family that hailed from land that was now part of Pakistan. At the time of Partition, her grandparents were forced to leave and relocate to Mumbai (like a good BJP girl she never once referred to the city as Bombay). She was born there and had spent all her life there. From a young age she liked the public stage and decided that when she grew up she would do something big. For a pretty girl in Mumbai, becoming Miss India was one way to stand out.

'It started when I was fifteen and I saw Sushmita Sen win the Miss Universe crown for India. It inspired me. I thought, why not put my height to good use? My parents said no. It's for dumb women, you're too intelligent, they said. Remember Papa? But at twenty I thought this is it. I told my parents I wanted to do something big with my life. I gave my pictures to the Miss India contest.'

She was selected.

'I read books on motivation, attended seminars on how successful people of the world achieved all they had. I worked day and night sculpting my body. Diet. Exercise. In two months I emerged a different person. I wanted to put myself in the oyster of the world.'

The car pulled up outside a hall. Flanks of short men with bulbous eyes and slug moustaches stood at the entrance, holding clipboards and scratching their balls with an air of affected indifference. A young man guided us through the scrum of testosterone, enlivened by the sight of such a glorious creature. We were led to the backstage of a cavernous hall, still only a quarter full even though the show was due to start in just fifteen minutes. Behind stage, screened off from prying eyes by green netting, we sat on plastic chairs and continued to chat under the sullen gaze of the lighting gaffers.

'Can we have some pani, yaa?' Yukta instructed the gofer. Her father sat to her right and I sat to her left. So, the oyster of the world—what did she mean?

'I mean, I had larger dreams about life.'

'What kind of dreams?'

'I want to be an icon for the younger generation, but women in general. For people to say: "She did great things in her life",' she said, eyes gleaming, enthused by her own patter. 'Someone not only strong but someone who will stand the test of time. I want to be remembered. You know, the way Oprah Winfrey is remembered, Princess Diana, Audrey Hepburn.' To the best of my knowledge, Oprah was still alive.

'Why these three?'

'These are women who used glamour for a purpose, brought about change, a history of change in the world. They will not be forgotten. That is the larger dream. I can't be someone who channelizes all her energy into clothes, hair and looks. I'd like to create a movement where people realize there's more to life than money.'

Only an Indian with money could make such a comment. In India money *was* life. Those who had it spent all their waking hours building fortresses of their homes to guard it, shutting out the grime and poverty of the rest of India in a gilded cage of A/C, MTV, DVD and 4X4. The underclass that didn't have it spent vast amounts of their day seething and plotting how to get it. Money consumed minds in India. There was no safety net and with more than a billion people, if you fell into the abyss it was a long way to the bottom of the heap. If ever there was a nation whose mantra was 'show me the money', it was New India. The Punjabi businessmen running that night's award show had showed Yukta the money for this show. It was a long way from the Big Dream, but it was a living. There were even reports in the newspapers that the BJP had paid its celebrities to jump aboard the Hindutva bandwagon. The word on the street was that Yukta's price was 1.5 lakh rupees a day (or 2,000 pounds). She denied all allegations of taking cash for campaigning.

A rather hurried-looking young man had been hovering around. Finally plucking up courage, he homed in and poked a television camera into our faces, interrupting the conversation. His head wobbled side to side in a state of anxiety. 'Madam, I am from *Punjab Today*. I am seeking just two minutes of your time, Madam *pleease*.'

Daddy examined the young man's press card closely and finally granted his approval. I moved aside to let the *Punjab Today* reporter cosy up next to Yukta. She was a consummate professional, staring deep into his eyes, articulating fluff about film and pageants in a husky voice.

I asked the father about when he left Pakistan. What did he remember?

'I left in 1948. Terrible. It was a tragedy. A bad, a harrowing experience.'

'Did it change your view of Muslims?'

'We loved the Muslims. We are the most secular people still. A lot of Muslims helped save our lives in Pakistan and we always had good relations with them before Partition. These views were inculcated in my time in Pakistan. Even in my job as a businessman I came across hundreds of Pakistani Punjabis when I went to the Gulf. When you speak to them in their language they love it. Language is the thing. As long as people can relate to one another, not knowing religious backgrounds, but communicate on the basis of logic, sense, then you can develop a relationship with any person in life.'

He thought a little further.

'Of course, cricket is also another form of religion,' his face creased into a smile. India had just won the first Test series against Pakistan in fifteen years. The Boys in Blue had shown that India was the best and the country erupted into days of celebration after the result. Language might unite the Pakistani and Indian Punjabi, but when it came to cricket, all bets were off. Mr Mookhey was right: cricket was religion in south Asia. Many in India had feared that if Pakistan won the series it would ignite communal clashes in India between Muslims and Hindus. Luckily for the Indian Muslims, India delivered a cracking victory.

'And are you a BJP man, Mr Mookhey?'

'I am not a BJP man. I am not *anybody's* man,' he said, humour evaporating. He turned to ensure that Mr *Punjab Today* was not getting fresh with his daughter. Mr *Punjab Today* was on a roll. It was the longest two minutes of Yukta's life. A gaggle of youths had gathered to watch, eyes swarming like flies over ripe meat. 'That's enough. She must focus,' said Mr Mookhey. Chastized, the Punjabi reporter packed his equipment, asked for an autograph and slunk into the darkness. Yukta prepared to go on stage and handed her orange leather handbag to her father. The crowd was filling up with Punjabi families here for a night of awards, music and dance. It was not a classy affair. The stage was lit with flaming torches, coloured lights and dominated by two huge, rather incongruous sculptures of Tamil gods, blue tongues hanging out and eyes protruding in a show of ferocity. The statues seemed out of place.

Rich young Punjabi girls paraded up and down in the aisles, casting sly glances at the boys, long silky hair swinging across their backs. Largely proportioned mothers, rolls of fat nurtured by years of ghee and rasmalai, gossiped in perfumed huddles. Their men congregated in large groups, pot-bellies distended under tank tops pulled tight over their trousers. The master of ceremonies, a short, wide man who looked like he'd escaped from the Big Circus Hall of Mirrors, introduced Yukta as the compere. Mr Mookhey and I sat in the front row and clapped as she emerged under a spotlight to a distracted crowd. She swung into action, beaming her smile and flicking her hair.

'Her bit should be over by 7.45 pm,' said her father in a whisper. On stage Yukta had mastered the crowd.

'And now to open the evening, it is my pleasure to present Zenith,' she said. A burst of applause filled the hall as a dance troupe bounded on stage. Four men in pink and silver trimmed catsuits that left little to the imagination and two girls in white hot pants. Piped Hindi pop songs blared from loudspeakers and Zenith swung into the first routine. Hip-gyrating and lip-synching, the dancers exchanged hot fervent glances to the beat of the tabla. The crowd was in an ecstasy that was difficult to fathom. It was a long way from Hepburn. And Hindutva.

After Zenith came the nadir. Punjabi dance troops in gold chain-adorned black turbans, dancing with dandas and bells. An old Seventies' film actor, eyes watering with emotion, came on stage to the wild applause of his fans as he received the special prize of the night for services to the industry. He wasn't the only winner. Everyone seemed to get a gong. Looking at the line-up of nonentities on stage, gongs in hand, with Zenith still gyrating with unbounded enthusiasm, I felt a pang of sympathy for Yukta. No wonder she had joined the BJP. It was the BJP or this.

Her set was over and she left the stage, taking with her the only grace and dignity the event had. Backstage, the testosterone crew was waiting. She became engulfed in a small mob of tight-trousered youth. The smile remained bright and constant but I sensed she had had enough. So had I, so I went in search of her father who was chatting to the organizer. Minutes later we were safe in the car and heading back to the hotel. We'd have a light supper in her room, he said. But later she had to work some more and host the official post-awards dinner that would go on until the early hours. I would make my excuses and leave.

Their hotel room was rather small and strewn with discarded clothes, makeup, flowers from well-wishers and baskets of fruit and chocolate with notes expressing ardent admiration. Mr Mookhey was immediately on the phone asking why they had not been moved to another room. He seemed worried. Maybe Yukta snored.

Yukta ordered room service: sandwiches, crisps and coffee. A homemade chocolate brownie was unwrapped from foil and laid before me. I liked the brownie, I even liked Yukta. But she worried me. Had she weighed up the implications of lending her name to the BJP and considered what the party stood for? Not just the party's PR glitz of the 'India Shining' economic campaign which had saturated the election media coverage, but the underlying philosophy. Why did she sign up?

'When one starts a journey, one has a plan. Okay, I've become Miss World, I'm very proud of my looks, of my Indianness and I do not want to be influenced by Western media, trends, clothes. My purpose of wanting to be a filmstar would be to use that glamour. Because when you're glamorous, people want to hear what you have to say. I've achieved a certain amount of stardom and so there is a natural graduation to politics and using my public persona in a different way.'

'But why the BJP?'

'When you start earning, paying taxes, you ask why after fifty years of Independence, why are we still a developing nation? Why not like Japan or Dubai? You tend to wonder about the great leaders we had like Gandhi, Nehru and think: look at the corrupt nation we are today. So shallow. It's great to be self-centred but not great to be selfish.'

She nibbled on the corner of a cheese sandwich, sipped at some water and pondered further as she sought to expand her philosophy. 'I truly believe India is a superpower. I respect what the Britishers left. Roads, rail. But why did they Partition us? There was no need. In my mind, India is a sleeping giant. The BJP understands this. It has done brilliant work over five years. We are well placed globally, we have a better image, we are seen as liberal.'

'What happened in Gujarat blackened India's reputation around the world.'

'It was definitely more than tragic and I'd definitely condemn what happened,' she said, her sing-song voice not skipping a beat. 'I definitely don't support fanatics whether Muslim or Hindu. There has to be balanced government leadership and Vajpayee's leadership is very balanced.'

'Vajpayee stood by and watched it happen.'

She lost her Miss World poise for the first time and looked over to her father, a small girl once more. Her father interjected. 'She's very tired. Let her eat something. Why don't you both eat something. Five minutes.' Yukta nibbled, eyes cast into her lap. A minute later she answered, having got the story straight. 'There will always be mistakes,' she countered. 'Tragedies. Definitely it will go down in history as a black patch. But let's not dwell on the past. A mistake was made, a blunder was made, but let's learn from it and look to the future.

'It happened and by sitting in your comfortable living room and pulling someone down, it doesn't help. There are bigger, larger issues. As there was a revolution during Independence era, the whole nation came together then, so we need to come together now to bring India forward.'

'Do you believe that Mr Vajpayee and his government stand for national unity?'

'I *do*,' she replied, eyes wide with sincerity. Perhaps she believed what she was saying. To me it sounded like Yukta was still painting the world in rainbow colours. Painting over the black with her Technicolor Dream. She was intelligent enough to know that people would be questioning her intelligence. It put her on the offensive, answering unspoken criticisms and the media mockery that plagued her efforts to become something more than the beauty queen. She struck me as someone with no strong political views, only good intentions and a desire for something more—more for her country but mostly more for herself. And what was wrong with that? Weren't we all like that? On the blank canvas of Yukta's political consciousness, the BJP could paint any picture it pleased.

'People say, what does she know of politics? I might be wrong and fine, I'd love to be proved wrong,' she continued. 'I need to help the younger generation to realize there's a need to do something and not just sit around and say, "The system sucks. I'm going to the US." It's very sad. If we channelized our energies in India we wouldn't need help from the outside world. I say to young people: you need to vote.'

There *was* too much apathy in India about the way it was heading and it was too easy to absolve oneself of responsibility. Tomorrow Yukta would begin a five-day tour of Rajasthan to drum up votes. Of course she was there to bring the showbiz factor to the stump. But what did she think about the issues themselves: the future of a country which faced the enormous challenge of opening up its economy while dealing with the terrible risks associated with the social changes that came with it, a country torn by economic, religious and ethnic divides? She bit her lip for a second and then smiled widely, as if the cameras were upon her. 'In my capacity as Miss World and a celebrity I will address younger women. I want to work for their betterment and upliftment. I should be able to put my good looks to good use. I see this as a platform to reach out to people.'

She seemed lost and in a way her singsong answers sounded the political death-knell for the BJP party strategists even before a single vote was cast. Yukta was a lovely woman with a passion for her country, but she had no idea where to take it, let alone where the BJP planned to take it. Hers was a hopeless answer which failed to address any of the issues which would decide the election in a few weeks' time. Perhaps it was a personally driven vision, rather than one the BJP had forced upon her, I had read somewhere that Yukta decided to enter politics because she wanted to be remembered in history. What did she want to be remembered for?

'Since a child I was read the great stories of leaders like Guru Nanak, Gandhi, Nelson Mandela. They were remembered not for being ministers or Prime Ministers but because they made a difference in history. A journey of struggle and hardship but with truth and sincerity. They got their message across.'

'What message do you have?'

'I want to influence minds of the young and women to do something wonderful in life. It comes from spirituality. When you die, you die by yourself, empty-handed, and only achievement counts. That's my vision. I hope by supporting this government it helps to uplift the common man. That's my dream.'

24

The Saffron Revolt

The common man did not share Yukta's vision of how to realise the dream. The BJP was voted out in May 2004. While Vajpayee and Co. had dominated Delhi's election campaign coverage with talk of an 'India Shining', of rising economic growth, 'upliftment' or whatever you want to call it, the villagers that Nehru once described as *real* India didn't see things getting better. They were the economically disenfranchised, the forgotten hundreds of millions who had seen little benefit from the booming stock market, telecom revolution, privatization bonanza and so on. For them, life remained a struggle and five years of BJP had done little to provide them with basics such as clean water, a reliable electricity supply or better health and education. More than thirty-five per cent of Indians still lived on less than a dollar a day and India continued to hold the dubious honour of being the country with the greatest concentration of the world's poor.

Then there was the communal issue. Always there, like an unhealed scab, itching and waiting to be picked off. India remains a country where the painful past has not been properly reconciled to its present. The 2002 Gujarat riots in which Muslims were murdered under the gaze of the government, in which the killers literally got away with murder, had scarred the conscience of many in India. Even those who were silent at the time could not forget. Whether out of defence of the secular ideal, or basic human disgust that such a thing should have happened in their country, in their name, many from the religious minorities and Hindus who believed in the true tolerant spirit of India chose not to vote the BJP back in.

There was always the fear that ultimately the election result could strengthen the Hindutva hawks. In the 2004 election campaign, Vajpayee had sought to take the BJP to the political centre-ground by shrewdly campaigning on economic development and peace with Pakistan, not on Hindu nationalism. But it was too little, too late. By the autumn of 2004, the BJP leadership torch was passed to Vajpayee's hardliner deputy L.K. Advani. The Hindutva hawks argued that 'moderation' had failed, the time had come to return to the real agenda of the movement: the Ram Temple, the creation of Hindustan. There were threats of the Hindu right forming a breakaway political party to replace the BJP because of its failure to address core issues like the Ram Temple when in power. Such threats were designed to bring the moderates to heel.

Advani promised his vote bank that the Hindutva agenda remained sacred. Despite the internal wrangles, a draft BJP discussion paper quoted by *Frontline* magazine in August 2004 made clear defeat had done nothing to change the core Family Credo:

'We should, in particular, mount a powerful and sustained counter-offensive against those ideologies and political forces, especially the Congress and Communists, who reject Hindutva as the basic identity of the nation, who have the perverted ideal

of secularism for their narrow political ends... and
in whose hands the destiny of our Motherland is
decidedly not safe.'

For now, the Hindu fundamentalist agenda remained intact.
For the Hindu Right it was a question of how to implement
it. Sometimes it would be through opposition, education,
media and mass religious campaigns; sometimes in the
corridors of power. The battle started by the RSS almost
eighty years ago continued. Clearly, the struggle for
Hindustan was not over.

But a ruthless internal battle rages over how to take the
struggle forward. The debate over the right path to Hindu
power has become an increasingly bitter one. By the end of
2005 the internal wrangles of the Hindutva family were
totally out in the open, dirty laundry aired to electoral
scrutiny. By then, Advani was viewed increasingly as a
caretaker leader, an elderly statesman ill equipped to lead
the next battle charge for power. The focus had shifted to
his possible inheritors and the jostling for the next succession
of the BJP had begun.

In November 2005, Hindutva's self-styled warrior
princess, Uma Bharti, was suspended from the BJP. It was
the latest spat with BJP leaders who had come to view her
as a loose cannon. Cornered, she told her tormentors: 'I am
the real BJP.'

Things had not always been so. Once she had been
exploited as the darling of the activists, a woman who had
shunned the traditional role of wife and mother to marry
the BJP cause. She had made her name as one of the leaders
who led the original yatra to Ayodhya—that spiritual
heartland of Hindutva. After the 2004 electoral defeat, she
positioned herself for the leadership by calling for a return
to hard-line policies instead of the placatory path of the

mainstream. It placed her on a collision course with the other potential successors of Advani such as Arun Jaitley. Jaitley was representative of another type of BJP leader, a slick lawyer who had once run the commerce ministry, a man committed to the cause yet possessed of a hardened realism and ruthless ambition. He courted the media in a bid to be portrayed as a man of the future, cultivating correspondents to tout him as a Prime Minister-in-waiting. Yet his lack of mass appeal and rather prickly way with the man on the street was a political handicap in a country where elections are won or lost in the villages, not the exclusive salons of New Delhi.

But while the Jaitleys of this world lacked Bharti's street appeal, they knew how to neutralize her power in the closed confines of party meetings. When Bharti was thrown into the BJP wilderness it was seen as the possible beginning of a predicted split in the party—she saw herself as someone capable of capturing the hardened Hindutva vote, leaving the BJP'S 'moderates' to court the centre-ground so vital to electoral victory.

In Maharashtra, its Hindutva dynasty was embroiled in a public feud over succession. Bal Thackeray, the old tiger, was by now sick and almost toothless. His Shiv Sena legacy was subject to a bitter leadership feud between his son Uddhav and nephew Raj that threatened to bring decades of domination to an end.

Strangely, the son was unlike his father. He was soft-spoken and more adept at backroom negotiation than public showmanship. Whereas, the nephew modelled himself on the uncle: a man of the masses, capable of firing up the crowds with oratory pyrotechnics. The son wanted to broaden Shiv Sena's appeal while the nephew stuck firmly to the divisive ethos of the party. It was indicative of a wider dilemma within Hindutva: how to evolve

The saffron mutiny within Hindutva's two most important political organizations—the BJP and Shiv Sena—threatened to undermine gains that had taken decades to build. It showed the movement at an ideological crossroads. While a populist divide had worked in the early days, the challenge now was different. There were elements within both organizations which recognized the limitations of mass-scale communalism in today's India. While the Uma Bhartis and Thackerays relied simply on communal tension, demonstrations, religious rallies and verbal fireworks to impassion India's Hindu masses, others saw a more calibrated approach was needed to build a mass appeal capable of delivering a stable government.

The new India is looking for a leadership which understands the formidable challenges of economic and social change ahead, not one purely seeking to avenge the religious wrongs of the past.

Those who believe in a truly pan-faith Indian identity see this as a hopeful sign. Hindutva began as a movement designed to straitjacket Indian identity within the confines of Hindu identity. So far, India has refused to be straitjacketed. Instead, I hope, India will force Hindutva to recognize its own limitations and to adapt itself.

Acknowledgements

Holy Warriors began to take shape when I moved to India in December 2001 to write for the *Financial Times*. In the intervening years, I benefited from the guidance, advice and generosity of many people both in India and the UK.

Firstly, I wish to thank those editors at the FT who gave me the chance to write about India, most of all John Thornhill and former senior editors including Edward Carr and Graham Watts.

I am enormously lucky to have publishers who are both inspiring and a joy to work with. In the UK, I wish to thank Philip Gwyn Jones of Portobello Books and his team including Laura Barber. In India, I wish to thank Penguin's Ravi Singh, Thomas Abraham and their team. Also, thanks to my literary agent Ayesha Karim at Gillon Aitken Associates for her unstinting support and good advice.

Along the way there have been various others who helped wittingly or unwittingly, including the staff at the British Library in London, the library at the Nehru Memorial Museum in Delhi and the Francis Xavier archives in Goa. Also, the staff of the Shahi Imam at the Jama Masjid in Delhi, the staff at the Golden Temple in Amritsar, the

Roman Catholic Basilica in Old Goa and those associated with the Ram Temple trust in Ayodhya.

Among friends in India, I wish to acknowledge: Shipra Biswas, Mario de Miranda, Tony Jesudasan, Narayani Gupta, Paran Balakrishnan and family, Jagmohan Singh, Fayaz Syed, Levinson Martin, Dr Eclito D'Souza, Tahir Mohiddin, Parvez Imroz, Gulum Butt and his grandson Majid Butt, Ashok and Rajni Hoon and the late General Hoon whose recollections of combat over glasses of Royal Challenge whisky will linger in my memory forever.

I wish to thank Dr Karan Singh and Brigadier Monty Madan who first told me of the plight of the Pandits, Professor Aswini Ray of JNU, Ashraf Buchson, Jacob and Molly John, Virat Bhatia, Ajai and Rita Singh and their daughter Manvi, Balmukand Singh, John Dayal and the late Bhupen Chakravarti. Last but not least, my Indian driver, the indomitable Gurmel Singh.

In London I wish to thank a few of those who supported me along the way, including my sisters Tania and Maria Fernandes, Jill McGivering, Jackie and Michael Porter, Brenda Smith, Paul Troop, Colin and Colette Crone. At the London School of Economics, thanks to Florian Lennert, Professor Henrietta Moore, Professor John Harriss and Dr Athar Hussain.

My love and gratitude to my husband Andrew Atkinson who at times must have felt his life had been invaded by a multitude of ululating extremists. With fortitude he accompanied me on trips to more temples, gurdwaras, churches and mosques than he cares to remember.

Last, to my parents Max and Elfina Fernandes. This one is for them, with love.

For news about current and forthcoming titles
from Portobello Books and for a sense of purpose
visit the website **www.portobellobooks.com**

encouraging voices,
supporting writers,
challenging readers

Portobello
BOOKS